Germans No More

Germans No More

Accounts of Jewish Everyday Life, 1933–1938

Edited by

Margarete Limberg

and

Hubert Ruebsaat

Translated from the German by

Alan Nothnagle

Berghahn Books
NEW YORK • OXFORD

First published in 2006 by
Berghahn Books

www.berghahnbooks.com

©2006, 2011 Margarete Limberg and Hubert Ruebsaat
First paperback edition published in 2011

All rights reserved.
Except for the quotation of short passages
for the purposes of criticism and review, no part of this book
may be reproduced in any form or by any means, electronic or
mechanical, including photocopying, recording, or any information
storage and retrieval system now known or to be invented,
without written permission of the publisher.

Library of Congress Cataloging-in-Publication Data

Germans no more : accounts of Jewish everyday life, 1933-1938 / edited by Margarete Limberg and Hubert Ruebsaat ; translated from the German by Alan Nothnagle.
   p. cm. --
Includes bibliographical references and index.
ISBN 978-1-84545-084-7 (hbk) -- ISBN 978-0-85745-315-0 (pbk)
1. Jews --Germany --History --1933-1945. Germany --Ethnic relations. I. Limberg, Margarete. II. Ruebsaat, Hubert.
DS135.G3315 S5413 2006
940.53/180922

2006042690

British Library Cataloguing in Publication Data

A catalogue record for this book is available from the British Library

Printed in the United States on acid-free paper

ISBN 978-1-84545-084-7 (hardback)
ISBN 978-0-85745-315-0 (paperback)

Contents

Foreword	vii
Introduction	1

Part I
Boycott—Don't Buy fom Jews!   7

1. "We Stood in the Trenches for Them" / *Edwin Landau*	9
2. Aryan "Justice" Against Jewish Firms / *Friedrich Weil*	14

Part II
The First Victims: Doctors and Lawyers   17

3. Devoted Patients—Opportunistic Colleagues / *Henriette Necheles-Magnus*	19
4. Patients as Extortionists / *Arthur Samuel*	22
5. I Was No Longer Considered a Front Soldier / *Karl Friedländer*	25
6. A Notaryship Is Revoked / *Siegfried Neumann*	30

Part III
Plundering and Ruined Livelihoods   35

7. The Department Stores Become "German" / *Hetti Schiller*	37
8. Aryanization Everywhere / *Kurt Sabatzky*	45
9. The End of a Wine Merchant's Business / *Friedrich Weil*	48
10. A Livestock Dealer Gives Up / *David Grünspecht*	51

Part IV
Friends Become Strangers   55

11. The Brutality Spreads / *Raffael Mibberlin*	57
12. I Would Have Liked to Dance, Too / *Gerta Pfeffer*	65
13. "Jews Not Welcome" in Hotels / *Leo Grünebaum*	68

14. A Witch Hunt Under Police Supervision / *Martin Gumpert*	71
15. The End of a Relationship / *Hans Kosterlitz*	74
16. Alone in Familiar Surroundings / *Heinemann Stern*	77
17. Good Germans, Bad Germans / *Joseph B. Levy*	80
18. A Rabbi Is Misunderstood / *Mally Dienemann*	84
19. A Mixed Marriage Beneath the Swastika / *Eva Wysbar*	87

Part V
Through the Eyes of Children 95

20. A Child's Suffering / *Hugo Wolf*	97
21. Segregation from a Child's Point of View / *Hans Winterfeldt*	99
22. I Want to Become a Nazi / *Ernst Loewenberg*	103
23. Jewish Schools as Refuges / *Heinemann Stern*	105

Part VI
German Culture Is *Verboten!* 111

24. Hitting a Wall / *Fritz Goldberg*	113
25. The Banning of a Music Critic / *Ludwig Misch*	115
26. The Kulturbund—Ghetto and Home / *Kurt Baumann*	118

Part VII
Self-help—Self-assertion—Self-discovery 129

27. The Jewish Wirtschaftshilfe / *Alexander Szanto*	131
28. From "German Maiden" to Convinced Zionist / *Luise Stein*	143

Part VIII
The Beginning of the End—The Reich Pogrom Night 147

29. Escape from Hell / *Max Moses Polke*	150
30. My Troubles Were Just Beginning / *Arthur Samuel*	159
31. A Failed Escape Attempt, a Devastated Home / *Siegfried Neumann*	163

Part IX
Farewell to Germany 171

32. Freedom! / *"Aralk"*	173
33. A Final Round of Theft / *Siegfried Neumann*	180
Biographical Information	183

Foreword

It all started with an extended radio broadcast. We had been reporting on new research concerning the lives of Jews in Germany in the years between 1933 and 1938, that is to say during the period between Adolf Hitler's appointment as Reich Chancellor on January 30, 1933, and the so-called Reich Pogrom Night of November 9 and 10, 1938, on which synagogues were burned all across Germany. This broadcast generated an unexpectedly large quantity of mail. In most letters people wrote that they had already heard and read a great deal about the Pogrom Night and the subsequent extermination of the Jews. However, they did not know to what extent Jews had also been shunned, stripped of their rights, and persecuted before 1938. They wanted to learn more about it.

That is why we decided to publish a "reader" on this subject in which the victims would tell the story in their own words. During our professional life we had frequently experienced how history becomes particularly tangible in the form of eyewitness accounts, and how an audience is more open to persons relating their own experiences than to mere document collections and statements of fact.

During our search for appropriate material for this project, we came across a previously unused collection of Holocaust memoirs in the United States. It was located in the Houghton Library at Harvard University. The individual reports from this collection proved to be particularly valuable since they were recorded only months, sometimes only weeks, after their authors' escape from Germany, making them more authentic than recollections written down later on.

This collection originated in a contest sponsored by Harvard University. In the spring of 1940, German refugees were asked to describe their "life in Germany before and after January 30, 1933." According to the contest guidelines, these texts would then be used "for a study of the social and psychological effect of National Socialism on German society and the German people."

The response was overwhelming. More than 260 refugees sent in reports from almost every country on earth in which they had taken refuge. Most participants came from the former bourgeois middle class in Germany, including many physicians, lawyers, teachers and merchants. But cattle and wine dealers, housewives and mothers also described their lives before their expulsion and escape. In order to paint the most representative picture possible of Jewish life in Germany, these texts have been complemented with some reminiscences from the memoir collection of the Leo Baeck Institute in New York, which is concerned with the history of Jews in Germany.

Our thanks go to all those who have encouraged, advised, and assisted us in this project. We are particularly indebted to the curator of the Houghton Library of Harvard University, Rodney G. Dennis, and his staff. Thanks to their unwavering kindness and patience, they made our search both possible and painless. Our thanks also go to the archivists of the Leo Baeck Institute in New York, who supported us in our search for additional material. Last but not least, we would like to thank our editor, Maria Matschuk, whose support helped make this book possible.

Berlin and Hamburg, 2005
Margarete Limberg   Hubert Ruebsaat

Introduction

On the day after Adolf Hitler's appointment as Reich Chancellor on January 30, 1933, the *Jüdische Rundschau* wrote: "A power which is hostile to us has seized control of the government." Nevertheless, few of the some 450,000 Jewish Germans were ready or able to see this event as the end of all emancipation and assimilation, let alone as the beginning of a process of persecution that would end in the murder of millions. Just like many non-Jewish Germans, many Jews also believed that, despite his strong words, Hitler would soon be done for. At the same time, they hoped that Hitler's coalition partners would have a moderating influence on him and at least cushion the blow. They listened eagerly to rumors of an impending military coup against the new regime.

After a long struggle for their political and social emancipation, German Jews finally believed they had achieved their goal: a guarantee of equal rights under the law. Just how firmly they believed this is shown by the numerous lawsuits Jews initiated against the injustice they experienced in the early years of the Third Reich. Jewish front soldiers particularly hoped for protection from Reich President von Hindenburg. They assumed that the former general would honor the Jewish veterans of World War I. Of course, the Jews also recalled the centuries of persecution they had suffered in Germany. In early 1933 they still hoped that the new government's anti-Semitism would soon run its course and that, as so often in German history, the phase of persecution would be followed by a phase of calm. After all, many of them argued, over the generations the Jews had amassed a wealth of experiences and skills which would help them survive these difficult times as well.

Most Jews felt themselves to be German to the core and wanted to remain German. This explains the various offers of cooperation and declarations of loyalty to Germany on the part of Jewish institutions and associations following the Nazi seizure of power—statements that sometimes outdid themselves in their servility. For instance, just days after the Centralverein Deutscher Staatsbürger Jüdischen Glaubens (CV) [Central Association for German Citizens of Jewish Faith] proclaimed: "The cultivation of German convictions in our ranks must be continued at all costs!" the Reichsbund Jüdischer Frontsoldaten (RJF) declared in October of 1933: "We shall stand with our German fatherland to the last!" And also in 1933, the Jewish congregation of Berlin actually sent a personal petition to Hitler stating, "In this hour, we once again declare our bond with the German people, whose renewal and elevation is our most sacred duty, our right, and our deepest desire."

Without a doubt, such statements expressed the feelings of a majority of German Jews who could not understand why they were being excluded as "alien elements." These assimilated and liberal Jews, who vocally distanced themselves from the Orthodox eastern European Jews and who were highly skeptical of Zionist demands to create and emigrate to a Jewish state in Palestine, believed that they had gained a legal foundation by virtue of the fact that many of them had already lived and worked in Germany for many generations and had even gone to war for their country. They saw themselves as Germans first and only then—if at all—as members of the Jewish people or of the Jewish religious community. They were proud that Jews had achieved great things for their fatherland as entrepreneurs, scientists, artists, physicians, lawyers, and teachers, among many other professions.

Because they felt emancipated and equal within the state and the society, they systematically combated all symptoms of a new anti-Semitism. The CV was founded already in 1893. It rejected the idea of a distinct Jewish nationality and increasingly transformed itself into a lobby for the liberal Jewish majority. Just how powerful this nationalist fervor was among many Jews, and how little these people differed from other German nationalists, became apparent in two organizations that arose following World War I, namely the RJF, founded in 1919, and the Verband Nationaldeutscher Juden (Association of German Nationalist Jews). This latter group was founded in 1921 as an offshoot of the CV, which even sought to cooperate with the political right. Like other Germans, Jews joined fire brigades and political parties, chess clubs and sports associations. As politicians, they rose to the highest positions and assumed nationwide responsibilities. One proof of how firmly Jews were integrated in Germany was the fact that the number of "mixed marriages" between Jews and non-Jews was on the rise. Many of the approximately 37,000 Jews who fled abroad immediately after the Nazi seizure of power or following the first Jewish boycott on April 1, 1933 returned after the situation had quieted down.

In any case, scarcely any of the Jews living in Germany could imagine that soon they would have to abandon overnight everything they had built up with such effort and hard work, that they would have to leave their homes and struggle to make a fresh start in a foreign country. For this reason too, the numbers of emigrants declined again after 1934. In that year 23,000 left and only 21,000 in 1935. By mid-1938 only about 140,000 German Jews had emigrated.

But in reality, the process that would soon transform Jews into "strangers in their own country" had already begun in 1933. In retrospect, the speaker of the German Jews at that time, Rabbi Leo Baeck, called this process a "martyrdom in life" that preceded the "martyrdom in death." After the Reich Pogrom Night in 1938, this first phase of a new persecution of the Jews in Germany moved smoothly into the second phase of the extermination of German Jewry. Anti-Jewish policies in the first years of Nazi rule were to some extent still unsystematic, selective, arbitrary, regionally varied, marked by chance, and fraught with contradictions, so that many Jews embraced the illusion that their situation was not entirely hopeless after all. During the first boycott measures against Jews, former front soldiers believed that they could appeal to reason by wearing their war medals. Repeated announcements by Nazi functionaries that the anti-Jewish laws had come to an end nourished such illusions. But this was pure wishful thinking. Within just a few years, the Nazis' "separation" of the Jews from the non-Jewish population was practically complete.

In order to achieve this, the state's legislative and administrative machinery was kept running at full tilt. As early as 1933 a total of 319 laws, directives, and proclamations were issued against the Jews. These included such regulations as the "Law for the Restoration of the Professional Civil Service," the expulsion of Jewish students and disbarments from various professions, the first laws banning Jews from public beaches and swimming pools, and the ban on spelling out Jewish names on telegrams. In their eagerness to anticipate the new regime's wishes, and in the subservient tradition of their forebears, non-Jews complemented government-sponsored measures with anti-Jewish activities in nongovernment spheres as well. Thus as early as April 1933 Jews were excluded from the matches of the German Boxing Association, and in July of the same year they were banned from the Greater German Chess Association. In 1934 the government issued 177 additional laws, directives and proclamations. By the time of the Nuremberg Laws of September 15, 1935—which among other things stipulated that Jews were no longer "Reich citizens" and thus no longer possessed any rights, and which banned mixed marriages—a further 140 were added. This trend continued until 1938, ultimately leading to such absurdities as the November 1938 ban on Jews' possessing homing pigeons.

In the economic and social sphere as well, the years 1933 to 1938 saw the development of a policy of excluding and displacing Jews. By the time of the Reich Pogrom Night, the destruction of the Jewish economy and numerous livelihoods had gone so far that now only "remnants" were left. As soon as April 6, 1933, the *Jüdische Rundschau* wrote, "Tens of thousands of us have been forced out of our livelihoods and our professions, and many independent businesses have been uprooted." On April 20 of the same year, the newspaper wrote: "The distress of dismissed Jewish employees, workers, and craftsmen is immense." In the private economy as well, more and more Jewish employees were fired, and Jewish companies themselves were put under increasing pressure. According to official statistics, in July 1938 only 9,000 of the 50,000 Jewish retail businesses that had existed in 1932 were still in Jewish hands. Out of approximately 8,000 Jewish physicians, only 3,000 were still practicing their profession, and only 1,750 out of 4,500 Jewish lawyers. According to a different set of statistics, in April 1938 more than 60 percent of all Jewish businesses no longer existed after having been "Aryanized" or liquidated altogether. For most Jewish congregations, this development was impossible to bear. Already in 1936, one out of five Jews was considered to be indigent. The greatest suffering could only be eased by donations, which other Jews in these troubled times were ill able to afford.

Many Jewish Germans were particularly embittered that the government's and Nazi Party's exclusionary and isolating tactics became increasingly noticeable in daily life. Non-Jewish friends and acquaintances faded away: old neighbors eventually stopped saying hello. Jews were asked to resign from clubs and associations or their membership was simply terminated, a step that longtime members only learned of in an impersonal form letter—if anyone bothered to inform them at all. In public, the Jews—to the extent that they were recognized as such—were exposed to insults and abuse. They were occasionally beat up. They usually waited in vain for assistance or even moral support from non-Jewish Germans. Even their children were affected: friendships collapsed when "Aryan" parents forbade their sons and daughters to associate with "Jewish brats." Jewish children were often beat up and were submitted to constant discrimination and insults from their teachers and fellow pupils.

German Jews were also increasingly excluded from cultural life between 1933 and 1938. Jewish artists were no longer permitted to work, and Jews chose to avoid attending cultural events, to the extent that they were not prohibited from doing so in the first place. In reaction to all of this, the first Jewish cultural association developed in Berlin around 1933, followed by numerous other such organizations in other German towns. They joined together in the Reichsverband der Jüdischen Kulturbünde [Reich Association of Jewish Culture Leagues] in 1935, which safeguarded the livelihood of some 2,500 Jewish artists by sponsoring numerous concerts, opera and theater performances, readings, and lectures until its dissolution in September of 1941. If nothing else, it provided many Jewish Germans with a feeling of security, consolation, common experience, and cultural gratification in a difficult period. It provided them with relaxation and restored a fragment of their human dignity. To be sure, the National Socialists restricted the activities of the culture leagues by banning some authors and composers and censoring the rest. And yet, even under this pressure the culture leagues became centers of intellectual resistance and a new Jewish self-awareness.

Without friends and allies at home and without effective support from abroad, Jews closed ranks, developed their own self-help networks, and often discovered a new Jewish identity as they were forced to face their Jewishness. Back on April 4, 1933, the editor-in-chief of the *Jüdische Zeitung*, Robert Weltsch, discussed the first anti-Jewish boycott three days earlier with its shop windows smeared with yellow paint, and proclaimed the slogan: "The yellow star—wear it with pride!" Under such outside pressure, a central Jewish umbrella organization was founded after internal conflicts had prevented this step beforehand. On September 17, 1933, the Reichsvertretung der Deutschen Juden [Reich Agency of German Jews] was formed. In 1935 it was forced to change its name to Reichsvertretung der Juden in Deutschland [Reich Agency of Jews in Germany], and it was replaced by the Reichsvereinigung der Juden in Deutschland [Reich Association of Jews in Germany] in 1939. This representative Jewish central authority, which encompassed almost all branches of German Jewry, became the mouthpiece of the Jews. It was also the opposite number in negotiations with government and Nazi Party agencies. At the same time, it organized a network of Jewish self-help facilities, including a Jewish business promotion center, a Jewish job exchange, and retraining and educational programs. In addition, at great financial sacrifice, it helped oversee the creation of a Jewish welfare and school system.

And yet the final result of all these efforts was a dream world where Jewish Germans sought to lead an at least partially normal life. But this had long since ceased being an option for them, as became dramatically visible in November 1938, when the Reich Pogrom Night introduced phase two of the extermination of German Jewry.

Part 1

Boycott: Don't Buy from Jews!

Many of the "old fighters" had hoped that the Nazi regime would strike at the Jews immediately after seizing power. They could hardly wait to eliminate their Jewish competitors, thereby enriching themselves with a minimum of exertion. In some areas, the Storm Troopers organized their own boycotts against Jewish shops. The regime chose April 1, 1933, as the start of the "Defensive reaction of the German people against the Jewish enemies of the people." This boycott was the first official large-scale anti-Jewish operation. The Nazis used it to show their impatient followers that they were still serious about the anti-Jewish slogans contained in the program of the NSDAP (National Socialist German Worker's Party).

The regime justified the boycott by pointing to an alleged "atrocities campaign against the New Germany." The action was decided on at the end of March and was set to begin throughout the Reich on April 1, a Saturday, at 10:00 A.M. At the appointed hour, Storm Troopers marched into the streets and demonstratively took up positions in front of German shops, department stores, doctors' offices, and lawyer's practices. Their posters bore such slogans as "Don't buy from Jews!" Customers, clients, and patients were intimidated from entering and insulted if they ignored the Storm Troopers and went in anyway. But there were still non-Jewish Germans who did not let themselves be bullied and defiantly shopped in Jewish shops. Some of them came through the back door, while others asked for extra large packages to show everyone that they had "bought from Jews." However, many Germans were in basic agreement with the boycott and with the new regime's efforts to exclude Jews from economic life. Finally the Nazis were following their anti-Semitic propaganda with deeds that "ethnic Germans" could join in on.

But they were not satisfied with a mere boycott. Jewish employees were fired in increasing numbers. Jews still tried to resist and some labor courts declared such summary dismissals null and void. Nevertheless, Jewish apprentices had scarcely any chance of finding non-Jewish masters to learn under, Jewish tradesmen were forced from their accustomed market stalls, and many small business owners panicked and gave up.

The boycott was tacitly ended one day later. The regime was still concerned with foreign opinion and did not wish to endanger the economic recovery. But other boycotts and repressive measures, less strident and less visible but all the more effective, soon followed. On April 7, 1933, the "Law for the Restoration of the Professional Civil Service" went into effect. According to this measure, all civil servants of "non-Aryan descent" were to be dismissed. For the first time since the emancipation of the Jews in Germany a new special statute was created for Jews, whose discrimination was now sanctioned by law. Jewish front soldiers and civil servants who had already been in office on August 1, 1914, or whose fathers or sons had fallen in World War I, were excluded from this measure until 1935.

The repercussions were felt far beyond the civil service. They also affected workers and employees in the public service sector and became the guideline for private employers, institutions of all kinds, and even clubs and associations. Some seventeen thousand Jews left Germany following the first boycott. But the majority were convinced that this horrific episode would soon pass and that it was just an anti-Semitic wave, one of many in German Jewish history. With this hope in mind, many of those who had fled returned to Germany after things settled down somewhat in the summer of 1933.

1

"We Stood in the Trenches for Them"

EDWIN LANDAU

On early Friday morning we looked out and saw the Storm Troopers marching through the street with their banners: "The Jews are our misfortune!" "Down with Jewish atrocity propaganda abroad!" Soon after, the Nazi guards began taking up positions in front of Jewish shops and businesses, urging each and every shopper not to buy from Jews. Two young Nazis stationed themselves outside of our establishment and prevented the customers from entering. I couldn't believe my eyes. I simply could not imagine that something like this was possible in the twentieth century. Things like this had only happened in the Middle Ages, if even then. And yet it was the bitter truth that two boys in brown shirts were standing outside our door, enforcers of Hitler's will.

And we young Jews had once stood in the trenches for this people in the cold and rain and spilled our blood to defend our nation from its enemies. Were no comrades left from this time who were disgusted by this behavior? We saw them pass by on the street, including many whom we had done many a good turn in the past. They now wore smiles on their faces and could scarcely conceal their satisfaction. Once people used to say, "Am deutschen Wesen wird die Welt genesen" [Germanness will heal the world], but what we were looking at now was Satanism—and it was only the beginning. I gathered my war medals and pinned them on, then I went into the street and visited Jewish shops, where I was also stopped. But I was seething inside; I wanted to scream my hatred into the faces of these barbarians. Hatred, hatred—when had this emotion first taken hold of me? A change had come across me in just the last few hours. This land and this people, which I had always loved and appreciated, had suddenly become my enemy. I was no longer a German, or at least I wasn't supposed to be one. Of course, it takes more than a few hours for that to happen. But all of a sudden I realized: I was ashamed that I had once been part of this people. I was ashamed of the trust I had placed in so many people who had now revealed themselves to be my enemies. Suddenly even the street seemed strange to me. In fact, the entire city was strange. There are no words to describe the sensations I felt in these hours. After returning to my shop, I went to one of the guards, whom I knew and who knew me, and I said to him, "Back when you were still wearing diapers I had already fought for my country." He replied, "Don't blame me for my youth, Herr . . . , but I have my orders." I looked into his young face and thought, He's right.—Poor misguided youth.

Despite all this, on the same day a number of customers, particularly Catholics, came to me, and there were also some who only visited me because of the turmoil outside. Even the district officer came just to shake my hand, as he put it. When I thanked him and said that he should not place his position in jeopardy on my account and that he should think of his family, he said proudly, "I am party member number twenty of the German National People's Party, so what could ever happen to me?" The poor idealist—he would soon find out that even this party, too, would soon count for nothing. But I thanked him from the bottom of my heart, because I was hurting inside. In the afternoon, two Jewish estate owners were arrested and the Catholic district officer was dismissed. I ran into the street and went to my Jewish schoolmate, who had a five-and-ten shop next door, and we walked up and down the street. At the door to his shop I asked him what he would do if the Storm Troopers stood in front of his door the next day. He answered me, holding his cigar in one corner of his mouth: "I will shut it down." I went back and the new guard would not let me in. I raised a ruckus, saying that he had no right to prevent me from entering my own business, whereupon some Storm Troopers came and asked the fifteen-year-old Hitler Youth why the Jew was raising such a ruckus. I then went into my shop without any trouble, and my wife closed it immediately. The staff looked at me sadly and asked whether they should come the next day. I said no. My people went away, and I felt broken inside. I just didn't care anymore.

At the flat my wife prepared for the Sabbath. I went to the synagogue like many other Jews. There I saw desperate faces filled with profound spiritual pain—pale, shaking. Never before did Jews pray with such fervor as on that evening. They all experience their Jewishness in the most fundamental way. My heart shook, too, and my soul cried secretly to its God: "My God, my God, wherefore hast thou forsaken me?" Christ himself, wracked with pain, had once sobbed these words on the cross. We, too, were being nailed to the twisted cross of the Nazis. The prayer gave me little consolation and I went home to my wife and our children just as shaken as I had left them. And as I began to celebrate the Sabbath in the circle of my family, just as I had always done, and came to the line in the prayer where it says, "Thou, who hast chosen us from among all peoples," and my children, who were looking at me with their innocent and questioning eyes, saw that I was losing my grip, the whole heaviness of this day discharged itself at once, and I could barely stammer out the last words. The children did not know or understand why I cried so loudly, but I knew that it was because I was taking leave of my Germanness; it was my inner separation from my former fatherland, a funeral. I buried forty-three years of my life. And even if this had been the only day when I experienced such things, from that day forward I would be a German no more.

And what was I now? Although I was a religious Jew, I was very assimilated. Now I was homeless. Hordes of Nazis marched through the town that night and rioted. On the next day, Saturday, they started searching the houses of Jews and Social Democrats. The brown mobs also visited the homes of many Jewish friends. The guards stood watch again. I couldn't look at it, I was at the end of my rope. That evening, some Jewish friends and I were sitting together, and suddenly one of them asked how long Hitler was going to govern, whereupon my friend, the owner of the five-and-ten store, said "ten years." The others protested and said three months or a year. We believed that the outside world could not tolerate such barbarism in the twentieth century. Where was England, where was America? What had happened to Christianity? John Simon delivered some protest speeches, but that's all there was and Israel remained entirely alone. Was God on its side?

What did the future hold in store? Things quieted down over the following days, and we began to come to our senses. I registered myself as the new chairman of the Jewish congregation at the district office. So many Jewish citizens had come to me, saying that I was the only one who could do something. That's why I went to the commissioner and was shown in immediately. He told me I should calm the other Jews down. The operation was now over, he said, and was only meant as a punishment for the propaganda of the Jews in other countries. I told this to my fellow sufferers and this gave them courage. But I had lost all confidence, and although I acted bravely and strong toward others, inside I felt frightened and alone. I visited the graves of my parents, grandparents, and great-grandparents and talked to them. I gave them back everything that I had absorbed and cultivated in the way of Germanness over the past three generations. I shouted to them in their graves, "You were mistaken, I, too, was misled, but now I understand that I am no longer a German. And what will my children be?" No answer came. The gravestones remained silent. Nor could my old teacher answer from the grave.

My other teacher, the popular principal at the girls' gymnasium, who was greatly esteemed by the teachers and pupils as well as by their parents, soon learned the truth. During the morning hours, in the middle of lessons, Storm Troopers appeared and started yelling at him in front of the pupils. "Clear out of here right now, Jew. You have no right to teach German children." He froze, and many of the girls began to scream and called out his name. But he said to them: "Dear children, I have taught culture for fifteen years. Now I am leaving you because the authorities demand it. Farewell." So he left, and his colleagues did not give him a parting glance. That was the gratitude he received for his self-sacrificing work. But he experienced one small joy. In the afternoon, some of his pupils appeared in his flat with flowers and other small gifts. This was the protest of a still unspoiled and uninfluenced youth.

On the following Wednesday my friend H., with whom I had spoken on Friday in front of his shop, was arrested. I was shocked. What had happened? I went to the first chairman of the Jewish Front League in order to find out how to free him. I went to the police commissioner, who was extremely decent to me, but he could not tell me why my friend H. had been arrested, saying that the police were now frequently helpless. The commissioner told me I should go to the district officer, because he had the power. I hurried there, but he had just departed for Berlin. His assistant was an official of my acquaintance, a friend of the office director with whom I had spoken. I was on my feet all day. That afternoon the commissioner called me on the telephone and said that I had to come to the police station to be interrogated. I hurried to him. He told me that my friend had been reported to the police because he had been overheard saying to me that he would shoot down the Storm Troopers the next day. A girl had heard it and told it to her grandfather, and he had reported it to the police. I replied that that was a lie and told them what had really happened. My friend had probably spoken somewhat unclearly because of the cigar in his mouth. But he had certainly said that he would *shut his shop down*. None of us could be such a fool as to threaten anyone with shooting. Then, after further deliberations, my friend was released that same evening.

The next day my shop was abruptly searched. Six men appeared, including a man from the Stahlhelm [a right-wing paramilitary organization]. He was very embarrassed and quietly asked me for forgiveness. He made a quick job of searching my office and the safe by himself and found nothing. Some of them searched through my ledgers and registry files. I gave them my revolver and the bullets and showed them my gun license. They called the commissioner to ask whether they should impound the weapon, which was denied. Then they went into the cellar and the flat. The piano and the violin case were opened. They found nothing and then left after seeing my black, white, and red banner in the attic.

On the following Saturday my friend C. was arrested. He had been a Social Democratic city councilman and, as the only Jew, had flown the black, red, and gold flag. Three or four Jews were arrested along with him and brought to the police station. A few Christian Social Democrats were there. They were well treated and were allowed to buy whatever they wanted. I busied myself getting my friends freed, filing petitions, and telephoning the main office of the Front League. But nothing helped. A few days later, a truck came and drove the whole group to a concentration camp. We waved good-bye. One of them did not return, and the others came back after three months.

In the meantime, the drop in business became noticeable. Customers stayed away. Some estimates were sent back because no one needed them at the moment. I also had to lay off some employees for lack of work.

2

Aryan "Justice" Against Jewish Firms

FRIEDRICH WEIL

On March 29, 1933, the members of the Retail Association in Frankfurt met in the hall of the "Gross-Frankfurt" restaurant to discuss ways of dealing with the impending boycott and its consequences for Aryan employees. The meeting had been duly applied for and approved by the police president. Soon after the meeting was opened, a troop of between twenty-five and thirty Storm Troopers showed up in their brown uniforms and announced that everyone there was under arrest. Under strict guard, the prisoners—nearly one hundred of the town's most distinguished citizens—were forced to march with their hands raised high down the middle of the main street to the police station and from there to prison.

I happened to witness this procession and I will never forget the sight. Without exception, the owners of the Jewish shops left their shops open on April 1, 1933. Some of the owners stood near the entrance, wearing their war medals. Although the Nazis had publicly declared the boycott to be "over for the time being" at twelve o'clock noon, the Party hooligans stayed on the street and attempted to harass, photograph, and beat up everyone who patronized the Jewish shops. Some of the arrested business people were released again after eight, fourteen, or thirty days.

People accused Jews from all strata of society of a violation or a crime, and in all businesses—and naturally also in all Jewish businesses—they set up so-called company cells with shop stewards who drew up Gestapo papers with some kind of punishable allegation against Jewish owners. These allegations varied: there was tax fraud, falsified weight listings in customs declarations and in purchases of consumer goods, particularly butter, substandard wages, income tax evasion, foreign currency violations, capital flight, punishable indiscretions against female employees, and so on. First, the business owners were arrested and brought to their knees both physically and spiritually during months of pretrial imprisonment. In the meantime, the newly founded National Socialist Judges' and

Lawyers' Association made sure that from now on "justice" would be served in Germany. The sole principle behind this was "Justice is whatever serves the Party."

I myself became a victim of this newly created judicial system. After three months of pretrial imprisonment, in which I was never once arraigned before a judge, I was sentenced to eleven months in prison and fined thirty thousand marks, plus an additional nine months in prison because of an alleged customs violation on December 15, 1924. The court chairman, State Court Director Messerschmidt, declared in his oral argument that the court had not sought the maximum sentence of twelve months because it could imagine even more blatant cases of such a violation and that for this reason the punishment would stay beneath the maximum sentence. However, the court had based its verdict on evidence provided by the customs authorities—even though not one of the thirty witnesses had confirmed the accusation. This evidence consisted of three protocols by the customs inspection office, which one of my former workers had signed there; for this he received thirty marks in "support" for his family. The customs inspectors confirmed this fact in the trial and the previously even-handed chairman responded to my attorney's objections by affirming that "this kind of evidence was legally recognized by the customs officials."

I would also like to cite some cases from my own close circle: Herr B., a Jew and banker, was sentenced to a year in prison because of a currency violation. He had failed to report a transfer of sixty Dutch guilders during regular business operations to the customs office within the required time period. His appeal to the Reich Court was successful: the Reich Court commuted his year in a penitentiary to a year in the local jail. The banker waited fourteen months for this decision without even one hour of it being taken into account against his sentence.

Herr St., a Jew, seventy years old. An Aryan customer owed him 2,300 marks for delivered goods. The debt was long overdue. St. warned the debtor personally that he should finally pay up. The customer laughed at him and said that he was now a member of the National Socialist Party and would never pay a Jew another penny. St. replied that there was no legal basis for such a refusal—it was July 1933—and that he would now be forced to hand the matter over to the courts. He did so and the customer was indeed forced to pay, but his Jewish creditor was arrested by the Gestapo on the very same day for allegedly saying, "This Hitler business won't last forever." St. was sentenced to ten months in prison in addition to his three months of pretrial incarceration.

A. Senior and Junior, father and son, Jewish cattle dealers from Hessen-Nassau, were charged and convicted to four and five years in prison, respectively. This was the case against them: fraud because of scrubbing their cattle before bringing them up to market, cutting their tail fur short, and polishing their horns. The Gestapo copied the customers' names from the business ledgers and worked on each and every one of these customers so they would tell the court that they felt cheated by their transactions with the accused. But not one of these customers stated under oath that he felt he had been deceived. Some stated that these cattle dealers had come to their farms for three and four generations and they had always had full confidence in them. The court dismissed these facts as irrelevant and punished the "fraudulent embellishment" of the cattle with the high prison sentences I have already mentioned.

The shoe wholesaler H., a Jew from the Rhineland Palatinate, was given five years in prison. He had also been charged with repeated fraud. The Gestapo ordered his house to be searched for supposedly hidden foreign currency. This search turned up nothing, but they discovered a customer list in his business ledgers. The court capriciously sent the Gestapo after each and every customer living in the Mosel Valley and in the Hunsrück region and made them sign affidavits where each customer confirmed that he felt deceived and cheated by the accused man's shoe deliveries, some of which dated back five or ten years.

The Jewish industrialist Fl., who owned an important chemical factory that produced special substances for tanning and dyeing leather, was arrested on the basis of a report by an employee who was an "old fighter" in the Nazi Party. First, they searched his home and business, even cutting open his mattresses, for alleged currency violations. After eight months the prosecution ran out of steam. During the investigation the employee filing the report was set up as a "commissar" in the firm in order to continue running the firm in the interest of the Aryan staff and workers. During Fl.'s imprisonment, the Party exerted enormous pressure to Aryanize the factory and eliminate its Jewish owner and rob him of his earned and inherited income and his factory too. When Fl. finally agreed to their demands, he was forced to leave Germany immediately.

A poor sixty-five-year-old Jew was given a six-month prison sentence for cruelty to animals. The facts of the case: As the caretaker of an old house, he had negligently locked his neighbor's cat inside, so that on the next day, a Sunday, the poor little creature could not receive its milk breakfast from its loving owner at the accustomed time. Then in 1938, because of this previous conviction, our "criminal" was given the opportunity to compare the Nazis' love of animals with their love of their fellow man in Buchenwald.

Throughout these years—1933 to 1935—the Party issued orders to classify as many Jews as possible as criminals in order to establish the necessary statistical basis to prove that Jews as a whole were criminals who were acting against the German people.

Part II

The First Victims: Doctors and Lawyers

Jewish doctors and lawyers were among the first victims of Nazi persecution. Anti-Semitic propagandists had already treated them with particular hatred in the past. After all, a proportionately large number of Jews worked in these professions. The census of June 1933 counted around 5,600 Jewish doctors and 3,030 Jewish lawyers. That corresponded to a share of 11 and 16 percent respectively, concentrated in Berlin and other large cities. A particularly virulent form of anti-Semitism had long been prevalent within both professions.

In March 1933 the Bund Nationalsozialistischer Juristen [League of National Socialist Lawyers] demanded that legal firms become "Jew-free." In Prussia and Bavaria—even before the first boycott measures of April 1— Jewish lawyers were prohibited from entering court buildings. Jewish lawyers and public prosecutors were strongly urged to take leaves of absence. Nazi squads occupied court buildings, hunting down and beating up Jewish lawyers. In Prussia, 60 percent of all Jewish lawyers lost their licenses on April 1. The so-called front soldiers, Jewish participants World War I, were temporarily allowed to continue working. But on September 27, all Jewish lawyers were disbarred. Only a few were allowed to continue working as "consultants" for Jewish clients alone. But the Jewish lawyers had long suffered from an attitude widespread among "Aryan" clients that a Jewish lawyer would only antagonize a German court.

Jewish doctors fared little better. Hospitals and other public health facilities dismissed their Jewish staff, even before the April boycott and the civil service law. In Munich, for instance, the slogan "Jews may treat only Jews" prevailed. On April 24, 1933, Jewish doctors were dropped from the public insurance system, ruining countless careers. The large private insurance companies soon followed suit, and the exclusive companies paid only for non-Jewish patients. In the summer of 1933 professional cooperation with non-Jewish doctors was forbidden. That is, it became impossible for Jewish and "Aryan" doctors to stand in for one another or to exchange patients. The Jewish doctors also lost their role as experts and advisors, and were no longer allowed to take part in professional training schemes. By the middle of 1933 nearly half of all Jewish doctors had abandoned their profession. Many emigrated, while others attempted to survive as masseurs, nurses, and midwives.

Those who still managed to practice were driven to ruin in other ways. Their non-Jewish patients abandoned them one by one. Some remained loyal for a time and came, if necessary, under cover of darkness. But the pressure placed on these patients grew stronger every day. They were threatened with dismissal from their jobs, insulted, and denounced. But there were also patients who attempted to exploit the doctors' situation by employing blackmail and false accusations. On September 30, 1938, all Jewish doctors in Germany lost their license to practice. After that, only a few hundred were allowed to care for an exclusively Jewish clientele as "patient caretakers."

But it was not the material hardships alone that drove lawyers and doctors to despair. The boycott, the disbarring, the discrimination and humiliation struck at a bourgeois class that had previously enjoyed high social status and had been particularly devoted to the idea of integration and assimilation.

3

Devoted Patients—Opportunistic Colleagues

Henriette Necheles-Magnus

Arriving at my practice that morning, I already saw from a distance two sturdy Storm Troopers standing guard at the entrance. Above the door hung a large poster: a black background with a bright yellow spot in the middle. I went through the back door into the consulting room and sat down at my desk. First I had to console my weeping receptionist. She said, "We are so ashamed of our fellow countrymen!" Her husband was a shipyard worker. Across the way was a small egg shop that was run by a Jewess. Her husband had fallen in the war [World War I]. The two "guardian angels" stood in front of her door, too.

My consultation hours began at nine o'clock. At 9:10 the first patient came in, upset, seething because they tried to prevent her from going to her doctor! "Have we gone back to the days of Nero?" At 9:20 there was noise at the door: "We want to see our doctor!" Storm Trooper: "She isn't there, she's made herself scarce!" Then my girl went to the door: "Frau Doktor is here, but you are not authorized to disrupt the consultation. You are only there to show people that she's a Jewish doctor."

And so it went. The patients came and came with flowers, with small gifts: "We want to show you what we think about this policy." "I'm not sick, Doctor, I just came to see how you are doing." I've still got a small piece of stitching, the "boycott quilt," here in my room. A patient crocheted it in those days to demonstrate her affection.

In the afternoon it started raining. Our protectors became surly and started stamping around outside the door. The patients started laughing and suggested that they go to the bar and play whist. Fortunately, it ended without a fight, because some of my patients outside in the waiting room were real "toughs."

My neighbor on the other side of the street had the same experience. She said she never sold as many eggs as on that day. The poor people had only enough money for one egg, and yet they wanted to demonstrate their solidarity. It didn't go this smoothly everywhere. The owner of a clothing shop in our street attempted to stop the Storm Troopers from blocking the entrance, because the regulations stated that the guards should only stand there as a warning. He picked a fight with the guards and naturally lost. There were no deaths in our little town. All in all, the boycott was unpopular and was ended after one day, since the population had not yet become accustomed to such spectacles. My pretty yellow spot was removed by an insulted neighbor. He secretly scratched it off overnight ("Poor Frau Doktor!").

On June 1 I said farewell to my practice. I felt like I was burying a beloved relative. Only the thought that I would soon give birth to a child kept me going. Each new patient who came, and there were many, reopened the wound. It was like the start of a funeral. The people—shocked and intimidated—did not know where to go. No one told them how they would continue their treatment. The insurance administration did not care about newly opened cases. It was pure politics and they couldn't wait to demonstrate how quickly they could shift gears from Social Democracy to National Socialism.

It was fascinating to observe how my colleagues reacted. In general, the older ones had seen so many governments come and go that they did not take the new regime very seriously. The Social Democrats had been extraordinarily unpopular within academic circles since they suppressed dueling and other student ideals and condemned militarism. So most of them thought they could tame Hitler. The chairman of our physicians' association, who had formally been a devoted monarchist, pledged himself to National Socialism and continued as head of the physicians' association in Wandsbek. But, predictably enough, his lukewarm attitude was soon noticed and he was thrown out in disgrace. The director of our hospital, an opportunist to the core—he would have shouted "Heil Moscow" with the same enthusiasm as "Heil Hitler"—enthusiastically did everything demanded of him and pitied me in private. A third doctor, the former first chairman of the German Democratic Party, who was excited by everything new, whether it was raw vegetable diets, Cubism, or National Socialism, was an instant convert and in the next parade he marched through the streets for hours. But these were only the new converts, opportunists who were viewed with suspicion by the old fighters.

Fourteen days after I gave up my practice Doctor K. appeared and rented my rooms. The first thing he did was to remove and destroy the sign indicating my new address. In Germany a departing physician was allowed to keep his sign with his new address on it at his previous residence for half a year. I had been offering private consultations together with my husband since losing my license to treat state-insured and welfare patients. Doctor K. commented that "the Jewish woman" did not need a sign on her door. When one of my patients asked where I was, he replied, "She's killed herself."

So there he sat and waited for my patients to arrive. A few hesitant souls appeared, and he basically examined their political views. One patient, as he told me beamingly later on, told my successor, "Doctor, I'm here because of my illness, not because of my political views," and disappeared. That is how it went for many, and after a short time my dear colleague had to close the practice. After this experience, no one else wanted to risk his neck, so the landlord called me up to ask if I would start over again without my insurance license. The patients would come to me privately. But I did not want to leave my small child alone and neglect my new responsibilities. Before Doctor K. withdrew, he told everyone who would listen that the lady doctor owed her success to unethical behavior. My patients' reaction was to come to me—I lived at the other end of town—and give witness: "We won't let you be insulted by such a lout!" I knew more about the power of a Nazi leader and about the prevailing sense of justice, and I simply thanked them for their devotion.

Shortly before this, I won an injunction letting me put my sign back up immediately and sentencing Doctor K. to a considerable fine. He had to pay the fine, because it was a court fine. But he sent me a threatening letter by way of the Gauleiter of the physicians' association, which prevented me from undertaking any further action. It is scarcely worth mentioning that after the failure of his own practice, Doctor K. became a military doctor, the head of the Red Cross and the independent examining doctor for the insurance company, that is to say, he was placed in charge of supervising his colleagues' work and thus no longer had to worry about earning his patients' affection.

In the meantime, I had rebuilt my life and replaced my husband in the consultations. Some of my old patients found their way to me. My husband fought to maintain his license as a physician in the insurance system. During the war he had been a doctor in a military hospital that, unfortunately, had not been located at the front. He had treated patients suffering from infections, but apparently not enough of them to replace a frontline field hospital.

They tried to interpret the front soldier law in such a narrow way as to exclude as many Jewish doctors as possible. When my husband left town for a few days on business, a rumor began circulating that he had killed himself. One patient came and asked me if he could arrange the funeral. How horrified he was when I went into the room and fetched my husband, who had just returned, to explain the matter in person. Of course, our attempts to continue working as doctors within the insurance system failed since people were afraid of the influence the Jewish insurance doctor had on his patients. But even so, many old patients continued to come at their own expense, since trust in one's physician cannot be decreed by the government.

4

Patients as Extortionists

Arthur Samuel

In 1928 the morphine-addicted, epileptic merchant Ludwig S. came to my office. He owned a rubber stamp company. For years he had been treated by university professors in polyclinics and by other doctors in Bonn. Since there was no law back then making it possible to lock up a morphine addict in an institution against his will, all attempts to break him of his habit were doomed to fail. One day, after a new injection was discovered, I decided to break him of his habit without his knowledge and without his consent. The new medication was called Pernokton. With the help of this substance I could put him into an instant state of semi-unconsciousness. Only now did the family consent to committing him to an institution. He soon broke his addiction. In order to ensure the success of the treatment, the doctor in charge kept him in the institution for several weeks. During this time he went to the district physician, showed him a box with a collection of empty morphine bottles, and demanded that I be reported to the public prosecutor for bodily injury through culpable negligence. I had made him into a morphine addict, he said. I had enriched myself at his expense and I had reduced him to beggary.

Before the court granted the plaintiff's request to initiate a civil suit against me, it demanded a legal opinion from the neurologist Prof. de Crinis of Cologne. De Crinis, a successor to the famous Jewish professor Aschaffenburg from Cologne, was a National Socialist. Prof. de Crinis prepared a thirty-page report and came to the conclusion that I had acted entirely correctly and that my accuser's claims were baseless. He was a pathological person, he wrote, and should not be taken seriously. This opinion is naturally in my file. But then something unprecedented occurred! The plaintiff introduced a private opinion, and this private opinion was by Prof. Poppelreuther. He demonstrated that the poor plaintiff was a victim of the Jews. The doctor, the lawyer and the experts were Jews. While some of the experts and some of the judges were Aryans, he said, they could not keep free of the Jewish influence. The thing that gave these events the imprint of their time was the fact that Prof. de Crinis from the University of Cologne declared his report, which he had just substantiated, to be null and void and signed on to Prof. Poppelreuther's report. Now all further efforts were in vain. Endless grueling deliberations ensued. The result: the Nazi morphine addict prevailed over the respectable Jewish doctor.

Another case: An Aryan patient, the daughter of a well-known innkeeper whose establishment the Nazis used for their meetings, poisoned herself with Veronal. The poisoning was deadly. For three days the patient lay in a deep coma. All my efforts to save the young woman were in vain. My first question, when I was called, concerned the origin of the poison. I knew the patient's heavy-blooded nature and I had avoided prescribing narcotics for her. Then, in his excitement, her brother-in-law spilled the whole story. The young woman knew an Aryan assistant in the psychiatric hospital. This man, a National Socialist who frequented the inn, brought her a large package of Veronal tablets.

It was up to me to draw up the usual death certificate. Cause of death: Veronal poisoning. The family tried hard to persuade me to record a different cause of death because they feared the legal consequences for themselves and they thought their establishment's reputation was at risk. Two days later I was summoned to the police station. What was it about? I don't have to emphasize how such summons to the police affected us Jews, since we never knew why an order was issued. I went to the police, they put me into a car, and I was driven immediately to the court building, where an old assistant physician working with the forensic specialist interrogated me like a criminal. I filled out a large questionnaire. Then the interrogating colleague "turned to the case at hand." "You treated Frau I." I affirmed this. "How did the woman get hold of the Veronal, a whole clinic package, which we discovered on the scene? There's no point in trying to cover up the truth; we can figure out by the serial number if you gave it to her or not." I responded curtly that he should not waste his time trying to make me responsible. Then he said, "We will consider you guilty until you can prove to us the contrary." "All right then," I said, "now I am forced to abandon all my professional courtesy. I do not like to inform on others." Then he said, "Tender considerations are now no longer needed." I told him what I knew about its origin, that the assistant physician at the psychiatric hospital, K.L., had provided her with the Veronal. I had to wait. Cars raced off and soon brought back the assistant and the dead woman's relatives. They confirmed my statements. I was released. I would have been lost if I had not known the source. I would have been accused of culpable negligence in the death of an Aryan.

Another case: I diagnosed a society woman with abdominal cancer. On my insistence, the woman underwent a radical operation by a gynecologist and was cured. She was grateful and said I had saved her life, particularly because I had insisted on the removal of the entire uterus against the opinion of the operating physician—an operation that the gynecologist had at that time not considered necessary. The biopsy proved me right.

The lady could not be shaken in her trust. She continued to come to me despite the unfavorable times. Some time later I cured her from a painful neuralgia with an injection of Novocain. She was happy. But how horrified I was when the same lady, who had recently proclaimed me to be her savior, now showed up in my consultation room, in pain and close to fainting. She said literally, "Ah, Herr Doktor, don't be angry with me. But I can no longer sleep. People have told me such strange things. You took away my pain with the injection. But back then, since I had to watch out for my husband's position, I went to another doctor and he said to me: 'The Jew took away your pain, but don't you know that the Jews have substances which may take away your pain for a while but that the people all die within half a year?'" The patient looked at me in horror. "Tell me, dear Doctor, what did you inject into me? Tell me so that I can sleep again and please swear I won't die!" I explained the treatment to the stupid goose. I had to for my own protection. Then I showed her to the door and told her never to come back.

5

I Was No Longer Considered a Front Soldier

Karl Friedländer

Life among Berlin's law community was never the same after the executive board of the lawyers' chamber, bowing to pressure from the Nazi lawyers, resigned without further ado and without any resistance. On the basis of an emergency decree by the judicial authorities, a new board was chosen without an election. Aside from individual exceptions, it was made up entirely of Party members. This was only the beginning and further steps soon followed. On March 30, 1933, a raid was launched against Jewish lawyers in the Berlin courts. At precisely twelve noon, NSDAP members of one sort or another appeared in the court offices and demanded that the Jewish lawyers leave the court building immediately. The demand was largely obeyed. In individual cases there were very unpleasant physical altercations.

I was just working with an elderly judge in a hearing when two Party members burst in and loudly asked if any Jewish lawyers were present in the room. In my place, the judge affirmed the question, adding that by virtue of his power and authority as a judge he would not allow the hearing to be disrupted. The lawyers would leave the room after the hearing was over, but by virtue of his authority as a judge he demanded that the rowdies leave at once to prevent any further interruption and disruption. The two young men then left the room. A few minutes later the hearing ended and I wanted to return to the lawyers' chamber to hang up my robe and go home. In one of the corridors I met a court usher whom I had known for more than twenty years. This old man had been informed about the events that had been unfolding in the court building since noon and was very upset. He could not imagine that a political party would ever dare to infringe upon and disrupt Justitia's holy trinity: inviolability, peace, and order. Worried, he shook his gray head and told me I should follow him on a special route through the corridors to the lawyers' chamber. He said he would use his keys to open any locked doors. He only hoped I wouldn't encounter the young rioters. He actually accompanied me all the way to the lawyers' chamber, and when I went in my Aryan colleagues were surprised that I was still there as all our other Jewish colleagues had already been forced to leave the building. Immediately, several colleagues came to me and offered safe passage, so to speak, so that I could leave the building unmolested. I resisted and said that if it was my fate to be molested, well, then these young people should do what they thought was right.

I left the lawyers' chamber and headed toward the exit. I noticed that one of the older colleagues, who was a member of the Party, actually went a few steps in front of me and whispered something to his Party comrades. What it was I cannot say. I only know that the gang of young Party followers who had assembled in the corridor parted in the middle, forming a passageway through which I passed, genuinely unmolested, toward the exit. Thus I can say that on March 30, 1933, I was the last Jewish lawyer to leave the court building on Grünerstrasse.

We Jewish lawyers did not know what would happen in the coming days. A commission made up of around ten Jewish colleagues formed immediately, and it made contact with the other side, meaning the colleagues who belonged to the Party. The first thing we were told was that the Jewish lawyers should under no circumstances enter another court building. Party members kept guard at the entrances, and they would use force to prevent the Jewish lawyers from entering. When we replied that the Jewish lawyers had all kinds of appointments with their clients and serious consequences would ensue if they, the Jewish colleagues, did not appear, we were told that the NSDAP had already contacted the judicial authorities about this; they had arranged that the relevant parties would not be prejudiced by the absence of a Jewish lawyer. The new National Socialist board of the lawyers' chamber would select some twenty-five Jewish lawyers. They would be permitted to appear before the court until the licensing of Jewish lawyers had been regulated.

These persons received an identity card that allowed them to enter the court building. They were obliged to stand in for those Jewish lawyers who were forbidden to enter the court building and to see to their court responsibilities. Altogether, as I recall, twenty-six Jewish lawyers were selected. What was decisive in this selection was not the lawyer's age or reputation, but rather—and this was the primary and sole condition for provisional licensing—this stipulation: the Jewish lawyer must have served as a frontline soldier in World War I and possess as many military citations as possible. Since I did not fulfill this condition, I was not included among the chosen.

Then came April 1, 1933. The NSDAP had announced a boycott for this day. For us lawyers it meant that all offices belonging to our Jewish colleagues, as well as to colleagues who were considered Jews from the point of view of the NSDAP, should be made visibly recognizable as such.

According to the guidelines for lawyers, all lawyers had to post a nameplate at the entrance to the building in which their office was located. The NSDAP had intended that our signs should be covered up, namely with a sheet of white paper in the middle of which was to be a large yellow spot. With this yellow spot they sought to evoke the so-called yellow badge that the Jews were forced to wear in medieval Germany.

I left the central city on the morning of April 1 and was not far from my office when I saw the NSDAP squad covering my sign with the boycott poster. In the office my office manager informed me that a member of the squad had left orders that no one was authorized to damage or remove the boycott poster; it had been put up on the orders of the NSDAP, and only the NSDAP had the right to permit any changes. I thought it in no way shameful or dishonorable that I was labeled as a Jew, since I have never made a secret out of my Jewishness and my convictions. Thus the NSDAP's intention to embarrass and insult me by hanging up the poster failed entirely. Furthermore, the Party itself seemed to have realized the impracticality and absurdity of its measures, because already the next morning they announced the end of the boycott and simultaneously ordered that all boycott posters, meaning all the white posters with the yellow spot, should be removed immediately.

The Reich judicial administration was completely aware that the situation caused by the expulsion of the Jewish lawyers could not be maintained, that instead some sort of order had to be established in the interest of jurisprudence, particularly because in the meantime the Jewish and non-Aryan judges had also been removed from office. Then came the famous law on the Restoration of the Professional Civil Service of April 7, 1933. This title is not entirely comprehensible, since in reality the law made it possible to remove all Jews, or such persons who were classified as Jews according to their racial arithmetic, as well as all undesirable elements from office or whatever position they might hold. This law was also interpreted as applying to the Jewish lawyers and notaries. Since I was politically clean, or, as we had to say back then, since I was a "decent fellow," I could not be removed on account of political reasons. Thus I would have to fulfill the general conditions necessary to remain a lawyer and notary. These conditions were: one had to have been a front soldier in World War I or else have already been a lawyer or notary on August 1, 1914.

The law of April 7 specified World War I veterans, and this was first understood to mean everybody who had been called to military service in any way, shape, or form. But since they realized that this interpretation was too broad, a consensus soon emerged that veterans were only those soldiers who had in any way participated in field combat. The others were not considered veterans, even if they had been called to military service and performed service in enemy territory. They did not fulfill the condition of active participation in military action against soldiers of the enemy powers. I scarcely need to emphasize that this interpretation brought with it a great number of disputes and borderline cases, and thus an executive guideline ruled that in cases where the Reich judicial administration did not recognize one's status as a front soldier, then the plaintiff could appeal to the Reich War Ministry, which would have the last word in the matter.

I do not know in how many cases the Reich War Ministry was asked to make a decision. I only know that individual Jewish colleagues fought with enormous energy to have their front soldier status recognized and that the Ministry faithfully examined every case. The material was substantial, since the affected persons often brought pages of testimonies and confirmations by former superior officers and front soldiers. Some testimonies were so vivid that the secretary in the War Ministry gradually assembled an absolutely realistic documentation of the battles and their combatants.

I had no need to wait for a decision in this matter. I had in fact served in the war and was a soldier, but I never experienced enemy combat. There was thus no doubt that I would lose my position as a notary as I had neither been a notary on August 1, 1914, nor had I been a front soldier. On June 16, 1933 I received the so-called blue letter, that is, the *lettre de congé*, my certificate of dismissal. I didn't have to worry my head over my position in the legal profession. I was a so-called old lawyer, because I had already been admitted to the bar in 1910. And so at the same time, in June 1933, the National Socialist government certified that I would continue to be allowed to practice as a lawyer at the Berlin district court. From this moment on I could again enter the court building unhindered and appear before the court as a Jewish lawyer.

By now the atmosphere in the lawyers' chambers had changed. If the colleagues were not Party members but were Aryans, they demonstrated a pronounced friendliness to us Jewish colleagues. If the colleagues were Party members, then business was attended to in the usual way. Only one National Socialist lawyer failed to uphold the rules of professional courtesy. There was always friction and confrontation between us. By contrast, our dealings with the judges in the hearings were invariably correct, whether they wore a National Socialist Party badge under their robes or not. And the old judges, who had already known us for years, outdid each other in the affability they displayed. But practicing our profession was no longer the joy it once had been.

With painstaking conscientiousness, our clientele was placed under surveillance. This was barely perceptible in the first years after 1933, but later on this surveillance assumed unpleasant forms. For example, for years one of my clients was an official receiver. He was an Aryan. I had to conduct trials against around a dozen tenants for this official receiver.

Some of these cases had already been decided in the official receiver's favor. Just when I was in the midst of a further set of cases and was in the middle of a hearing, my receiver came into the court dripping with sweat and told me the following: "It's all over! It's all over! We can't continue. I have just been categorically informed by the authorities that I may no longer be your client because you are a Jew. Please cancel all further hearings today. I'll come to you personally and give you more of an explanation."

The receiver kept his promise, and what revelations did his further explanations provide? One of his fractious tenants had taken steps against the receiver because he had allowed himself to be represented by me, a Jew, and the receiver risked losing his position if he did not change this. That was the answer to the riddle, and that is why the receiver had to say farewell to me, his legal advisor of many years.

Although the loss of this client was of no serious material importance to me, the manner in which this relationship ended was characteristic enough to make me skeptical of the future. But I do not know the real reason why I disregarded this event and returned to business as usual. I am not exactly sure whether it was a sort of hesitation on my part to recognize reality with all its cruel consequences for a Jew, or whether it was my faith in Germany, in the order and future it represented, that kept me from pondering this further. The fact is that despite this bolt out of the blue in 1934, I remained in Berlin and continued to practice my profession. I was busy, perhaps even more than busy, and therefore I didn't take the time to ponder what the future held in store for me—not that I had any lack of opportunities to do so.

6

A Notaryship Is Revoked

SIEGFRIED NEUMANN

April 1, 1933, arrived, the day of the boycott and the day on which the Nazi Party cut the bonds linking itself to civilized humanity. However, this matter was sold to us as a measure to protect the Jews against an enraged populace. In a small town in Pomerania, where everyone knew everyone else, the boycott guards asked my wife's brother-in-law to serve them warm coffee "because they had to stand around outside so long in the cool weather."

When the newspapers wrote that the boycott was basically over, I drove back to my office. I had an appointment at the court and I kept it. I was surprised that everyone there stared at me in amazement. But no one said anything. I did not know that in the meantime—by administrative means—Jewish lawyers had been banned from entering the court building, thanks to the house rules of the justice authorities. Oblivious to this, I went to my appointment. Just as I was making objections to a witness for the opposition, the latter replied that he did not need to answer my questions. The judge emphatically stated that he himself would decide what the witness would answer or not answer. I then heard that the supervising judge had enquired from the director of the boycott committee and had received the answer that the local Nazi Party had no objections to my appearance before the court. So I kept my appointments over the next few days. Then one of the officials or colleagues—I suspect it was the latter—made a complaint to the district court. I was suddenly prohibited from entering the district court on the district court's instructions. Nevertheless, only one client, himself a Nazi, who had only come to me after Hitler's accession to power, came to me to retrieve his files. The others remained loyal. The trial lawyer was decent enough to discuss matters with me by telephone. For a time my colleagues covered for me, particularly the director of the boycott committee, who had worked for me as a clerk. Cases in which I was involved as an attorney were postponed.

At this time a directive from the Justice Ministry was disseminated through official channels calling for each non-Aryan notary to make a voluntary declaration that he would cease performing his services. Otherwise, we were told, there was no guarantee that the people's rage would not make it impossible for others to continue tolerating the distribution of official documents by Jewish notaries. Naturally, if I wanted to save myself from the concentration camp or worse, I would have to make the desired "voluntary" declaration. My emotional turmoil at that time cannot be expressed in words. In those days we were still working within a state under the rule of law, a state we had known since birth. And then the justice ministry, of all institutions, comes up with the idea of sending common extortion letters through official channels because they had not yet found a legal way to exclude their Jewish notaries.

As a volunteer who had gone to the front at age nineteen and who had fulfilled the greatest duty to the state—military service in time of war—my pain was intense. I sat down and wrote a registered letter to Hindenburg. In it I appealed to the feeling of comradeship in this old soldier, beneath whose flags I had stood on the Eastern Front. I was and remain convinced that he knew nothing of these extortion letters from the justice ministry. I took the letter to the post office immediately. When I came back and sat down at the table—we still lived with my mother-in-law—my wife and her mother became extremely upset. Did I want to ruin us all? I should go straight back to the post office and try to get the letter back before it was sent. At first I did not want to go. I could not imagine that anyone would intercept the Reich President's mail. Finally I gave in and retrieved the letter.

Now a series of struggles began. The first concerned my attempt to be readmitted to the court. At first I was told that the president of the lawyers' association would decide the matter. I asked the director of the boycott committee and the police captain for certificates stating that I had never engaged in Communist activities. I arranged for the police certificate to state that, on the contrary, I had been a member of the German Democratic Party and had occasionally chaired its meetings. I believed that this was the best way to counter the accusation of Communism. It turned out that this latter request was a mistake. Our supervisory judge, a German nationalist but not a Nazi, refused to draft this certificate, saying that he could not know something that never happened. Since we had seen a great deal of one another socially, this was my first personal disappointment. I then threw in some military documents and sent everything to the lawyer's association in Potsdam. But nothing happened. Then I was told that I had to prove that I had taken part in at least one battle.

The central registry office in Spandau, which prepared the corresponding documentation, could scarcely keep up with its duties. After all, the number of Jewish front soldiers was quite large, a fact that took only the Nazis by surprise. After all, that had been a time of universal military service. I gained the impression that the Nazis, who themselves had wanted to exempt the Jewish front soldiers from all special regulations, were so surprised by the large number that they would have preferred postponing their readmission indefinitely. Now that the law concerning the legal profession had been promulgated, clearly stipulating the status of the front soldiers and the conditions required for this status, the justice ministry tried to draw things out. The Reichsbund Jüdischer Frontsoldaten [The Reich League of Front Soldiers] supported our cause with feverish activity. Above all, Hindenburg had stood up for the Jewish front soldiers. It took extreme pressure from this side to force the justice ministry to abandon its delay tactics. A directive appeared that nullified the directive of such and such date. It was not explicitly stated that we would be allowed to appear before court again. I presented the supervisory judge with an affidavit concerning my front soldier status and referred to this directive. After a suspension of almost three months, I was once again allowed to practice at the district court.

During my first hearing, I was shocked that a colleague of mine who had once made fun of the Nazis now refused to hear the case with me, saying that I had no right to be there. I explained that it was not his decision, and if he did not wish to hear the case with me then I would sue for a judgment by default. He replied that I could call up the ministry for clarification. I refused, saying that there were no clear directives concerning this matter. After all, it was possible that the ministry would secretly attempt to revoke what it had been forced to concede publicly. My "colleague" ran angrily to the supervisory judge but soon returned. I later heard that the judge refused to pay any attention to newspaper articles; he only followed official decrees. The colleague now attempted to intimidate the trial judge, a young assessor. This judge allowed me to participate in one hearing and asked me to bring an authorization for my readmission within a week's time. All of this took place during a public hearing before the eyes of the public. No one stood up for my colleague, not even the other lawyers. One of my Christian colleagues later told me that clients of his who were present at the time found the colleague's behavior appalling. (The racial question had revealed itself to be a cash question.) A few days later my colleague stopped me as we were walking out of the courtroom. He asked me how my wife and children were doing. I said I was astonished that he first wanted to prevent me from practicing law in court, only to turn around and ask me about the well-being of my family. He replied that the situation was so crazy that people no longer knew what they were doing and I shouldn't take offense.

Finally, in June or July, a directive appeared according to which I would once again be allowed to practice my notaryship. Once again in possession of my lawyer's status and my notaryship, I believed that I could now face the future with few worries. Of course, I had to considerably reduce my staff of six employees. But in one respect I was at a great disadvantage. In those troubled times the poor law cases were critical, since the state paid a large proportion of the legal lawyers' fees, and often the entire fee had to be collected from one's opponent upon his defeat. There was apparently a secret decree stipulating that Jewish lawyers should no longer be hired to defend the poor. The official laws had nothing to say about this. Some courts, such as the superior district court in Marienwerder, obeyed the law and hired Jewish lawyers in accordance with the poor laws. I could not assert this right in our court, not even when my clients requested it. Another lawyer was appointed, even if I prepared the case and made the application of the poor law, which already assumed that the trial had a good chance of success, possible in the first place. Of course, in this way I lost a great many clients. Back then, a boycott was even less noticeable, particularly since I was now more successful than ever. The reason for this was that I could now spend more time on individual cases than had been possible previously with my wide-ranging activities. The—in my experience—unfounded observation that you cannot win a case with a Jewish lawyer only gained currency among the public later on. The best times had passed for the notaryship, since the Prussian ancestral estate law had been passed and new mortgages slowed to a trickle.

On September 30 the deadline for notaryships expired. I had felt safe up to now. Then on this day the following appeared in my office: the inspector general of the justice ministry and an usher from the local court with a locksmith in tow. I interrupted the discussion I had been having. The inspector general wore an expression on his face as if he were on his way to a funeral. Now I had known this old official for the past ten years. He presented me with a directive from the justice minister: "According to section 4 of the Professional Civil Service Law, I hereby dismiss you from the office of notary." The court usher or justice guard had come along to attend to the delivery; the locksmith was there in order to remove the stamping machine on the spot. I had to give him my stamps and notary registry. All notary files went to the local court for storage, the same procedure as when a notary died. Thus at the last minute fate caught up with me after all. No reasons were offered. I merely stayed calm and continued the disrupted conference with my client. I turned to the Reich League of Jewish Front Soldiers, of which I was a member, and was soon informed that of all the cases it had taken on, mine was the only one where an appeal had been allowed.

The procedure to regain my notaryship made no headway. I was always informed that some information or other was still lacking. In November 1934 I was informed that my petition had been finally rejected. I filed suit against the state, demanding a small sum in damages. In such suits against the state the Reich Court was the final authority, regardless of the amount of the sum in question. I based my suit on the fact that, as a front soldier, I was licensed and that section 4 did not apply to me. The state, as the defendant, refused to provide reasons, stating that the agency in question was not required to do so. There were cases in which the court could suspend the case in order to bring about a decision by the administrative authorities. In my case this regulation did not apply. Nevertheless, upon the defendant's request the Berlin district court suspended the case. The responsible administrative authority in this case was the police president of Berlin: retired Admiral von Levetzow. Old soldiers generally had a soft spot for the Jewish front soldiers. I assume that the position he took on my behalf was not unfavorable, because after a short time the defendant declared that, as I had already argued, the suspension of the suit was not permissible and requested that the suspension be halted. He limited his defense to stating that the authorities were not required to provide reasons for my dismissal. I lost. The defendant agreed that I could circumvent the court of appeal and take my case directly to the Reich Court. But no lawyer was willing to do so. Thus I had to ask the Reich Court to appoint a lawyer to prosecute my case. The Reich Court rejected my petition, since the appeal had no chance of success. That is how the matter ended.

Part III

Plundering and Ruined Livelihoods

Eliminating Jews from economic life always played a key role in anti-Semitic propaganda. Economic boycotts looked like the most effective means of forcing Jews to emigrate. At the same time, they allowed thousands of Nazis, important and unimportant, to enrich themselves by legal means. New research has shown that by 1937 the economic position of the Jews had already been seriously undermined and "Aryanization," that is, the transfer of Jewish property to non-Jewish owners, was well advanced. Thousands of Jews lived off public handouts, many from their savings.

In early 1933 there had been some one hundred thousand companies in Jewish hands throughout the German Reich. These included corner shops, department stores, one-man operations, and large-scale companies. By the spring of 1938, some 60 to 70 percent of these firms had either ceased to exist or had become "Aryan property." Of the more than 50,000 retail stores in early 1933, only 9,000 remained by July of 1938, including 3,637 in Berlin. At least half of all Jewish workers and employees were unemployed by early 1938. The economic historian Avraham Barkai has called what happened after the pogrom of November 9/10 the "final stage in a continuous process of liquidation and looting."

The National Socialist policy of expulsion and plunder affected a Jewish community that was already in economic freefall at the end of the Weimar Republic. Inflation and the Great Depression had impoverished vast sections of the middle class. Jewish employees were laid off more frequently than their non-Jewish colleagues since, on the one hand, many worked in the crisis-plagued garment industry and, on the other, they had already been the preferred target of the anti-Semitic employees' associations in the late 1920s. In Berlin, one out of four Jews was living on welfare in 1933.

The economic structure of the Jewish population had changed over the decades, but it was still lopsided. The Jews continued to concentrate in certain areas. In 1933, 61.3 percent earned a living from trade, 23.1 percent worked in industry and trades, and 12.3 percent worked in public services. Forty-six percent were self-employed, but many of them—particularly small shopkeepers, peddlers, traveling salesmen, and craftsmen—had nothing more to do, had no income, had to sell their property or else lived off their savings. The Jewish community was also aging and was concentrated in just a few large cities. About a third of them lived in Berlin. In the countryside the economic position was even more one-sided, since in some areas 90 percent of Jews worked in the livestock trade.

At the beginning of the Third Reich many Jews still believed the frequently cited statement by Reich economics minister Hjalmar Schacht that there was no Jewish question in economics. But that was an illusion. From the outset Jews were forced into a constant and desperate defensive struggle. Government orders evaporated, officials and employees of the public service sector were forbidden to buy from Jewish shops, other non-Jewish buyers gradually withdrew, welfare recipients were not allowed to use their food coupons in Jewish businesses, and local newspapers were forbidden to print advertisements from Jewish companies. Using threats, blackmail, and open violence, the Nazis finally crushed small and medium-sized companies. In their dealings with the large companies, however, the new regime at first took job security and foreign trade into account. They did not want to lose any foreign currency income.

It is remarkable how long some Jewish businesses continued operating under such conditions. Jewish livestock dealers, for instance, remained the farmers' preferred business partners for years. They paid their bills promptly, and that often had more impact than the pressure from the Party and the Reich Nutrition Estate. In addition, the rate of plundering and exclusion varied. Some people refer to the period between 1934 and 1938 as a "closed season." Avrahim Barkai, on the other hand, has noted that boycotts and looting were pushed forward relentlessly. The supposed "closed season" was in reality an "open season for the little Nazis."

Things were particularly bad for the unemployed. Many officials, lawyers, physicians, and managerial employees ended up as street peddlers, traveling from one town to the next, while their wives served meals from their homes, took on paying guests, or else sought jobs as household servants just to survive.

In the spring of 1938 the regimentation, isolation, and dispossession of the Jews was far advanced. A flood of regulations continuously restricted the Jews' freedom of action and created the conditions for the final phase of systematic expropriation and looting. Property exceeding 5,000 Reichsmarks had to be reported, all Jewish companies were registered, and Jews were no longer permitted to work as traveling salesmen and agents. This left the unemployed with virtually no earning opportunities. Final bans on physicians and lawyers followed. Jews lost control over their cash, their stocks, and their jewelry. Finally, on November 12, 1938, the "forced Aryanization" of the remainder got under way.

7

The Department Stores Become "German"

Hetti Schiller

Immediately after Hitler's seizure of power the three largest German department store chains were Aryanized: Karstadt, Hermann Tietz, and Leonhard Tietz. The large banks were told to cancel the department stores' credits on a short-term basis so that they would be forced to sell out. Since the Schocken firm did not have any bank credits but rather a bank balance, this pressure could not be brought to bear against it. Instead, the Party organization in the towns where Schocken department stores were located forbade their members from shopping there. Soon, middle-class people and officials no longer dared to go into the department stores for fear of being seen by their acquaintances who were Nazis. But the workers did not care about such bans and said, "We'll shop where the merchandise is good and cheap." Since the newspapers were no longer allowed to print advertisements, the company recorded a decline of about 15 percent compared with earlier years. But it was so well organized that it could bear this loss well. It still had a surplus and would continue working over the years under normal operating conditions.

Since the company was among the largest taxpayers in Saxony, its work was scarcely disrupted. Nevertheless, the Party office gave it plenty of pinpricks, which the management constantly had to fend off. The central office manager, who served as the chairman of his Nazi Party cell, was required to discuss all occurrences with the managing director, and it was essential that the director not make an enemy out of this man, who received his orders from the Brown House. The central office manager was one of those people who immediately do as they are told.

Within the company itself the Aryan employees behaved decently and in an orderly manner toward the new "non-Aryans," but they increasingly avoided being seen with them on the street or associating with them privately. One of the long-standing directors, a Russian by birth, was once addressed in an unfriendly way by one of the minor employees. An Aryan colleague replied to this person as follows: "But Director G. is extremely capable and, after all, Jews are people, too." This answer cost him a fine by the Party.

A non-Aryan grocery purchaser was presented with a small jubilee certificate upon completing ten years of work in the company. He wanted to celebrate the occasion and invited a few of his Aryan colleagues, including some girls, for coffee and cakes and entertained them in the company building. The matter was reported to the Party by some particularly patriotic Nazis, upon which the Party demanded the employee's immediate dismissal. The managing director refused, whereby the cell chairman said that he could not guarantee that the young man would not be horribly maltreated. The managing director told him that he would see to it that a peaceful atmosphere was maintained within the company; nevertheless, he gave the purchaser a leave of absence. In the meantime, the Party collected material against the purchaser to the effect that he had run his department in a disorderly manner—and got him fired. Now this apparently successful method was systematically applied by the Brown House through the cell chairmen. They played the same game with another Jewish employee, who had "outraged" the rest of the staff. He had allegedly once yelled at a lazy apprentice, and had once touched the arm of his secretary, who was an Aryan, in the corridor, whereupon he was later informed that he had committed offenses against a "German youth" and a "German maiden." The matter ended up in court, where the judge, who thought the whole thing was nonsense, found the young Jewish man innocent.

In this situation the managing director traveled to the Reich Economics Ministry in Berlin to request protection from such chicanery. Since the majority share of the company's stocks had been sold to an Englishman, he explained the alienating impression such methods must have on the English shareholder. In the meantime the Brown House in Z. had thought up a new trick: the young man was indicted by the disciplinary court of the Reich Labor Front in order to remove him from the company in this way. The disciplinary court consisted of a National Socialist judge, an employer, and an employee. A witness appeared who claimed to have seen everything, but his testimony was so muddled that the judge declared him to be unreliable and acquitted the young man. Then a new accusation was brought against the employee: encountering a friend of his on the street, he had raised his fist as a joke. This was interpreted as a Communist salute and he was sentenced to four weeks in prison. By the time he won his appeal he was already long gone. Then the Reich office intervened and prohibited all such arbitrary actions until further notice.

Of much greater concern to the company were the tax conflicts with the revenue office. This example illustrates how the Third Reich undermined the laws. The National Socialist leaders called it "bringing the laws close to the people." The new Nazi tax law gave the revenue offices the right not to tax transactions according to the legal terms of a contract but rather according to the economic purpose that they pursued. The following is a typical case: when the manager of a business emigrated, but still remained the business's chairman, the company was forced to shoulder considerably higher taxes. Those were the legal regulations. However, the company's owner, Herr Schocken, was no longer the chairman of the company following his emigration. Before moving to Palestine he had arranged his affairs by appointing his son and his nephew as chairmen and hiring an Aryan manager. Now the tax officials of the Z. revenue office came to the head office and stayed there for three full months, eight hours a day, in order to scrutinize the company by conducting conversations and inspecting all the documents they could find. Since the company was the largest taxpayer in all of Saxony, the revenue office thought this was worth the effort. After checking out everything from top to bottom for three months, they added an extra million to the company's tax bill, stating, "Herr Schocken may no longer be the chairman, that is true. But we find that he is still tantamount to a chairman, since the current chairmen solicit his advice in all important and complex matters; if he is not needed in daily operations this can be attributed to the fact that he organized everything down to the last detail before his emigration to Palestine." The company won the case since the Reich Finance Administration considered it to be practically impossible to assert constant influence and carry out any meaningful management functions from Palestine. The highest court authority for economic matters thus contradicted the municipal revenue office's attempt to change the legal regulations through an arbitrary interpretation; however, in theory the Reich Finance Administration did not reject this weakening of the law as such but only noted that genuine management was not possible from such a great distance. The law clearly stipulated an "emigré who has formally remained a chairman." This was clearly not the case. Nevertheless, the revenue office set a tax sum "as if" it were the case!

Toward the end of 1937 the pressure from the Nazi authorities in economic life became so powerful that the owner of the Schocken company and the English majority decided to sell the company as a whole. All suppliers were compelled to be members of the Nazi association, which forbade them from supplying Jewish shops. While individual suppliers had refused to comply with these regulations until the last moment, or else quietly ignored them, as the raw materials became more scarce and the inspections more frequent, they gradually lost interest in supplying the despised non-Aryans. After all, they were now selling their merchandise right and left. Thus the non-Aryan shops received no more goods, and their turnover declined rapidly. At the same time, customers were threatened and stopped by the authorities if they continued to buy from Jewish shops instead of from Party comrades. In Saxony, the Party simply shut down two small stores for several weeks, and it did not help when the Aryan manager complained to the specially established authority in the Berlin ministry. We were informed that the Party administration felt compelled to take such measures because "the spontaneous outrage of the people" demanded it. Our Nuremberg store was closed down just in time for our busiest season, right before Christmas. Finally the Reich Party office in Munich ordered it to be reopened after ascertaining that sales negotiations were already in progress. After the house was reopened, our "spontaneously outraged" customers flooded through the doors in such numbers that the staff did not know how to handle them.

One of Holland's largest private bankers emerged as the purchaser of this large property. He wanted to sell the company to German bankers or to another department store group later on. For many weeks a staff of the company's experts busily worked through all our books and prepared the contract. But the sale would only become valid when it was approved by the Party and had also received the permission of the Reich Economics Ministry, which centrally processed the entire matter for all nineteen towns in which Schocken department stores were located. The Dutchman went to the Reich Economics Ministry in person to submit the contract to the official in charge for approval. After the latter had spent several days going through the matter, he asked banker K. to come to him and the following conversation ensued: "So why do you, a banker, want to buy this department house group?" Herr K. replied that he viewed the sale as an intermediate deal, but did not have any other purchaser as yet; that would take a long time considering the size of the property. The official said, "It is very simple; the large German banks will buy the group from you. It will be taken care of very quickly. I will bring the chairmen of the large banks together with you in a meeting, and everything can be arranged there." "Yes, but will the banks be prepared to purchase it and will they agree to your suggestion?" a surprised Herr K. asked. "The banks will have to buy it, just leave that to me," came the amazing reply. Herr K. objected that he himself would have to pay the purchase price to the group's owner in foreign currency, even if it was on a controlled currency basis, so that he himself was only interested in a purchaser who could pay him in foreign currency. "Of course, of course," the official assured him, "if it means bringing the Schocken group into German hands, that's worth a million in foreign currency to us!"

The meeting was held in the presence of so many people that they had to reserve a large hall in the ministry. Alongside the entire complement of officials from the individual agencies, the chairmen of the Deutsche Bank, the Dresdner Bank, the Handelsgesellschaft, and the Reichskreditgesellschaft appeared as interested buyers. In addition, the group's chairmen were there with their lawyers together with Robert as the owner's representative, as well as the Dutch banker with his lawyer. The bank chairmen declared, "Of course we will buy the group immediately." They had no reservations since the statistical material had been prepared and arranged in such an excellent manner! Then the representative of the foreign currency office stood up and declared, "The currency office will make a million marks in foreign currency available to ensure that the group remains in German hands." And he demanded that the group's owner deliver half of his share in the purchase sum to the Golddiskontbank. After all, when he left Germany in 1934 he had transferred his funds under good conditions, and Herr Schocken should take an idealistic view of this matter and make a sacrifice to ensure that his life's work could be carried on in Germany. After this statement, a silence fell across the hall. Finally, Robert said that he regretted he was compelled to inform the gentlemen that Herr Schocken would never agree to this. The chairman then asked Robert, "Are you implying that Herr Schocken is free to choose whether to sell or not?" "This is indeed my opinion," Robert answered. "Then you are sadly mistaken," the chairman informed him. "This is by no means the case. If Herr Schocken does not sell, then the group will be liquidated as non-Aryan property and Herr Schocken will receive nothing." Robert smiled and pointed out that for Herr Schocken it made little difference if he lost the suggested 97 percent or 100 percent. Then the Dutchman stood up and asked the chairman, "If I understand you correctly, Herr Oberregierungsrat, then it is the opinion of the foreign currency office and the Reich Economics Ministry that a Jew must surrender practically everything he owns to the German Reich when he emigrates. Is that your opinion?" "Yes," said the Regierungsrat, "that is our condition, and if Herr Schocken does not agree to this then the responsibility for the group's ruin will fall upon those who could not persuade him." The Dutchman intervened once more: "Excuse me, Herr Regierungsrat, the responsibility for impossible conditions always falls upon him who sets them, not him who rejects them!" The mood was icy. Finally the representatives from the currency office and the ministry gave in and suggested that they should all reconsider the affair in a "benevolent" manner. The result of the negotiations was that the owner had to transfer only a quarter instead of half of his share to the Golddiskontbank.

The sale of a second department store also occurred under dramatic conditions. In Erfurt one of Herr Schocken's nephews and a further relative owned the Roman Emperor department store, which was known throughout the region. Since the Roman Emperor was aimed more at civil servants and the middle class—whereas the Schocken department stores had mostly "the common man" and workers as its customers—its sales declined rapidly. Hardly anyone from the middle class wanted to risk being seen shopping in a non-Aryan department store. The owner searched high and low for serious buyers. He mostly found small business people with little cash. Herr V., who later provided the group with his services and his good connections until its sale, was advising such a group of purchasers. This man played an unusual role in the Nazi economy. He served as a sort of unofficial representative of the central Party office in Munich. Thanks to this relationship he could be useful for both sides in "Aryanization" operations, and he was usually successful in ensuring that such sales remained fair. He was then compensated for his services—likewise on an unofficial basis. The times being what they were, it was virtually impossible for non-Aryan buyers to navigate all the restrictions, while this man with his Party connections could open every door.

The department store owner, with Robert as his legal advisor, then waged a bitter struggle with this man over the sale of the department store. After a long search they finally hit on a serious buyer: a former lawyer who had once played an important advisory role in the Karstadt group. Since then, he had become an entrepreneur in his own right by using bank credits to buy up Jewish department stores whose previous owners had been driven out of business. He started out with nothing, but by now he already owned ten stores with an annual turnover of thirty million marks. Of course, he was hopelessly in debt, which did not bother him since he owned nothing himself. He and his partners offered the owners in Erfurt a fair price, only a quarter of which they wanted to pay in cash while paying the rest in long-term installments. The owners of the Roman Emperor agreed to this and the contract of sale was drawn up.

First the town's mayor had to provide a so-called retail guarantee authorization; then the new owners had to be approved by the Party and confirm that the company would remain "purely Aryan" from now on. Both authorities then demanded that the purchasers immediately pay the entire price to the previous owners—for otherwise the department store would still be in non-Aryan hands! Since the purchasers were not able to do so, the problem seemed insurmountable. Then Herr V. activated his connections and managed to transfer the entire remaining sum to a Berlin firm of accountants who now became the official "purely Aryan" creditors and would manage the clearing with the previous owners. Without a doubt, Herr V.'s daring coup was quite brilliant; it had never been attempted before, and it was actually approved by the Party office. With this authorization, Herr V. and the buyers went to the city council in order to receive the other necessary endorsement. A councilman looked at the order from the Party office and said, "Well now, everything is in order. You can pick up the mayor's authorization tomorrow."

Everyone breathed a sigh of relief when they saw that everything was signed and sealed. The purchaser group immediately put an ad in the daily paper and hung up signs in the store windows saying that the store would be closed for two days for inventory and then would be reopened under "purely Aryan" ownership. When it was time to pick up the authorization from the councilman, the latter was very embarrassed and stuttered that the mayor had refused the authorization and that it would be better if the gentlemen would go and discuss the matter with him personally. The mayor had only recently assumed this office, which he had been given because he was such a zealous, 150 percent Nazi. In the meantime, the local retail store owners had besieged him, plotting against the reopening of the department store. As long as the department store had stood under boycott and had been losing vast amounts of money, its turnover dwindling, the retailers had nothing against it. But now that it was to receive new Aryan management, the turnover would rise again—once again providing competition for them, the retailers. That could not be allowed to happen. Even Adolf Hitler had spoken against large firms in his book *Mein Kampf*. The situation for the purchaser group was as bad as it could be. As they had already advertised that they would open on Monday, with all the necessary preparations in place, they would be humiliated throughout Erfurt.

Thus Herr V. went into a meeting with the mayor while the purchasers waited outside the door. He later provided a vivid account of this dialogue. There, in a hall of immense dimensions, high upon a podium, sat the mayor at a long table, flanked by his councilmen to the left and the right. Herr V. stood below and had to look up to the elevated mayor from a respectful distance. He presented himself to the mayor as the intermediary in the sale. He was not offered a chair. Instead, he was made to stand throughout the proceedings, and Herr V. reported that he felt as if he were undergoing a court martial. The mayor was as ill-tempered as a despot who had breakfasted badly. Then he informed Herr V. that he had decided to refuse the authorization. Everything had gone much too quickly, he said. He would have to study the case first—whether the purchase price was appropriate, whether the new purchasers were honest and reliable people, and so forth. Of course, his investigation would take a very long time. If the new purchasers decided to open the store anyway, he, the mayor, would send the police to close it down again. Of course, he would also keep it closed down if the old management remained in place, since following all the newspaper advertisements the public would have been deceived, being led to believe that it was now an Aryan store. So one way or another the store would remain closed! Herr V. responded angrily, "Herr Bürgermeister, you know that the Party has approved the takeover of the store by the new purchasers. The Party administration in Munich has also been informed and asked me to take on this case. If I have not received your authorization by one o'clock this afternoon, I will board the train to Munich and report that you have sabotaged the Party's orders!" The mayor, beside himself with rage, screamed that he would not be blackmailed. Herr V. said coldly that he did not care what the mayor did not want to be; come what may, he would board the Munich train if he did not receive the authorization by the early afternoon.

The authorization arrived at noon—but it was only a temporary one! Furthermore, the mayor wanted to set two more conditions: first of all, the department store had to do away with its grocery section (in a German department store, groceries are a large and important sales department). Herr V. declared that this condition was unacceptable and baseless as long as all other department stores in Germany continued to run grocery sections. The mayor quickly dropped this point. But there was still something else: the large Freemason globe on the store's roof had to come down. The Freemason globe was the registered trademark of the Tietz group, to which the department store belonged. This triviality, Herr V. said with a smile, could naturally be removed.

But now the bank—faced with a "temporary" authorization—refused to extend the credits that represented half of the agreed-upon cash sum. Robert now faced the fateful decision of whether to let the store go for half the agreed price. In the end, this was done, the firm changed hands the same day, and after three weeks everything was finally set. The new owners approached the old ones, shook their hands, and assured them that they would maintain the good old tradition and honor their life's work. With their Nazi Party badges stuck in their buttonholes, they said: "We can't do anything about the times!"

These transactions illustrate how formerly prosperous Jewish merchants who were forced to emigrate ended up with only a ridiculous residue of their fortune after selling their stores. This was not because the new purchasers were unwilling to pay a fair price, but because the revenue office and the foreign currency office squeezed immense taxes from the purchase price on the most unbelievable grounds, so that such transactions assumed the character of confiscations. If a merchant emigrated, he had to pay an additional Reich Escape Tax. The rest of his fortune could only be transformed into foreign currency through a so-called controlled currency sale, whose rate amounted to just 6 percent in 1938! If, for example, a merchant received a million Reichsmark (RM) for his company, which corresponded to $100,000, then after all the deductions and conversions he was left with a mere $12,000 in foreign currency. The situation was even more blatant for a medium-sized merchant who managed to get 100,000 RM out of his company—only to receive $1,200 overseas.

8

Aryanization Everywhere

Kurt Sabatzky

In Leipzig we had a number of large Jewish publishers. I said to myself that these publishers could only be saved by exploiting the National Socialist regime's Achilles heel, namely the foreign currency problem. I asked the publishers to supply me with figures from their foreign currency income. This amounted to several million marks. Armed with this figure, I went back to Herr von Buch at the Saxon economics ministry. I informed him and his book trade consultant, Regierungsrat Podlich, that this foreign income was entirely due to the fact that the owners of these publishing houses were Jews. Foreign countries could just as easily order their German-language books or sheet music from as yet unannexed Vienna or from Zurich. The foreign booksellers only continued buying from Leipzig because they knew that the large publishers I represented were Jews. If the Saxon economics ministry placed any significance on retaining this share of foreign currency, then it was essential that Jewish owners not be driven from their positions. Herr von Buch promised that the Saxon economics ministry would intervene with Reich Economics Minister Schacht, who worked closely with Reich Propaganda Minister Goebbels in regard to all questions concerning the Reich Chamber of Culture, to influence Goebbels accordingly. This intervention was a complete success and the Jewish publishing houses managed to hold on because of the foreign currency income they generated—until the "Jewish action" of 1938. Only then were they placed under trusteeships and finally Aryanized in 1939.

The Reich Nutrition Estate under Darré took powerful steps against Jewish traders in agricultural products, particularly against Jewish livestock dealers. The Reich Nutrition Estate did not have an Aryan clause, but it did have a regulation stating that merchants involved in rural trading had to be politically reliable. If a dealer was declared politically unreliable, he had the option of appealing to an arbitration court of his own professional group. A system emerged in which Jews in general were declared politically unreliable because of their background. The arbitration courts took the same position and also took away the Jews' right to continue working within the framework of the Nutrition Estate. These decisions amounted to the complete destruction of their economic existence.

A genuine witch hunt then ensued against Jewish traveling salesmen and itinerant workers, whose commercial identity cards and itinerant licenses, which they needed in order to practice their professions, were often confiscated by industrial inspectors. When this happened one could appeal to the Prussian district administrative courts or to the district authorities in Saxony. These appeals were frequently denied. In other cases, appeals made to a number of Prussian administrative courts were successful. And then an appalling thing happened: the police administration, which had been legally compelled to return a Jew's identity card and thus to permit him to return to work as an itinerant worker, issued him a new card. He was then asked to go into another office in the same building, where another official wished to speak to him. There sat an official from the Gestapo who promptly confiscated his legally prepared and issued card and thus effectively prevented him from plying his trade. This behavior even went too far for the Prussian Supreme Administrative Court. It passed a decision that citizens would be shaken in their sense of justice, along with their trust in the authorities, if on the one hand the police administration is ordered to issue a commercial identity card, while on the other hand the Gestapo can take it away again. In actual fact, this ruling, which was genuinely objective, had no effect whatsoever. The Gestapo remained stronger than the highest administrative court in the Reich and continued to confiscate freshly issued identity cards.

The most blatant case where a Jewish business was confiscated also took place in my district, namely in Suhl. In political terms, Suhl belonged to the Prussian government district of Erfurt, but it lay in the Gau of the Thuringian Reich governor Saukel, whom the locals preferred to call "Saukerl" (bastard). Suhl was the home of the Berlin-Suhl gun and vehicle plant of the brothers Simson. The Simsons had been indiscreet enough to appoint their authorized signatory as the company's trustee as early as 1933 and without any urgent need to do so. However, this trustee turned out to be an infamous traitor, who lined not only his own pockets but those of Gauleiter Saukel as well.

Now, with the help of police commissioner Gomlich in the Thuringian interior ministry, Hoffmann set about confiscating this business without compensation. Although the Thuringian interior ministry was in no way responsible for Suhl, since this town was Prussian, Gomlich constructed an artificial suit with Hoffmann's support. According to this accusation, the Simsons had pocketed unjustified profits from the supply of guns and machine guns for the Wehrmacht and the Schutzpolizei, and had also delivered shoddy weapons. Here it is important to note that all contracts with the Reich Army Ministry and the Interior Ministry had been drafted by Hoffmann himself and had been examined by ministry officials and officers. Furthermore, every weapon in the district had been tested for effectiveness by officers specially assigned for this purpose. Even before the trial began, the entire operation was confiscated and transformed into the Friedrich Saukel Foundation, from which Saukel himself and also Hoffmann and Gomlich drew a vast income. Hoffmann and Gomlich received special honors for this theft; both were appointed as senior civil servants in the Thuringian ministry of the interior. The Simsons were taken into "protective custody," then set free after paying a high bail. They managed to flee to Austria and from there to America. Fortunately, they did very well for themselves there, despite the theft of their family fortune.

The Nazi courts gradually arrived at a consensus that companies in which the German Reich had a capital stake of 51 percent were to be placed on the same footing as state owned companies. The Simsons are supposed to have used this legal argument to impound the giant steamer *Bremen* belonging to Norddeutscher Lloyd, in New York harbor by means of a temporary injunction. Since the Reich had a greater than 51 percent stake in Norddeutscher Lloyd, the New York court issued the temporary injunction to impound the steamer. The Reich was now forced to bail out the *Bremen* for several million dollars.

Like most other German newspapers, the *Köthener Zeitung* had declared that it would not accept advertisements from Jews. The local merchant Simon wanted to sell his rabbits, and to do so he had to advertise them first. He asked an Aryan friend to place the ad at the newspaper's office and not provide the name, just the street and house number. By chance people found out anyway that the seller of these rabbits was the Jew Simon. That moved the public prosecutor's office to file suit against both Simon and his Aryan friend. The local court in Köthen sentenced Simon to six weeks and his Aryan friend to four weeks in jail. He stated that it was an insult to the National Socialist advertisement director for a Jew to dare to deliver an ad through an intermediary. The middleman, he said, was also guilty of such an insult by helping the Jew to deliver this covert ad, so that a spell in prison—the Jew, of course, receiving a longer sentence—was the proper punishment for the two of them. I initiated an appeal. I have followed the entire administration of justice in regard to the Jewish question and I can only recall this one case in which an appeal was successful and a higher court did not follow the decision of the lower. The appeals court in Dessau cleverly distanced itself from this matter without making waves with the Party and the Gestapo. It declared that the previous judge had failed to examine whether the insulted party had reported an offense in the first place. As this was not the case, both of the accused were released without a fine.

9

The End of a Wine Merchant's Business

Friedrich Weil

From August 1935 to May 1938 I worked as a wine commission agent, primarily in the Rhineland and in the southern German wine-growing regions. My work consisted of continuing the wine commission business my father had founded and which my two late brothers had been running. After my own wine business was destroyed during the Nazi hate campaign, I devoted myself once more to the family business. This gave me the opportunity to work closely with both the wine's producers and its large-scale consumers, particularly Germany's sparkling wine manufacturers. For the producers I was the purchaser and for the sparkling wine manufacturers I was the supplier. It was my responsibility to distribute the right wines for their respective purposes. I served as an agent for both sides, and because of my more than forty years of practical experience I enjoyed everyone's complete trust. I am certainly not exaggerating when I say that this trust, particularly that between the wine growers and me, can almost be called patriarchal. The trust continued to show itself in the final years, from 1935 to 1938, when all economic activity on the part of Jews was suppressed in a wave of unparalleled ruthlessness.

In order to practice my profession I needed a so-called traveler's identity card, which I received from the responsible authorities every year until 1935. In 1936 the now entirely politicized police refused to give me the card without offering me any explanation whatsoever. When I filed an oral complaint, I was given the rude response: "You are a Jew, and as a Jew you cannot be trusted in the exercise of your profession." I turned to the chamber of industry and commerce, and after five days a policeman brought my new identity card to my office.

In 1937 I had the same problem. This time my complaint resulted in a thorough search of my office and my private rooms during my absence. They slit open my mattress. My office assistant—who had left my services six months previously—was interrogated for hours about my business ethics, my personal relationships, my foreign contacts, and where the hidden foreign currency could be found. After eight days I was once again given an identity card.

In this way I remained active in the German economy until I was suddenly sent to a concentration camp along with two thousand other German Jews on June 13, 1938. Up to this point I had been working the same way I had over the previous forty years. In recent years I had had to deal with bigger and bigger problems. I embraced the struggle out of a sense of justice, but tyranny won the day, and justice had to hold its tongue. Leading sparkling wine companies, with whom I had maintained the most cordial relations for more than forty years, invited me to private meetings in which they explained to me in the frankest possible manner how they had been forced to dissolve this decades-old, pleasant and proven business relationship. For instance, in 1937 the Henkell Trocken company in Wiesbaden informed me through its first chairman, Director Ickrath, that it could no longer maintain its contacts with its Jewish suppliers. The personal relationship they had to the regime, namely through the marriage of one of the owners' daughters to Foreign Minister Joachim von Ribbentrop, left the company no choice. They not only expressed their personal regret over the necessary dissolution of this business relationship, but also confirmed to me that the Henkell Trocken company would suffer a greater financial loss than I would, since they had always had the greatest confidence in me and knew that the company always received the best and most suitable wines. But now the company had to send a task force of six to eight of their own people into the production areas to test the wines on site, and I could imagine, they said, that this could not occur "without damages" to the company. Other equally large firms suggested that I hire an "Aryan" as camouflage, so that the company could present itself as an Aryan firm in its invoices, shipping bills, and so on. I refused categorically.

After receiving not a single order from my Aryan customers between December 1, 1937, and March 1, 1938, I decided to emigrate to America, where my three adult sons had been working for many years. On April 16, 1938, I sold my house in Frankfurt am Main. On May 8, 1938, I traveled to the American consul in Stuttgart to enquire about the necessary formalities. I did not neglect to mention that I had already been convicted by the Nazis, and I brought the conviction with me. The vice-consuls showed great interest in my case and promised me—in a nonbinding manner, of course—that they would take a sympathetic look at my application. I should provide a good affidavit, and then the case would not be a problem.

Upon my return to Frankfurt am Main I received a printed form from the Party office asking me if and when I would sell my business to Aryans, liquidate it or otherwise dissolve it. They demanded an answer within eight days. Instead of giving them an answer, I went to the local court the next day and had my firm extinguished. At the same time, I reported this fact to the responsible chamber of industry and commerce.

At the end of the proceedings, the court secretary, who issued the certificates, asked me into the adjoining room. He said he wanted to place the official stamp on the document, but in reality he wished to speak with me for a few minutes alone and without witnesses. After the door shut behind us, he told me how sorry he was to have to extinguish this highly respected firm; but I should realize that, deep down, not all Germans thought the way they were unfortunately forced to act. He gave me encouragement and wished me the best of luck from the bottom of his heart—and said he hoped I would soon witness "the retribution of the German people!"

I said farewell privately to some of my clients, and some of these visits became quite dramatic. They deeply regretted my decision, which they recognized as the only possible option open to me under the circumstances, and they basically asked me for forgiveness. Three times I was told the following in the private offices of the heads of large firms: "You should be glad that you can leave; I would be delighted if I could change places with you, because then I would leave this dump in a minute and travel abroad, but we Aryans of draft age are no longer given permission to travel overseas."

At the same time, I saw plenty of evidence of virulent hatred on the part of the Aryan population toward the current brown regime. An old farm woman could not help shouting a pure German-style curse against the brown plague so loudly that I had to ask her to be more cautious in the future.

While I was speaking to this woman in front of her house, more and more farmers and their wives joined us. When they learned that I was emigrating to America, they were at first very quiet, but then the most prominent among them said, "Who will see to it that we can sell our wine every year?"

Each of them asked me to come to their homes to drink a glass of wine with them. Since time was short, I had to refuse, but within a quarter of an hour eight women appeared, and each of them had a farewell present under her apron: butter, eggs, bread, kirsch, and a freshly slaughtered chicken. I was deeply touched by all this attention, and at the moment I said farewell and thanked them and was about to get into my car, the mayor's daughter brought a bouquet of fresh mayflowers for my wife.

I still look back fondly on that hour in which old Germany sought to show me its true face one last time.

10

A Livestock Dealer Gives Up

DAVID GRÜNSPECHT

Relations between the Jewish livestock dealers and the farmers were still good. The livestock from our area mainly went to the livestock market in Fulda. During a livestock market in early 1935 the following occurred: business was going well, a portion of the livestock had already been sold and was tied up waiting for loading. Suddenly, a horde of Nazis in civilian clothes arrived in trucks, cut the sold livestock free, and drove it away. In the meantime, a huge brawl developed, during which the already frightened Jewish livestock dealers were beaten with rubber truncheons. Many of these livestock traders were beaten bloody. An acquaintance of mine, Gustav Levi from Fulda, bled from many stab wounds and required medical attention. The police looked the other way. The next day, the *Augsburger Zeitung* printed the following: "Because of the provocative behavior of the Jewish livestock dealers, a group of young farmers was compelled to take decisive action."

Among my few loyal customers was a small farmer from a neighboring town who also looked after the local post office. On the same farm there lived another small farmer, whose son was a fervent Nazi. Whenever he saw his neighbor heading out to his farm buildings—they shared a barn, separated by a partition—he would irritate him by singing: "When Jewish blood spurts under the knife." The farmer despised this, but since he did not dare say anything he would begin singing the church hymn: "O father of the faith, see the distress in which we find ourselves." But then the constable from Wüstensachsen, whom the Party dispatched to us, would appear and tell the postal agent to stop singing and not to buy from the Jew anymore, or the post office would be taken away from him.

I sent my son Eric to the post office on his bicycle. A boy of the same age rode up on his own bike, pulled up next to Eric, spat in his face, and said: "You goddamn Jew, aren't you in Palestine yet?"

A farmer from Frankenheim sold me a calf, which I then fetched in my wagon. While passing the house of a close acquaintance, I stopped and jumped out to say hello. Hearing voices outside, I came out again and found the constable standing beside the wagon. "Is that your wagon?" he asked. I said that it was, and he continued, "I will report you for cruelty to animals, because you have tied the calf up contrary to regulations." "But officer," I said, "don't you see that the calf is chewing its cud, a genuine sign of well-being? Where is the cruelty?" "Shut your mouth," the constable snorted. "You want to kill me with talk, which is the custom of your people! Clear out of Frankenheim, and don't let me see your face again anytime soon."

Extortion was the rule of the day. Debtors demanded and received receipts for sums they never paid. There was no use in going to court. Jewish lawyers were not allowed to practice, and Christian attorneys did not dare to defend Jews. I personally asked a debtor, in the politest of terms, to make a partial payment of a long-overdue sum. His answer was: "Don't be so cocky. I remember you saying something once, and if I tell that to the Party then just wait and see what they'll do!" When I asked him what it was I said, he replied, "You once said that everything will be different one day, and by that you can only have meant that the Communists would take power." I never received a penny.

They took away the Jewish livestock traders' licenses. Jewish grocery and textile stores were boycotted. The Jewish business people were systematically deprived of their livelihoods. For example, the new allocation system meant that Jewish butchers received no more slaughtered livestock. When we complained to the district farmers association, we were told, "We can only send some to you after you supply us with the names of your customers." After a second complaint, we were told: "Because of the new purchasing patterns among the customers, it is no longer necessary to supply you with meat. The Aryan population has enough opportunities to buy from Aryan shops." After I complained a third time, I was allocated one animal per month.

In June 1937 I was having a conversation with the seven-year-old son of a Christian neighbor and happened to admire his blue suit. Looking down upon himself, the little one said, in dialect, "I have a much prettier one." I said, "What kind of suit is that?" The lad said, "I won't tell you." "But you can tell me." "I won't tell you. Well, all right. It's a yellow one. It's hanging in the attic, and there's something hanging there with it." "What is hanging there with it?" "A rubber truncheon is hanging there. Boy, when I put on my Storm Trooper uniform and take the rubber truncheon in my hand, then I'll go into the Jews' houses, and boy, there'll be hell to pay." "So where are you going first?" "Not to you. First I'll go to the Jewish schoolteacher and then to the Liebmanns."

I will never forget how I went walking past a display case of the *Stürmer* around Easter 1937 and saw a picture of a "ritual murder" on the title page. Two women were standing in front of the case, looking at the picture. I heard one of them say, "Isn't that dreadful? Who would have thought of such a thing? And it must be true, otherwise the Jews wouldn't put up with it!"

You can imagine how glad I was when my emigration papers for America arrived. When I went to say farewell to a relative of mine in Bavaria, I saw a votive column at a crossroads. It was carved from wood and depicted a Jew lying on the ground, being beaten by a farmer with a stick. Underneath were carved the words, "Here, Jew, goddamn you, here's your long-earned wages."

I kept my impending emigration secret to avoid unpleasant incidents. One last time I wanted to look at my home, the beautiful area with the hills and valleys, the forests and meadows, and bid farewell to it in my mind. I was about to depart from my home, where I had been born, in which generations and generations had spent their entire lives. Hitching up my horse and wagon, I drove down the Ulstergrund to Hilders, then back to Batten and up the Brandgrund. As I was driving through Brand, innkeeper Gensler was standing at the window of his inn. We had always been good friends. I stopped and climbed the steps to the barroom. I had seen a car parked in the courtyard. There were only a few people in the bar. A strange man sat alone at a table. I ordered a cognac and exchanged a few words with the innkeeper. Then I heard the strange man say, "It smells of garlic in here." I acted as if I hadn't heard him. Then the stranger said: "Innkeeper, is there a garlic field nearby? The stench is intolerable." The innkeeper remained silent. At that moment the innkeeper's son appeared in the bar carrying a rope in his hand. "That's a nice rope you've got there," said the stranger. "Soon all the Jews will be hanging from ropes like these. Our Lord God has sent us a leader, and he'll soon take care of this lot!" I could stay silent no longer and said, "You seem to have studied the *Stürmer* closely." "What?" he shouted. "You goddamn Jewish swine, I'll get you, I'll show you the *Stürmer*." He pulled a knife out of his trouser pocket, a straight-edged knife which he now flashed at me. Since I was standing at the bar, near the door, I took off and raced down the steps, this fellow at my heels.

I ran across the road to the farm of farmer Breitung, who was just coming out of his barn with his manure fork. He quickly gauged the situation, then approached the knifeman and said: "Not another step, or I'll ram this manure fork into your belly. What do you want from this man? Get lost, and be quick about it!" Upon hearing this, the man withdrew to the inn. I thanked Breitung effusively, then I fetched my horse and wagon and drove full speed to Reulbach, the next village. I stopped at Büttner's inn, tied my horse to the linden tree in the courtyard, and—since I was on the alert—I went to the farmhouse of some friends from where I could survey the situation. It did not take long before a car pulled up. The knifeman got out, a half-meter-long lead pipe in his hand. As I heard later on, he went into the bar, saying, "Where is the goddamn Jew?" But the innkeeper and some of the guests told him to keep quiet, or he would have to deal with them instead. Then he withdrew beneath their catcalls. I then went back to the inn and returned home in a roundabout way.

When I went to visit the graves of my deceased parents and relatives a few days before my emigration—the cemetery lay in the beautiful region around Weyhers on the plateau—I found the iron gate wide open. Deep tire tracks led to the small basalt sphere in the center of the cemetery. Someone had taken the headstones for road building.

Part IV

Friends Become Strangers

Daily life also changed for Jews after January 30, 1933. Jews became increasingly isolated when non-Jewish Germans, with whom they had been acquainted or who had even been their friends, withdrew—sometimes abruptly, but usually slowly and silently. The vast majority of Germans feared reprisals and both professional and personal disadvantages if they continued to cultivate their previous contacts with Jews. Only a very few were courageous enough to put aside such fears. Close neighbors talked less than they had before. Even good acquaintances stopped saying hello to one another. This was particularly hard for older people who had long lived in familiar surroundings and now felt rejected, and for Jews for whom involvement in clubs or organizations had been a central component in their lives. They had worked long and hard for other people, and now they were expelled or were asked to resign. The social climate was poisoned. Jews, when they were identified as such, were increasingly insulted and even abused in public. In store and restaurant windows, as at the entrance to towns, there were more and more signs with the slogan, "Jews are not wanted!" and park benches were labeled with the words, "Aryans only!"

The situation was particularly difficult in the countryside, where a considerable portion of the Jewish population lived in 1933. For instance, about half of all Jews in Hessia and around a third of all Jews in Baden-Württemberg and Bavaria lived in rural areas. While Jews living in the anonymity of the large cities were more likely to find or maintain contact with their fellow victims, those who lived in the countryside suffered more from social isolation and ostracism, since in some towns there were few or no other Jewish families. For this reason, aside from the increasing social problems, more and more Jews moved to the cities, thereby making the situation even more difficult for the already hard-pressed Jewish communities.

The continuing threat from the state and society in general promoted a climate of constant fear and deep mistrust among Jews. As they withdrew into isolation, the sense of segregation and alienation toward a hostile or indifferent society increased. Jews suspected informants and spies everywhere and scarcely dared to express their thoughts, even among their remaining friends. This inevitably resulted in the loss of any sense of self-esteem. Reports from this time show just how desperate the situation was. We can read touching descriptions of even the most trifling friendly words from non-Jews, along with affirmations that not all Germans were anti-Semites but that this or that "good German" could still be found. For many Jews, such scattered positive experiences and impressions were like straws at which they clutched desperately but in vain.

One of the most fateful intrusions into the private lives of many Jews was that represented by the two so-called Nuremberg Racial Laws, which were promulgated on November 15, 1935. They were aimed at removing Jews from the "body of the German people." The Reich Citizenship Law stripped them of their Reich citizenship and with it all their political rights. The Law for the Protection of German Blood and German Honor banned marriages between Jews and non-Jewish Germans, extramarital sexual relations between them ("racial defilement" in Nazi jargon), and the employment of female non-Jewish women under forty-five years of age in Jewish households if a "non-Aryan" man was present, and banned the raising of the Reich flag. Violation of these laws was punishable by severe jail and prison sentences. Numerous such sentences were passed and in individual cases the death penalty was applied in cases of "racial defilement." More than any other, this law plunged countless people into misery. Many non-Jews used the law to inform on friends and neighbors, acquaintances and strangers on charges of "racial defilement" in order to throw them in prison. In mixed marriages, non-Jews succumbed to pressure from the state and divorced their spouses, either out of fear or for personal benefit.

11

The Brutality Spreads

RAFFAEL MIBBERLIN

I was standing on a little square, waiting for the streetcar, when the door to one of the houses opened up and a corpse was carried out and placed in a hearse. Behind me I suddenly heard one man call to another, saying, "Who's dead?" The other replied in a loud and derisive voice, "Oh, not to worry, another Jew has kicked off, that's all. Now, thank God, we've got one less Jew to worry about!" It wasn't hard to recognize that the dead man was a Jew, because some Jewish gentlemen were waiting around the hearse, ready to accompany it. My streetcar arrived and I jumped on board. From the platform I saw from the expressions on the faces of some of the individuals how offensive they thought this comment was.

Soon afterward I traveled to a nearby large city. The streetcar was filled to bursting. Then a somewhat corpulent "middle-aged lady" climbed aboard. I was sitting nearby and instinctively rose to my feet and offered her my seat. Her response: "I don't sit anywhere that a Jew has been sitting." And she turned up her nose. But I burst out with the comment: "Well now, everyone wears his character in a different place!" All the people sitting nearby had to bite their lips to keep from laughing, and the lady's situation was certainly more embarrassing than my own. She soon climbed out, and not only I but also the others in the car doubted whether she had ridden as far as she had intended.

Another time, on one of my frequent visits to a nearby large city, I experienced the following rather humorous episode: A Jewish lady of my close acquaintance lived in a happy mixed marriage with a man who on the exterior represented the typical blond Teuton. He was also unusually big and strong. Their marriage produced a boy and a girl, both blond and blue eyed, and the girl had long pigtails. The father once took a long streetcar ride with these two children. The four-year-old boy sat on his lap, and across from him sat his seven-year-old sister, her best friend alongside. But this child from a "pure Aryan marriage" was dark complexioned, and not nearly as attractive as her blond school friend, the half-breed. Then, after they had been riding for a while, a Hitler worshipper climbed aboard, with a big swastika on her jacket, and anyone could tell at a glance that she was a Nazi propagandist. They were a frequent sight on trains, streetcars, and buses. This lady sees the man and his two children, and after some admiring glances she starts to talk, "This just goes to show that our Führer's racial teachings are correct. Just look at these prototype Aryan children with their typical Nordic skull structure, their blond hair and blue eyes—it is a genuine pleasure to gaze on such children. And then look at this little, clearly non-Aryan child." With that she was referring to the dark-haired Aryan girl sitting next to the man's daughter. At first the father, my acquaintance, wriggled uncomfortably in his seat. In the meantime, the tactlessness shown to his daughter's friend provoked him so much that he could not restrain himself from saying, "I fear, dear lady, that I must disappoint you. My two blond children have a Jewish mother, and the little dark-haired friend is descended from 'pure Aryans'!" Touché! Everyone in the streetcar grinned, and our embarrassed heroine also got off at the next stop.

But such provocations in the streetcar could also backfire on their instigators, as shown by the following anecdote, My wife went to her dentist for treatment. She apparently looked somewhat worn out. In response to his question as to why she had become so slim, she said that the times were so unsettling. He said, "Well, you can go anywhere you want, because no one would ever take you for a Jewess. Let me tell you what happened to my wife the day before yesterday. You know, of course, that, what with her somewhat stocky build, her dark hair and pale complexion, she is not exactly a model Aryan. We were riding in the streetcar, sitting across from each other. A gentleman climbs aboard the full streetcar and has to stand, right across from my wife. Giving her an unambiguous look, he expressed his discontent as follows, 'This fat Jewess here could certainly stand up when other people can't sit down!' He soon received a fitting reward for this rude affront. I rose to my feet and gave him a powerful slap in the face. Of course, the case was soon cleared up, and this lout will have to pay closer attention to his 'racial science.'"

A former medical orderly, who had worked under me in a large military hospital during World War I, had been hired as a prison guard. In those days a disproportionate number of Jews were being held in the prison, for this or that offense, usually on the orders of the Gestapo. This exemplary guard frequently engaged these prisoners in conversation. For example, he talked with a patient of mine who had been accused of "racial defilement" and who was soon found innocent and released. When my patient A.A. remarked, "What kind of impression must you have of the Jews with so many of them here in this prison?" the guard replied. "Believe me, I know what's going on." And he whispered into his ear, "Today they're bringing the decent ones in here, and they're allowing many scoundrels to run around free outside. But that will change one day."

On the basis of Hindenburg's well-known Front Soldier Decree of 1934/35 exact statistics were collected on all Jews who had fought for their fatherland on the front during the War. After all, following the war Reich President von Hindenburg created the Cross of Honor for Front Soldiers, stating explicitly that all front soldiers should receive it regardless of their rank, class, and religion. Of course, although the Nazis did not want to believe it, there were many, many Jews among this group. The certificate of award contains the following words, "In the name of the Führer and Reich Chancellor. In commemoration of the World War of 1914/18, and pursuant to the regulations of July 13, 1934, Dr. . . . has been awarded the Cross of Honor for Front Soldiers created by Reich President von Hindenburg." Doesn't it sound like a bad joke to receive a cross of honor whose certificate of award begins with the words, "In the name of the Führer and Reich Chancellor," and that in a time when every day, in print and in public, the Jews were being abused as shirkers, as cowards, as traitors and all the other nice terms they came up with for us?

A cousin of my wife's once noticed a dog that was about to chase after a young kitten on the street. In order to protect it, he pushed the cute kitten to the side so that it could escape. This was without a doubt a harmless, everyday story. Who could have imagined that there were people who could exploit such a trifle in such a way that it would end in a man's death? How was that possible? Our cousin did not know whom the dog belonged to. The owner was a well-known Party agitator. She ran out and spouted the crudest imaginable invective against our cousin. As always, a crowd assembled, people took opposing sides, there was senseless yelling, there were anti-Semitic threats. A policeman who was happening by chose not to clarify the situation then and there, but rather to take our cousin into protective custody—"for his own protection," which was the diabolical justification they always gave. In plain language that meant that the person in question was taken to a police jail. One would expect that after a thorough interrogation he would then be released. With a bit of goodwill, the ridiculous harmlessness of this whole affair would have been cleared up immediately. Instead, he remained in custody for days. They refused to give him any information and his wife was not permitted to speak with him. Desperate and exhausted, he tried to slit his wrists with a nail file. Because of this wound he was taken to the hospital as a "police prisoner," that is to say, he was kept under constant surveillance and his door was locked. A few days later he was finally supposed to be taken from the hospital to the court building to be arraigned. His nurse had only gone to the nearby clothing room to fetch his clothes to dress him in. The completely innocent prisoner used this brief moment out from under police observation to open the window. A leap from the fourth story down to the pavement put a quick end to his life. On a slip of paper that the nurse found in his bed and which she gave to his widow was written the following, "As a decent person I can no longer tolerate the lawless and defenseless life of a Jew in Germany." It was no easy duty for me to accompany his body from the hospital to the cemetery that evening. Concerning the woman who caused this drama, permit me to add that she soon threatened another Jewish family of my acquaintance over another such triviality. And not only that: On her front door she had conspicuously placed a sign reading, "Caution, do not drop off any packages for us next door, and leave no verbal messages—THOSE ARE JEWS!" The last three words were underlined in red.

That teachers in the performance of their profession could forget themselves to such a degree as to turn even small schoolchildren against their parents is shown by the following macabre incident. A poor widow had been working for many years as a servant in a Jewish household. She was pleased to have such a good job, because she earned a good wage and was well treated by my acquaintances. She was also given somewhat faded but still wearable clothes from the daughter of the house for her own child. It is understandable that such a woman, who needed to work for her living, was devoted to this family even during the Third Reich. In addition, at the time when this event occurred there were no legal regulations affecting this employment. One day, the poor woman came to her employer, tears streaming down her face, and said, "Just imagine what has happened to my child, Frau S. You know that my little one attends the primary school, and when she came home yesterday she was confused and angry. It took a long time before she would speak, and then she told me, 'During class our teacher made me stand up from my desk. I had to stand in front of the whole class, and then he said, "Now look at this child, whose mother still cleans house for Jews. For shame!" When the teacher said that she was very ashamed. Her mother wept bitterly, saying that someone in the house must have informed against her, and that for her child's sake she was going to give up her old position, as painful as it was for her.

Once again, a racial fanatic chose the wrong victim: One of my patients, the very model of a decent Christian with unusually thick, dark, and wavy hair, who really looked as if he belonged to the Semitic race, crashed his elegant convertible into another car. Of course, a well-dressed man looking like that and driving such an elegant car could only be a Jew. After the police had ascertained that my patient was not responsible for the accident, his clean-cut adversary now thought he could turn the tables in his own favor by saying, "This crooked Jew should be banned from driving altogether." He was more than a little surprised when it quickly turned out that the supposed Jew was a Christian gentleman of high standing in the community! The racial teachings of the Nazi press seem to be very incomplete and overly hasty when it comes to the traits of the "Aryan" race!

For us the Nuremberg Laws meant that we had to part ways with our loyal house servant. She was under thirty-five and a Protestant. She let go a stream of epithets against the new National Socialist house servant law, including a genuine bouquet of anti-Nazi curses in superlative form. She had been cut to the quick by the knowledge that she would be forced to give up the position she had come to love so much. But we had to beg her to tone down the volume so that nothing would seep through the walls. Indeed, this was the only trouble we ever experienced from her throughout all her service with us. If a Nazi had heard only a fraction of this abuse, the Gestapo would have grabbed this loyal soul within fifteen minutes. Her tearful departure on New Year's Eve, 1935—this date was prescribed by law—was long forgotten, but our loyal Lina continued to visit us, displaying a touching devotion and interest for our well-being and that of our children. Shortly afterward she took a position in an "Aryan" household, where she was unhappy from the beginning, and where she only stayed on because her employer's wife was ailing. She continuously hoped the Nuremberg Laws would be lifted so that she could return to us the very same day!

Her successor was an honest and orderly woman, long known to us, who had surpassed the age limit set by the law for servants employed in Jewish households. This loyal person provided us with important information on the already growing disappointment and disaffection within various levels of German society over these Nazi methods and the steadily growing Nazi terror.

Not everyone was lucky enough to have persons of good character in their employment. A good friend of my wife's in town experienced the following deep disappointment. She had also had a house servant for many years, whose honesty she swore by. As affable, talkative, good-natured, and trusting as this lady was, she was careless enough to discuss political matters with her servant during the Third Reich, making the occasional facetious comment. When the lady's husband suddenly died and she then no longer needed the large flat, she transferred part of it to her servant, whose first name was Marie, upon the latter's request. Marie wanted to get married. She and her husband now lived comfortably and peacefully in the lady's flat as subtenants. But her generous nature would soon be ill rewarded.

This lady's friends frequently warned her against such a close relationship during these times, but she always laughed and replied, "My Marie is as good as gold." This is how good she really was: After they had lived together for some time, Marie and her husband exploited a sudden wave of anti-Semitism to make exaggerated demands upon her concerning the flat. They fell to arguing, and what do you know: a few days later, the lady was arrested in her flat. What happened? Believe it or not, months before the slippery subtenants had begun listening to all the lady's comments on the Nazis, noting them down word for word and recording the exact date, in order to use them as a weapon against her at the appropriate time. They then reported the lady to the Gestapo. This time there was a trial, in the course of which—as her greatest offense—my wife's friend was accused of telling her subtenants a joke about the Nazis. Although the lady could credibly prove that she had heard this joke word for word in a broadcast on the Leipzig radio station, she was sentenced to five months in prison, effective immediately. The presiding judge declared the following in his sentence: The Jewess's behavior was a malicious libel. Even if Jews merely spread harmless political jokes, he said, they do so in order to discredit the new state. It was a different thing entirely if a radio station of the Reich broadcast such jokes!

This was a time when, under the pressures of the time and because of fanatical agitation against Jewish businesses, many entrepreneurs tried to liquidate. This usually occurred in the form of a short-term liquidation sale. To carry out such a sale one needed permission from the Nazi authorities. For example, a large textile company put up window signs announcing a total liquidation sale. The press had not accepted any advertisements from non-Aryan businesses for a long time. At the beginning, the customers flowed like water, whether they were the wives of Nazi officials or of SS or Storm Troopers, because the prices had been reduced enormously. With prices like that, people didn't care who they were. Of course, this made the competition seethe. So they complained, and before long the Party started posting *Stürmer* hawkers and Storm Troopers at the entrances with boycott posters warning people not to enter. Yes, and to make their threat really effective they brought in people with cameras to take pictures of the people who still dared enter. They shouted out that these photos would be published in Streicher's newspaper. They didn't want to let the non-Aryan shops live, but they didn't want them to die decently either! Of course, the flow slowed to a trickle at once. A few undaunted souls went in anyway, running the gauntlet of the jeering crowd.

My wife came by on such a day, and outraged at this illegal boycott of the liquidation sale she felt genuinely inspired to go shopping there. After my wife had bought a trifle, the Aryan staff advised her to leave by a side exit and pointed out that, if she were a Jew, to yell it to the crowd immediately. If she did so then they would probably leave her alone. But by the time she left the store, a huge crowd had assembled in the back alley, and they greeted my wife with catcalls, spat on her, tore off her hat, and started attacking her physically. But she cried out, "What do you want from me, I'm a Jew!" They didn't believe her at first because of her appearance, then they shouted, "That's a lie, she just wants to slink away like a coward!" Only after her vigorous reply, "Goddamn it, that's not true, I'm a Jew!" the leader of the group commanded, "Hands off, let her through!" and she was permitted to go. But a policeman, who had been standing nearby and saw everything, didn't lift a finger . . .

One of my wife's acquaintances had a much more unpleasant experience at almost exactly the same time. This time the consequences were far more serious. She was married to an Aryan colleague and they lived together harmoniously. Their sole child was raised as a Catholic, as befitting a Catholic father. The boy went to an ordinary primary school. When he saw how many of his schoolmates joined the Hitler Youth, while he was rejected as a half-breed because of his Jewish mother, he had his first conflict with her. The boy was as robust as his mother was sensitive, and she took everything so much to heart that she actually considered doing away with herself. Her exemplary husband cut the Gordian knot with a correct and quick deed: For his wife's peace of mind and in order to remove his son from this corrosive atmosphere, thereby restoring the family's previous harmony, he abandoned his previously flourishing physician's practice and emigrated to America.

The number of mixed marriages had grown enormously during the years of assimilation. I observed a great number of them, and as a physician I had a more profound view than most. As long as the times were good, the majority of these marriages were also good. But when the ordeal of the Nazis theories and the fanatical agitation against the mixed marriages began, creating an artificial breach between spouses, many marriages began to wobble. One such case appeared in my own family. Years previously, a childless widower in his so-called prime, known for his elegant appearance and disposition, the co-owner of a successful factory before the Nazi coup, well-traveled and worldly wise, fell in love in with a somewhat younger, beautiful, skilled and charming Christian lady. She had a delightful little daughter from a brief liaison with an officer, pretty as a picture and charming in her own special way. This man's love for this woman was so great that despite the child's background he decided not only to accept her into his family but also to adopt her outright. In this way he wanted to give her his name and identity. For years these three lived together as a model family. In town people said that it was an aesthetic pleasure to see them together. The man provided his daughter with every kind of education, and no expense was too great. Even when the factory's profits declined following the coup, he fulfilled his daughter's fervent wish to attend a university. Her letters to her mother and father from this time are touching. The father may have loved this daughter more than he would have loved a child of his own. The little daughter now developed into a beautiful blond university student. Now among her fellow students there were also some who were fanatical followers of the Nazi movement. Young students were particularly intoxicated by such political terms as "pure national character" and such things. At first, the girl was not particularly susceptible to this agitation, but in the long run she succumbed to its suggestive power. To make a long story short, she let her Jewish father continue paying for her studies while at the same time she began to persuade her mother to divorce the Jew. The energetic daughter won out over her less energetic mother. They exchanged the Jewish marriage name for the previously embarrassing illegitimate name. It was better to be illegitimate than have "Jewish in-laws"! But the man's heart nearly broke, he aged rapidly, he fell silent. None of his relatives or friends dared to mention the names of his wife and daughter.

The next case had a much more tragic ending. It occurred in my practice. A nice young lady from a well-to-do Protestant family had once fallen in love with a Jewish gentleman during her dance lessons. She soon overcame her parents' objections. The two young people became a happy couple and had two pleasant children. After the coup in 1933, the young woman retained her absolute loyalty to her husband, even after the Nazi laws began to destroy his livelihood. The relationship with the woman's parents had become so good that they took the daughter together with her husband and the two children into their own household when their economic situation deteriorated. His parents had died in the meantime. When the young husband was just about to be thrown out of his profession on account of the new laws, he decided to travel abroad with his wife and children in order to make a new beginning. His wife agreed to this immediately. But not her parents. While they wanted to give their daughter and son-in-law the economic means to emigrate, they insisted on keeping their beloved grandchildren with them until the parents succeeded in establishing a foothold abroad. Now they debated back and forth. The man saw how his wife suffered. Finding herself in the most profound emotional dilemma, she felt torn between her children, her husband, and her parents. In order to smooth the way for both his wife and his children, he decided to sacrifice himself. In a lonely moment he put a bullet through his head, and all that was left for me to do was to record his death. He left a note saying that in this way he felt he was doing the best thing for his wife and children, since his in-laws had a good financial standing.

12

I Would Have Liked to Dance, Too

Gerta Pfeffer

The new department for upholstery design was becoming more and more successful. While I was at first worried that I might lose my wonderful job, the boss did everything he could to keep me. He received fantastic orders from countries all over the world, countries whose taste I was well versed in.

I had nothing to complain about in the company. Every morning my boss greeted all his employees with "Heil Hitler," saving a "Good morning" for me. The others followed his example. They all took their breakfast break in my office. One of my colleagues was our bookkeeper, a fanatical Nazi who was tempered by southern German easygoingness. He was too easygoing to insult me personally, and so he kept to jokes about Jews and Marxists. There was also a former Social Democrat who talked all day about how wonderful the Führer was. He had been a bundle of nerves since the seizure of power. Apparently to convince himself, he spoke constantly of Hitler's greatness. I didn't believe a word he said, but I kept my mouth shut. When it looked as if I was going to lose my job, I spoke to him of my worries and he repeatedly tried to reassure me, despite his convictions. During Hitler speeches, which were broadcast live in the factory, the employees who made the biggest show of singing the Horst Wessel Song, raising their arms and shouting "Heil Hitler," were invariably those who had once belonged to a left-wing party. Fear was probably the motivating factor.

Following the Nuremberg Laws I became increasingly nervous. I was afraid to address acquaintances on the street for fear of being reported for something, and I also could harm the people I spoke to.

I couldn't stand sitting alone in my own four walls, and I stayed out every night until midnight. Sometimes I sat down in a corner of the café and either read or observed my surroundings. I would have liked to dance, too, and young people always enjoyed dancing with me, whether they were in the Party or not, but it always meant danger and so I finally ended up turning down all offers.

I was once sitting together with my colleagues in a restaurant. I laughed again for the first time in ages. The atmosphere was pleasant and I failed to notice the people seated at the next table. The next day, I noticed that the restaurant owner was acting differently somehow. "What's wrong?" I asked, terribly upset. The people at the neighboring table had told the innkeepers that if they saw the Jewess laugh again, they would throw her out onto the street. They used many crude expressions, which the innkeepers did not wish to repeat.

The SS were renting an office in the same building. They now demanded that the innkeepers mount a sign on the entrance stating that Jews were not permitted in the inn. My innkeeper refused. I was his favorite patron. I had long been bringing guests from the factory and, strangely enough, other guests also asked about me. But after the SS rented their office in the building, I was always afraid of walking in and encountering one of their black uniforms, because in their meetings they sometimes talked about how they would like to bump me off. I'm convinced that it was the factory's heating engineer who was pulling all the strings behind my back, even though he was always friendly to me face-to-face and never physically harassed me.

I often came home very late, rarely before midnight. The street lights were already extinguished by this time. My heart would start pounding every time I approached my door. Once I saw a man standing there with a lighted cigarette. I didn't know who he was. My whole body shook, and when I heard my name being whispered I realized that it was my boyfriend. Sometimes I met him in the woods. We spoke very little. Even so, I listened for a long time to make sure nobody was around. I was afraid to go home alone at night because I always feared encountering a group of unwanted admirers. By daylight they cursed me as a Jewess, and at night they wanted to kiss me. They were disgusting.

In order to get out of town on Sundays and holidays, I often hitched rides with cars on the highway, asking their drivers to take me with them for a bit. It was dangerous, but I kept doing it. Every town in the district already had posted the "Jews not welcome" sign. I was always nervous when we sped past these signs, because one glance at the sign could touch off a political discussion. If we did start talking about politics, I changed the subject. Most drivers did not recognize me as a Jew, and those who did so were extremely kind to me.

It was customary for the colleagues in my factory to have parties together. I myself celebrated my birthday and invited fourteen people. These included Nazi Party members, who also danced. The next day there was a scandal. The Nazi chairman in our town wanted to publish some photos taken at my birthday party in the *Stürmer*. I was more frightened than ever. I now ate my meals alone in a separate room next to the dining hall.

I entered the room cautiously, so as not to meet anyone, gulped down my lunch in ten minutes and then disappeared. When I walked onto the street, I first took a long look at the passersby to be sure I was in no danger.

A Labour Service camp had been built in a nearby town. The fellows who were employed in building the Autobahn often came to the café in my village. Among them was a beautiful person who asked me to dance with him. I explained to him that I was a Jew, but he said that he cared for no such distinctions and that I appealed to him very much. From then on he came to the café often, and the people knew that he only came on my account, although I scarcely ever talked to him. One day he was attacked by a gang of Nazis and beaten bloody. All because he refused to hide the fact that he liked me.

13

"Jews Not Welcome" in Hotels

Leo Grünebaum

I remember how my friend, Director Helten of the Concordia Life Insurance Bank in Cologne, told me in a shamefaced way that he had become a member of the National Socialist Party because—mostly for business reasons—he simply had no other choice. "Dear Grünebaum, this may be to your benefit someday. I may some day be of help to you, if you should ever come into a difficult situation, because I already have good relations with the Party." I reminded him how, in the days of democracy, when Hitler was already on the way up, he often blamed the Democrats for having too many party bigwigs. Only their party membership cards counted, he said, and that was the cause of the state's sorrows. And how modest was the number of Democratic Party bigwigs compared to the Nazi system! But his statement that he could someday help me in dealing with the Party, as if he were somehow standing outside of it, was naïve but heartfelt. He could not have imagined how bitterly the Jews would suffer later on.

We met again over the next few years, and saw each other no more after around 1936. Up to that point he would sometimes call me up to drink coffee in a public place. When I once asked him if he was not running a risk by being seen with me, a Jew, he said, "I'd like to see who can keep me from meeting you, considering that we have business to discuss." So he already had an excuse at the ready, and that persuaded me to meet him less often and finally to stop seeing him altogether.

When I tried to reach him a few times in 1937 and 1938, whether because of my insurance policies or some other reason, he was nowhere to be found. He had always just left the office and he never returned my calls. We had worked together a great deal in the pre-Hitler days. I arranged many insurance policies through his company, and he often visited my family as a private guest. And after he remarried, I visited him in Cologne-Ehrenfeld together with my family. In the pre-Hitler days he had worked hard to arrange a group policy for one of the Jewish *Chewrots*. These Jewish associations were mainly designed to provide for the material and spiritual needs of their members in sickness and death. But Herr Helten was soon out of the running, and one of the special Jewish companies that emerged at that time, the *Familienschutz,* was given the commission instead.

Despite years of Party agitation, the Christian shops on the main business street in my town had not yet begun displaying the signs with the slogan, "Jews not welcome." They had long been a fact of life in other towns. I remember seeing the most blatant examples of this in Frankfurt am Main, alongside Jewish shops smeared with crude anti-Semitic slogans. One could see them in Cologne, too, although only sporadically. They would occasionally pop up in one street or another, only to disappear soon afterward. In brief, it was plain that a systematic Party agitation was at work which, despite the efforts of the government machine, never really took hold. And so one day some people came to see our good merchants in the autumn of 1938 and demanded that they put up signs with the slogan, "Jews are not welcome here!" Of course, they had to pay the Party apparatus: each poster cost a mark, it had to be bought on a voluntary basis, and every shop had to have one. When I passed by, one or another of the Christian merchants invited me in to apologize, and both our egg and butter seller and our barber said, "You have always been an excellent customer. I hope you do not take offense at this poster. We're forced to put it up and have no choice." The egg seller brought his merchandise to our house twice a week, and I cannot say that he treated me with any less respect than his Christian customers—even when eggs started to become scarce. On the contrary, he supplied us well and we suffered no shortages. When we came back from six weeks of summer vacation in the summers of 1937 and 1938, he had always kept a special supply for us, our unused ration and one or two extra. Two businessmen, butcher Wolf and his neighbor the fish seller, refused to put up the sign. They were taken to the police. The signs appeared the next day, but twenty-four hours later they were all gone again. The Brown Shirts had to intervene again and again to ensure that the signs stayed up.

I took advantage of a trip to Stuttgart with my wife and children to visit the birthplace of my wife Beate, née Oppenheimer. This was Göppingen, a town located a half hour by train from Stuttgart. We had great difficulty in reserving hotel rooms in Stuttgart. I had already had bad experiences of this kind on my previous trip there. While there were already some scattered hotels in Cologne that refused to accommodate Jews, the situation in Stuttgart—a town that, because of its consular offices, was being used to provide visas to Jews living within a radius of more than 500 km (all the way to Cologne and beyond), which meant that everybody was looking for rooms—was much worse. Almost without exception, the restaurants and hotels there were forced by the local Party authorities to refuse accommodation to Jews. On my last visit to Stuttgart I came to the Schwabenbräu, one of the last hotels in Stuttgart that still took Jews and did not bear the ominous sign. Using a Jewish gentleman from Stuttgart who was known to the hotel as a go-between, I was able to reserve a room for myself and a friend from Cologne, Herr Kugelmann.

When we arrived at the hotel, the house servant informed me that by chance the room that had been promised to us and that was supposed to be free would be kept another night by the previous guest and his wife. And since two large international conferences were taking place in Stuttgart, there were no other vacancies. But after a great deal of telephoning he managed to reserve a substitute room in a nearby hotel and gave us a pass for it, but he apologized in the hotel keeper's name and added, "There is no other reason for it. We aren't the way you think." And I was convinced of it, it was written on the man's face. The other hotel did display the ominous sign. But it was eleven o'clock at night, the hotels in town were occupied, so we had to pull ourselves together. We went in. Yes, the rooms were reserved. But as we were filling out the registration form, where we were asked our names and whether we were Aryan or non-Aryan, we responded truthfully. Then, in front of other hotel guests, the young hotel employee shouted out, "Non-Aryans cannot stay here!" and tore the registration form in half. I could not help responding, "That's nothing to be ashamed of," and then, red faced, we turned our backs on the wretched Hotel National.

Of course, we went back to the Hotel Schwabenbräu. The house servant (who was also the night porter) was terribly upset. "This is a scandal. Someday they will be happy to have had such decent people staying with them, these louts . . ." He again telephoned from hotel to hotel, but there were no vacancies. But he was so deeply hurt, this simple but decent man, that he finally brought in his boss, whispered with him, and thought for a moment. "We have to accommodate these people, that is more important," I heard him say. Finally he said, "So, come with me. We have freed up a room. The single woman, who has not yet arrived, can be put somewhere, if she even shows up. If she doesn't like what we offer her, then she can jump in the lake as far as I'm concerned. But now you need a good night's sleep after all this excitement." We entered a flawless double room, and when the porter brought in our hand luggage he really got going, "These scoundrels, this wretched government, they have no idea what fine people there are among the Jews. They have always been our most decent customers. Well, when the shoe is on the other foot someday . . ." Upon our departure we thanked the hotel keeper and promised to send customers from Cologne his way, which we did. The night before I received our visa I stayed there with my family. But the next afternoon the hotel keeper informed us that starting that day he was no longer allowed to accommodate Jews, that he had to put up the sign and, to his regret, we could not spend another night there. So that evening we traveled on to Göppingen, where we had relatives and friends.

14

A Witch Hunt
Under Police Supervision

Martin Gumpert

One evening I went strolling down the Kurfürstendamm and sat down in a beer garden belonging to one of the many cafés there. Hordes of young men gathered on the street. No doubt about it: these were Storm Troopers. The previous evening a new anti-Semitic film had premiered in one of the big film palaces. Some of the viewers protested, and the newspapers printed stories about Jewish insolence. The crowds grew larger and larger; a number of police cars appeared and positioned themselves at the intersections. Finally it started. The first victims included some Italians, who had been sitting near me and who were mistaken for Jews because of their dark appearance. They were chased away with bloody faces. Shopwindows were smashed and bits of glass lay strewn across the pavement. A procession formed and forced its way into all the restaurants on the lookout for Jews. Someone was carrying a distorted caricature, showing an old Jew with bloodshot eyes and wild curly hair drooping from his head. The toughs bawled out one of their Party songs with monotone voices but with a sort of religious passion, "When Jewish blood spurts under the knife, everything will be better." On the next corner I saw a man with a golden Nazi Party badge kicking an old Jewish woman. An old man was struck down and hauled away. A young man with a pince-nez on his nose ran panic-stricken across the street, a howling mob in pursuit.

About a thousand gangsters took part in this riot under the command of their leader. A much larger crowd stood on the sidewalks and watched. They didn't say a word. The expression on their faces alternated between curious amusement and revulsion. I stood alongside these people and felt safe because they would never mistake me for the Jews in their shameful caricatures. Only those people who ran away and displayed their fear were observed and hunted down. One of the criminals stood beside me and proudly showed us all a steel rod that he kept hidden in his glove. He explained that he used it to strike people from behind in the back of the knee and then would bludgeon them with it once they were lying on the ground. The most appalling sight was the police, who had apparently gathered to protect a crime. The policemen sat expressionless in their cars and did nothing when someone called for help or collapsed onto the pavement.

The next day the *Stürmer* appeared in showcases across the city. This insane newspaper, published by Julius Streicher, a former teacher, was packed with sadistic pictures, pornography, and obscenities, all of which revolved around the Jews. The *Stürmer* was distributed in the schools and teachers had to discuss the texts with their pupils. There were special editions for small children, showing the greatest obscenities, in full color, of a kind no one before would ever have dared put into print. There were three of these showcases in the quiet street where my daughter lived with her grandmother.

It would have been a crime to allow a child to grow up in this lunatic atmosphere. I had to give up. I could occasionally still write and publish something, and I viewed the survival of a small but at least existent opposition movement as a justification for my continued presence there. But even that was no longer possible. For the second time I decided to leave this country.

This was a very difficult decision. I felt like I was tearing out my own heart. I loved Berlin, I loved Germany, I loved Europe. It is difficult to recognize the moment when you are no longer of use to your fatherland, and to decide whether to admit your defeat or else to insist on your right to lead a dignified life free of threats and unbearable restrictions on your freedom. The events of this year had profoundly alienated me from myself, but also from the people around me. They made me realize that I would be insane if I sacrificed myself for them. It was really a decision between life and death: whether I was willing to witness the destruction and decay of all human values in a state of complete helplessness, or whether I would gather up the last remnants of my free will and cut myself free from the bonds of origin, tradition, and emotion to which I had dedicated myself. I knew that this latter choice was the best option and that it would be final.

There were Jews who returned after the first wave had passed, and I saw them when I visited Germany again. But can something like this ever be truly over? Not for me! I am certain that they will live to regret their decision. There were others who simply could not imagine giving up their property and valuables. I have seen people who later walked with open eyes into the gas chambers because they couldn't bear to give up their furniture, which apparently meant more to them than their lives. I pitied them from the bottom of my heart, but I understood them. Our civilization has made us so dependent on material values, on bank accounts and real estate, that the average person feels lost, naked, and on the verge of death if he loses his property. He'll lose his mind if he loses what he has gathered over a lifetime of drudgery or what has been collected over generations as the basis for his prestige and social status. Modern man is poorly equipped for upheavals in which he must derive his sense of self-worth from nothing more than his physical and psychological strength. I did not have many possessions, I believed in my abilities, I had a responsibility toward my child, I had lost all faith and all hope in Germany. Thus I saw no choice but to emigrate as long as it was still possible.

In the end, my life under Hitler brought only a boundless sadness, a sadness that could not be grasped by the mind, which was more or less an instinctive defense against the physical and psychological destruction awaiting us in this country. I had found a meaning to my existence: to survive the end of the tyranny. That was all. I had no hope for the future, nothing bound me to a world that was dying, even if it seemed not to realize it. I had only one great need, which was to see this earth liberated from the degradation around me, and to witness retribution for all the crimes that were committed.

15

The End of a Relationship

Hans Kosterlitz

The seizure of power changed nothing in my relationship to Trude. Of course, we occasionally read in the newspapers that here and there Jews who had had relationships with Aryans or who had Aryan girlfriends were abused or even sent to concentration camps. We thus became more cautious, meeting each other every evening far from town at different, prearranged places. Even so, we suspected that some people in the store knew about us. Later we were certain of it. The only thing these persons did not know was the extent of our relationship.

We had intended to get married as soon as I was granted the promised managerial position in another branch store that had yet to open. But thanks to the new ban on opening new retail stores, our plan fell through. Under these new circumstances we had no hope of marrying in Uelzen, let alone living there as a couple. Although mixed marriages were not yet illegal, and weddings between Aryans and Jews were still going on in Berlin and other large cities, the situation in Uelzen was such that marriage was unthinkable, unless I wanted to risk my position or even my freedom.

Today I believe it was the courage that is born from despair that led us not only to continue our meetings but even to ride off together on my motorcycle every Sunday. In fact, we even spent Pentecost and Easter together on the Baltic coast. Today this sounds to me like the legend of "The Ride Over Lake Constance," where the judge discovers that the smooth, shiny snow he had just ridden across was not a field but a frozen lake, whereupon he falls dead from his horse.

We were truly playing with fire, but we were blind with passion. We were attempting something that in our situation amounted to challenging destiny itself. We both knew that it was only our passion, spurred by danger, that kept us together and that in my case went so far that I failed to take advantage of an opportunity to emigrate to Chile in 1934. We also knew that once this passion had cooled nothing would remain, and in many a moment we only pretended to each other and to ourselves that this astonishing intoxication of the senses, this awareness of common danger, was really love.

The crisis of my relationship with Trude began in the fall of 1934 and reached its highpoint in February 1935. Word of our affair got out, as it had to, and there was no lack of whispering and insinuations. Although each member of the staff tried to act as if he or she knew nothing, I became uncomfortable at the thought of what it all could lead to. Nevertheless, I never thought of giving up Trude, since I believed that, from what I knew of my staff, there were no informants among them. On October 1 I hired a new salesman and made the unpleasant discovery that he had started becoming very interested in Trude. This young man, called Koch, came from outside and was, as I later learned, an SS man. Trude often complained about his pestering, but I could do nothing about it as long as he stayed within bounds. Besides, I had to be extremely cautious in my actions. When I gradually started noticing that Trude didn't seem to mind Herr Koch's "pestering," I confronted her on it, and she responded that she had to pretend not to mind so as not to endanger our relationship. It was scarcely edifying for me to hear this, but I tried to take her at her word. We continued to meet, although with the utmost caution. I moved closer and closer to a nervous breakdown, since I could no longer bear these secret encounters, the fear of being seen, let alone the knowledge that I might have a rival.

As the situation was becoming intolerable for both of us, I repeatedly suggested to Trude that we separate, but she begged and pleaded with me not to leave her, since "the thing with Koch isn't serious" and she only loved me and so on and so forth...

And so things went throughout the fall and winter. My brother was planning to get married on December 31, 1934, and I decided to travel to his wedding. I spent a few sad days with this emigré wedding party in a refugee hostel. I saw my brother, to whom I was devoted, for the last time. A month later he and his young wife went to Palestine.

I returned to Uelzen, only to hear from Trude's own mouth that she had betrayed me with Herr Koch in an alcoholic blur on New Year's Eve. I did not yell, I did not scream, I did not strike her. I only looked at her, the way you look at something that once belonged to you, that you once loved very much, and that you now have to surrender for good. Then I turned around. Nobody can ever know what I felt inside. I finally gave in to Trude's written and oral requests for a meeting. She assured me that she had not been in control of her faculties, that she had been under the influence of alcohol, and that she had only met Herr Koch by chance in the bar where she had been celebrating New Year's with her girlfriend and her sisters. She swore that she loved only me and begged me—"for our safety's sake"—not to object if she occasionally went off with Herr Koch. And I, fool that I was, believed her and promised to agree to everything if only I could hold onto our spare, secret hours of love. And so it went for several weeks. We met at the home of a Jewish seamstress who worked for Trude; we met on lonely country paths. Then one evening, as I was making my way home, I encountered Herr Koch, who had been spying on us. He brashly demanded to know where I was coming from. I refused to be spoken to that way and told him it was none of his concern. The next day he wrote me a letter, saying that unless I dissolved my relationship with Trude on the spot, he would report the case to his SS group. I wrote back that, as far as I knew, there was no law forbidding me to associate with Aryan women and that I intended to marry Trude. In any case, I wrote, the decision lay in Trude's hands.

That same day, the company's Party cell chairman took me aside and urgently warned me about Koch, who was already turning his comrades against me. He advised me either to break with Trude at once or else to marry her in Berlin without delay. In my blindness, as if I was trading horses, I agreed to Koch's suggestion that the three of us sit down together, and when I asked her if she was prepared to marry me on short notice, she answered "no." I left without a word, but the same day I received a letter from Trude explaining that she only said "no" for my sake, because Koch had threatened to have me arrested immediately. I left it unanswered and refused to accept any more letters, and then I saw how right I was, because at Easter "my" Trude went off with Koch for good.

Now let me say that in spite of all this I do not believe she is a bad person, only a weak one, and that her already weak character was broken by the atmosphere in which she was living. As for me, I had rescued my freedom, but at what a price! I felt like a pitiful coward. I cursed Hitler and his bandits, who reveled in extortion, even when it touched the most personal relationship a man can ever know: love.

16

Alone in Familiar Surroundings

HEINEMANN STERN

This story takes place in the wonderful Silesian mountain resort of Reinerz. Half an hour from the resort gardens, at the end of a splendid forest promenade, lies the Schmelze, an idyllic coffee restaurant, which is filled with memories of Mendelssohn-Bartholdy. At its entrance stands the Mendelssohn House, and in the middle of the garden one can see a mighty block of stone, the Mendelssohn Monument. An iron rod, cemented into the ground, once bore a plaque with the inscription, "Here, Felix Mendelssohn-Bartholdy composed his song *'Wer hat dich du schöner Wald aufgebaut so hoch da droben.'*" When I was there in 1936, all of this was still unchanged—but a year later, the plaque had vanished. Once again, I sat drinking my afternoon coffee in the Schmelze. As always after drinking coffee, I discretely headed toward a certain back room. But this time, when I sought to enter the special precinct marked "for gentlemen," I encountered an unexpected obstacle: next to the entrance hung a great big, brand-new, shiny enamel sign with the polite comment, "Jews are not welcome!" Now we Jews already had a long acquaintance with such gentle kicks in the backside, and we had become accustomed to them, as to so many other things. But I had never before encountered such a thing at this particular place. I must have stood there looking confused for a few moments, because some gentlemen, who came in after me, first saw the sign, then me, grinned, and disappeared through the door of the little house. I soon heard peals of laughter coming out of the windows. As far as I am concerned, I have always felt Jewish pride, and I have never been pushy. But this time the necessity that brought me there in the first place won out, and I did what I had to do. Upon my return, word of the incident must already have spread, because I encountered many smiling faces pointed in my direction.

I waved to the waitress and paid for my coffee. But I could not resist the temptation to comment on this matter—arousing the considerable interest of the other guests in the process. Finally, I asked that the innkeeper be told to express his dislike of Jewish guests at a more appropriate location so that we would not be tempted to drink his coffee in the first place. Two days later, the sign hung next to the main entrance. But the background to this affair turned out to be anything but funny. The restaurant was municipal property and the innkeeper, as its leaseholder, was not at liberty to do as he wished. The sign had been sent to him by the city administration—as was usually the case—and he had no choice but to do as he was told. On the other hand, he did not want to lose his numerous Jewish customers, and thus he came up with the absurd idea to solve this dilemma in the manner described above.

Private social relations—or, to be more precise, human relations in general—between us and our surroundings tore, loosened, vanished. The result was isolation, and in the end isolation is just another word for slow death. In a Jewish community the size of the Berlin congregation the death struggle took longer than it did in Hamburg, and in Hamburg it hung on longer than, for example, in Marburg. However, one should understand—so as to avoid any self-deception—that vegetating is not the same thing as living. For me, living in Berlin, it was of little consequence if Herr Schulze or Frau Müller, residents of my house, whom I only occasionally met on the stairs or on the street, chose to pretend I no longer existed, or even if Frau Schw., our old friend, gradually stopped calling on us. But my fellow sufferers Cohn and Levy in Schildberg did not enjoy the luxury of such indifference if their neighbors Müller and Schulze, whom they had always lived with and worked alongside, stopped associating with them. And just think of Frau Joseph in Fünfhausen: for ten, twenty, thirty years she had been working in her garden, and for ten, twenty, thirty years Frau Schmidt had been doing the same in the next garden over. And throughout all these years and decades, they have not only worked alongside one another, but they have been talking and gossiping, too. And suddenly they no longer know each other. Not today, not tomorrow, never again. No one can bear such a thing, particularly when you add up all the other things you are suddenly expected to bear. It can drive you to madness or to suicide. Or take Herr Goldberg in Merzbach, a tenured teacher at the little town's secondary modern school. The only friends he had were the handful of colleagues with whom he got along quite well. When disaster struck, they all pledged their loyalty, "We'll stand with you whatever happens!" But man proposes and the Party disposes. Problems arise. Colleague Luther cancels a visit. Old Professor Johannes cannot join him on their scheduled walk. "That's funny, today I could have sworn that Müller turned off onto a side alley when he saw me walking down the main street." Three days later, they meet by chance, but he only waves from a distance . . . And then one day it's all over, and they pass each other as strangers. Pure fantasy? Hardly! It happened to Dr. W . . . sohn from S. in precisely this way. One should never underestimate such "tragedies of everyday Jewish life," and one should not forget them when tabulating the crimes committed against us.

We in Berlin and our fellow sufferers in other large German cities knew how to take care of ourselves. We still had our congregations. We had our families and our friendships. And it was the latter that gave us strength and posture. We pulled closer together and created a new community life for ourselves. In fact, it was a beautiful life. And if the economic axe struck down the doctor one day and the lawyer the next . . . well, the next day they stood right back up on their own two feet, perhaps not as self-assured and stolid as before, but they were standing all right. And I just have to keep on saying what I have said all along: the fact that Hitler was so thorough about the whole thing had its good sides, too. If we had to let go of our grown children, at least they went away to freedom. And if our young children were kept from the schools, then at least their minds were not crippled and their characters were not contaminated. And is it of so little account that we old ones did not need to yell "Heil Hitler!" when deep down we were thinking "down with Hitler!"? That we did not have to pretend to entertain convictions and perform actions that we despised? How many times did I report the following strange opinion of an Aryan friend and colleague, "You Jews think only of yourselves and leave the rest of us to roll in our own filth!"

But how different things looked in the countryside! In 1935—that is to say, back in the so-called good old days—I was visiting my hometown. No one had lifted a finger against the people there. But they were lonely, lonely. They only left their houses if they had no other choice. Not out of fear that something could happen to them, but rather so they would not have to keep experiencing how people avoided them. I, as a stranger and visitor, could still afford to go into my old friends' houses. They, the established Jews, could do so no longer. Some ten to fifteen families still lived in L . . . dorf. I made some visits. At Frau S.'s house I witnessed the story I just told about Frau Joseph. I visited others, too, all my old comrades from the religion school. They sat around together, in twos and threes, at morning, noon, afternoon, evening. They chewed the fat three times, four times a day, always the same thing, only to start over the next morning. For a little variety, they did the same thing at M.'s house today, at J.'s house tomorrow. Yes, and don't forget the card games! The women had their daily grind, but the men—just the sight of unemployed men hanging around—ghastly! It's a good thing that scarcely any young people were left. The only hope these people still had was emigration or a move into one of the large cities. Yes—but what did they live off of? "Our savings." But the question was, how much longer?

17

Good Germans, Bad Germans

Joseph B. Levy

It should not be forgotten that the attitude of a large part of the Christian population, perhaps the majority, toward the Jews was basically friendly, often kind and sympathetic. We frequently heard expressions of profound disapproval, even strong rejection of the measures taken by the authorities and the Party against us and our friends.

In 1933 and 1934 we had a house servant who displayed a thoroughly decent attitude, often regretting and condemning daily events and the newspapers' excesses, our distress and anguish. Then she became engaged to a Lufthansa employee who had a reputation as a loyal Nazi. He frequently came to our flat, allowed us to entertain him, and accepted our invitation to a farewell party for his bride. While in the past he had often appeared in a uniform displaying his Party badge, he arrived at this formal affair in a normal suit without the badge, and our farewell from both of them occurred in the most heartfelt way, with the warmest of wishes on both sides.

Our L. was followed by M. Like virtually all of our Christian household servants—the only kind we had in all the years we maintained a household—she became a genuine member of our home and our family, even more than the others. She supported my ailing wife in the household, attending to the kitchen and rooms with a rare integrity and personal devotion. At no moment, not in a single action or on a single occasion did she ever show any form of dislike for us or for the Jews who always visited us in great number. She shared our joys and sorrows. She was often pressured by Party members and agitators to leave the "Jew house" or at least to join the "Labor Front" and attend its meetings. She was warned of the unpleasant consequences that her refusal and her apparently contrary attitude could have for her. She rejected any kind of cooperation with the Party organization and was jeered at on the street, yet she gladly bore all insults and threats. Then came the Nuremberg Rally in September 1935, which made it illegal to employ non-Jews under the age of forty-five as household servants, thus requiring M. to leave our service. Since my frail wife could not work, we had to give up our independent household and move to a pension. This was a sad event, both for us and for M. She cried endlessly, but the separation was unavoidable. M. remained a good friend over the next three and a half years, she visited us often, secretly at the end, since her new employer must not find out about this friendly relationship with Jews.

Our grocer came to us under cover of darkness, because our dear neighbors were afraid, and brought us merchandise that we could no longer buy in his shop. I could cite many such examples from our daily experience. The opposite, namely the refusal to make deliveries, was a rare exception. One tragicomic event occurred when I once tried to buy a cake in a large pastry shop. Then, when I asked for it to be delivered and supplied my name and address, the saleswoman whispered to me that she was not allowed to deliver anything to Jews. In another bakery the owner asked me to remain her customer, even though she also had a sign saying "German shop" or even "Jews not welcome." She did not approve of such slogans, she said. Instead, she, like so many others, had been forced to put it up.

Personal relations with "Aryans," even when it was a matter of saying hello on the street and in public, dwindled more and more. Even former close friends and acquaintances, colleagues, and wartime comrades shied away from talking to us, greeted us in secret, and excused this behavior with their fear of persecution or other difficulties. The following example is just one of many.

An elderly lady, whom I at first scarcely recognized, waved to me on the street from a distance. She at first seemed happy to see me. She was a colleague from one of the public schools where I had worked decades ago. We approached one another, but we had scarcely exchanged the first words when my eyes fell on the Party badge displayed on her dress. Following my gaze, the lady turned pale and left me without saying another word. She had suddenly realized that she, a prominent "people's comrade," had actually been standing face to face with a Jew and had nearly gotten herself thrown out of the Party.

To be sure, we were still counted among those rare "decent Jews"—a questionable compliment that was invariably expressed to us and to others with the words, "Yes, if only they could all be like you!" The German people were simply misguided: the constant drumbeat of dreadful propaganda, the same old slurs against the Jews over and over again, the way the actions of individual lawbreakers were generalized to encompass us all, the insults, the comparison to murderers and criminals, to Communists and Bolsheviks—all of this dripped the poison of hatred into the hearts of otherwise well-meaning people, it poisoned or at least intimidated them. This especially applied to the intellectuals—they had to remain silent and only expressed their convictions and positions to us in private. Here are some examples from my personal experience.

One of my granddaughters, who lived in Wiesbaden near Frankfurt, was compelled to leave the public school in order to enter a newly founded Jewish one. She gave her teacher an album with the request that she write a little verse for her. The teacher was happy to do this small favor for her eleven-year-old favorite student. A few days later, my daughter (her mother) was called in to see the school principal. He asked her—apparently ashamed of his own words—to remove the page from the album, saying that if the supervisory board discovered such evidence of affection for a Jewish child it could damage the teacher's career.

In the course of my charitable activities I frequently had dealings with a Christian notary, a mature and respected legal official. I visited him often; when I came to him after the terrible days of November, he rose from his chair, pressed my hand, looked into my eyes, and said with great emotion, "Please allow me to express to you and your Jewish friends my deepest compassion and sympathy." Then, shortly before my emigration, when I went to his office to have some copies of my personal papers notarized, he suddenly realized that I was being forced to emigrate. He closed the connecting door to his anteroom—since he had to keep his political opinions secret from his secretary—then slammed his fist onto his desk and shouted out, red faced, "These scoundrels, these charlatans, these fire-raisers! To drive a man like you, whom I know to be a man of honor, from his fatherland! Oh, if this would only end!"

One of the most frightening developments was the elimination of all Jewish physicians; the whole of Frankfurt, with its large Jewish population, was left with a mere five of them, now bearing the contrived title of "Jew healers." Thus we also lost our own family doctor, who was driven from a previously thriving rural practice as early as 1933. We then turned to a young "Aryan" doctor who was recommended to us and who proved to be a shining example of impartial love of one's fellow man. He took charge of my wife, who was succumbing more and more to the pressure and distress of these years, with admirable devotion. He was there for us anytime, day and night; he brought and sent expensive medications from his personal supply without any payment. When we asked about his fee, he would reply, full of goodness and kindness, "In these terrible times I can accept no payment for my services from Jews. I only perform my duty as a human being and try to compensate for the sins others have committed against you. Give the payment you intended for me to your poor persecuted coreligionists." He paid his last visit to my wife in the company of his own spouse, who brought the patient the first lilies of the valley from their own garden.

Such frequent signs of sympathy were made in secret, while in public they were kept hidden, even denied. Even our supposed friends feared one another and pretended to have an anti-Jewish attitude. Thus in the streetcar one could notice the icy silence that gradually edged out the formerly cheerful atmosphere. No one dared speak loudly, no one dared utter a harmless comment to his neighbor. No praise or criticism of the events in the city and the country, at the market or on the streets could be heard. Terror, cold fear dominated the internal and external life of ordinary people, who had previously lived in a world of naïve harmlessness, affable sociability, and love of their fellow man.

There is no denying that, alongside all the bad and even horrific things we experienced, we Jews experienced a great and bitter disappointment in these years. We could hardly expect that the National Socialists would treat us any better than they did. But none of us could have been pessimistic enough to imagine that Germany's great and greatest minds, aside from a few exceptions, would demonstrate so little courage and would not express their disgust at all the horrible things that occurred before their eyes and continue to occur. They quietly allowed German justice, German freedom, German culture, German morality, German human dignity to be trampled and destroyed. We do not believe that the majority of the German people are Nazis, but we did expect more courage, more decency from the intellectuals. What happened to their sense of charity, their humanity? What a heavy burden of guilt lies upon the shoulders of the silent!

18

A Rabbi Is Misunderstood

Mally Dienemann

My husband's professional work had grown much more difficult. There were so many people to help, console, and advise. Our house was filled with people seeking advice from my husband in these difficult times. He believed that he could give the people of his congregation a sense of security by teaching them lessons from our Jewish history. He wanted to show them that we had gone through similarly hard times and that our congregation had never broken down. He held frequent history lectures, and so in December he delivered a talk on the time of King Herod and the figure of Jesus Christ. His talk included this passage: If, after so many centuries, we now ask ourselves why the wonderful teachings of Christ did not convince and enthuse all Jews, our answer must be this: Jesus taught in a time that was politically restless and excited, a time in which people believed that the end of the world was at hand. It is irrelevant who is ruling you; concern yourselves only with the salvation of your souls! Nationally minded Jews had no understanding for this teaching. "Just imagine," my husband said with his special way of helping his listeners better understand past times with an example from the present, "if someone had stood up during the Ruhr occupation and had said to the people, 'It is completely unimportant who is ruling you. Who cares if it's a French general or a German police president? All that is important to you is the salvation of your souls.' You can be certain that a speaker like that, as pure as his own convictions may have been, would have encountered resistance."

Soon after Hitler's seizure of power it became customary for no lecture of any kind to take place without being spied on by the police. During my husband's lecture, two stupid-looking officers sat in the last row of the hall and slept most of the time, only occasionally jerking back into consciousness. My husband probably noticed them, but he had grown accustomed to the presence of such individuals at his lectures.

After the lecture was over, we made our way home without a second thought. The next day, we were sitting in my husband's study toward one in the afternoon when someone started ringing the doorbell. I opened the door and saw two gigantic young men in SS uniforms. Without any preliminaries they asked, "Is your husband at home?" I said yes and led them to my husband's room. They went immediately to the bookshelves, looked at the books, and confiscated utterly harmless volumes. Then they opened the desk and helped themselves to innocuous scholarly studies. They went into the other rooms, opened cupboards and drawers in our bedroom, but they didn't see my diary. They stayed for an hour and then they left, taking my husband with them. They didn't say where they were taking him or why. I waited several hours, and then when my husband did not return I notified the chairman of our congregation, Dr. Guggenheim, who was as helpless as I was. At six o'clock I went alone to the police to ask where my husband was and what it all meant. They refused to answer but merely shouted, "Get out!" That same evening, Dr. Guggenheim and I went to a lawyer, who promised to take charge of the matter. The next morning, on Friday, Dr. Guggenheim came to tell me that the lawyer could not take the case. While he didn't say so directly, we could tell that it was too dangerous for him.

I went back to the police and asked them at least to tell me the reasons for the search and the arrest. They replied: the arrest was made on account of a lecture my husband gave. He had supposedly said that it was of no importance for a nation if it was ruled by a French general or by a German police president. I tried to set the record straight, to say that it was very difficult for these people to understand this material. The man responded that the officers were reliable. My husband would be taken to a concentration camp the same evening. I could bring him some warm clothes that he could then take with him.

I hurried home, packed the things and managed to speak to my husband for a moment before he climbed into the car that took him away. It was a December day, minus twelve degrees Celsius, he was riding in an open car, and in this cold the blanket I had brought him was not big enough. He was taken to Osthofen, a concentration camp near Worms, and that was a two-to-three hour drive. My husband was fifty-eight years old and received frequent medical treatment for his heart condition. He spoke to no one in the court, no one had interrogated him, no one had told him why he had been arrested. At least I could tell him—right before he got into the car—that his lecture was the alleged reason for his arrest.

Then we set about trying to get my husband out of the camp. Some of the persons who had attended the lecture put together an exact summary of his remarks and witnessed through their signatures that the officers had misunderstood the lecture and that my husband had said nothing that could be construed as antinational. This report was sent to the head of the Offenbach police, police director Käss. I petitioned Herr Käss personally and attempted to clear up the mistake. I subsequently received the following response, which I am recording here in order to show the nonsense the two officers reported. I do not know if anyone really believed this rubbish or whether they were just pretending:

> We took Rabbi Dr. Max Dienemann into protective custody because he made the following comments in a lecture on December 12, 1933, in the house of the Jewish congregation:
> "According to historians, Herod was a Jew, but one could say that he was a feared man who could only assert himself through his brutal barbarism. Herod was a barbarian of Arabia. He had no fewer than ten wives. He had his first wife executed. His grandfather and his two sons also died by his own hand. Do you want to hear more? Let us go back to the time before 30 BC and to ten years before today, when the French were on the Rhine. Do we care whether we are ruled by a French general or by a German police president?' The turn of phrase in the last sentence in the context of the comments on Herod represents a rude insult and slander of German police presidents, who have been placed in authority to guarantee public peace and safety. In these comments he also exhibited an extremely anti-state attitude.
> "As a result of his behavior, which has become known to the public, such a hostile mood has arisen within nationally minded circles that attacks upon his person must be anticipated."

To me, the nonsense that was distilled out of my husband's lecture, the nonsensical links between Herod and a French general and a German police president, are a classic example of bogus reporting and stupid misinterpretation. The newspaper accounts of his arrest repeated the nonsense. Our hands were tied. We were not permitted to publish any corrections in the newspapers. They wouldn't have been printed.

Five more difficult days passed by, filled with petitions, visits to the police with hat in hand, and attempts to persuade people to use their connections to free my husband. An old Party member with a low membership number, who as a physician was horrified that an old man was transported in an open car in such cold weather, gave us anonymous support. On Friday morning, after my husband had spent nine days in custody, I went back to the top police official, police director Käss, a very young gentleman. He listened politely to what I had to say, then picked up the telephone in my presence and issued the release order. That was in the early morning, and in the afternoon we picked my husband up from the train station. He looked terrible. We then traveled to the Giant Mountains, where my husband gradually recovered his strength.

19

A Mixed Marriage Beneath the Swastika

Eva Wysbar

Aside from the absolutely highest levels of the Party, no one was supposed to know in advance that these laws would be announced at the Nuremberg Rallies in September of 1935. The two most significant features of the law were the bans on mixed marriages and on illegitimate relations between Aryans and non-Aryans—"racial defilement," which was punishable by the most severe penalties.

Informing on people began to assume unimaginable dimensions, and those people who had kept up their friendships and social relations with one another without regard to racial considerations now had to stop if they wanted to survive. A man and a woman could be suspected of racial defilement by merely sitting down to a cup of coffee together. People were exposed to malicious slander at all times and in all places. Disappointed spouses were handed an effective means of extortion, and dismissed employees were free to take revenge. No outside observer can even begin to imagine the total effect of this intrusion into the twisted labyrinth of human relationships.

For my husband XY and me there was nothing more to decide. Our livelihood and careers were utterly unimportant. We had only one thought left: to get out of Germany and go anywhere. Just get out! Up to this point my husband had been convinced that a purifying storm would break above our heads and that afterward a new dawn would shine forth for Germany. Equally strong was his conviction—shared by a great many people—that every non-Nazi was doing his part to help prepare this dawn. How mistaken he was. The sun did not rise. It sank over Germany, and the red glow of dusk meant blood. Icy horror tightened its grip around Germany's future victims.

At this time, XY was the last filmmaker who still lived in a mixed marriage and continued to work. Everyone else to whom this applied had either long since yielded to pressure and divorced or else—and this was a tiny minority—left the country together. Since only 100 percent Aryans—both in terms of origin and marriage—were allowed to work in the film association, and since everyone in the film industry had to be a member, either XY or the company he was working for had to apply for special permission allowing him to work on a film. This permission was randomly issued by Goebbels on the basis of his own personal desires and could be withdrawn at any time. This practice applies everywhere, and even today one can find Jews, or at least half-Jews, in leading positions, still employed thanks to the special permission of the minister in charge.

We had reason to believe that XY's filmmaking days in Germany were numbered. It was unlikely that Herr Goebbels would be good-humored enough to ignore the fact that, despite separate flats and surveillance by the Gestapo, we were expecting our second child. It had been my greatest wish to have this child. The more danger I saw around me, the more strongly I felt the need to protect my family and to support the existence of our first child with a second one.

In October 1935 my husband applied to renew his expired passport—he finally received it in October 1938. We tirelessly fought for three years to get this piece of paper. Three years in which my husband, condemned to immobility and silence, sat helplessly in the Nazi trap; three years in which I traveled through all of Europe and half of America on a quest for the key to this trap. It was a gigantic struggle, paid for with everything that makes life beautiful and only rendered bearable by the idea for which it was fought. The fact that his passport had expired and he was not permitted to renew it at first appeared to us as an irritating fact that would delay our departure but could certainly be attended to. In view of the international nature of his profession it would not be difficult to find a plausible reason for XY to travel abroad. As the director of several successful film productions, he was in a considerably better position professionally than he had been two years before, and we had no doubt that he would be able to continue his career abroad. Our plan was to arrange an "invitation"—a real or simulated one—for him as a guest director of a foreign production. Since all foreign currency wages had to be sent to Germany, international relations were promoted energetically, and there was no doubt that Goebbels would give his consent to such an invitation.

We soon noticed that correspondence did not help us toward our goal. It was too dangerous. Despite our caution, an opened letter, an overheard word, a tapped telephone conversation could spell our doom. Our greatest hopes lay in Switzerland, since the previous owner of the Terra company, who had since departed from Berlin, was trying to build up a new production firm there. We hoped that a personal visit by me would help us along toward our goal. As the happy holder of a passport that was still valid for a number of years, I traveled soon after the birth of the baby to Switzerland with both children and our loyal nanny. If our plan succeeded, it would be better to be outside Germany's borders with the whole family.

It would go beyond the bounds of this report to describe the suffering that led me from one city to the next, from Zurich to Paris, from there to London, and after many detours back to Rome. One disappointment followed on the heels of another, and I finally had to accept the fact that the brief fourteen days that most countries allow for a visit made it impossible to retry failed attempts. If the time had not been so short, and if I had not been caught and worn down by the infamous "Paris Group," then I might have succeeded in overcoming the one deadly argument for which I was least prepared, "We have neither any use nor any assistance for a man who is still living and working in Germany." "The wife is Jewish? Then she should get a divorce!" On this point my Jewish friends and my Aryan enemies were of one mind.

The suggestive power of the Third Reich transcended its borders. Even these German emigrés were guided by it and essentially did what the Nazis did, although the other way around. In Alexander Korda's Denham Studios I was told, "With a name like yours we won't even let you cross the threshold." But I did cross their threshold, two days before my English visa ran out. I was sick and tired. I did not speak to Korda. I spoke to no one whose name had any importance. An "invitation" from some German emigré would likely have made little impression on Goebbels. It had to be a foreign producer, and my acquaintances could not point me to one. I had failed outright—the obstacles in the way of survival, the suspicion and hatred were more powerful than I was. I left Denham on the hour-long trip back to London together with an UFA (Universal Film Corporation) agent for South America. He said, "Your husband makes wonderful films, but I can't sell them to my people. Too German and too highbrow." "That bodes well for the future," I thought.

In the meantime, my husband's position in Berlin had deteriorated rapidly. As we anticipated, the birth of our second child had finally demonstrated his "unreliability," and it was unthinkable that Goebbels would provide him with further work permits. In view of his decision to leave Germany, this end to his professional career would not have frightened XY if it did not also likely mean the end of his personal freedom.

Starting in the spring, all men of draft age were required to report to the military authorities. On this occasion, XY was given particularly unwelcome attention. A former officer with special training in technical units, which were now to include expertise in film and color film technology, was of great interest and value to the army. There was no doubt to what use they would have put XY the moment he stopped making films. But as soon as he put on their uniform, there would be no escape for him. We had to gain time somehow.

In the midst of this crisis, our rescue came from Hitler personally. At that time, two special copies were made of every German film. One went to the Propaganda Ministry, the other to the Obersalzberg. Hitler watched every film, but almost never interfered with Goebbels's competence. He would show the films he liked best to entertain his guests. At some official function or other he selected one of XY's films and referred to it as the very model of a good German film—very much to Goebbels's embarrassment. Goebbels, who had panned the same film just a few weeks earlier, rushed to award this film—which had already been out for more than a month—the highest honors and paid the producer a so-called premium of 150,000 Reichsmarks. XY was on top once more. He was given a new film project—but now under the final condition that he immediately file for divorce.

When I returned with the children to Germany in the late summer, I went directly to our lawyer in order to file for divorce on the basis of "insurmountable aversion." The lawyers representing me in the divorce suit had their work cut out for them.

In and of themselves, Gestapo clients were not popular, since even the most harmless of citizens feared becoming entangled with this institution. My first lawyer begged me to transfer my case to a colleague, since the numerous telephone calls and letters from the Gestapo requesting information on the divorce's progress were keeping him up at night. We drove our second lawyer to despair through our cleverness in avoiding the "reconciliation hearing" for a whole year. According to German law, this deadline is not mandatory, but it can be demanded by the plaintiff. Only when no reconciliation occurs by this hearing, at which both parties have to be present, is the divorce confirmed at a later late. Of course, I insisted on this "reconciliation hearing," but every time it came up it turned out that either my husband or I had convincing reasons for not attending.

After the reconciliation hearing had been postponed for the third time, the court declared that a renewed demand for the hearing would be viewed as a provocation, and my frightened lawyer asked me to transfer the case to yet another colleague. And I did so.

Desperate after the failure of my efforts abroad, XY tried a different way of securing a passport. After showing up at his office two or three times with threadbare excuses, one of the film association officials made a biting comment that revealed his suspicions. We would have to be extremely cautious in the future. We had picked out Italy as the goal of our new efforts, since in these years it was eagerly endeavoring to develop its own film production companies. A travel agreement between Germany and Italy made it possible not only to stay there for an extended period of time but also to transfer moderate sums of money. And yet, this money was not enough to permit the children and me to stay in Italy, so we decided to remain in Berlin.

However, my departure was unexpectedly delayed by the fact that my brother, who wanted to emigrate with us, had to undergo a serious operation beforehand. According to the 1935 law, which forbade female Jewish household servants for Jewish men, my brother, who had returned as an invalid from four years at the front, was forced to move out. For my husband's sake I was not allowed to hire non-Aryan staff, and I did not want to give up our nanny, whose loyalty was beyond question. It was simply grotesque that I ended up living alone with the children in a three-story house, while my husband and my brother lived in hotels. As a result of all this I ended up staying longer in Berlin. In the meantime, my husband had given up his hotel room so as not to leave the children alone in the remote house with the staff. During these weeks we lived together. With the sense of having performed our "duty" by filing for divorce, and with the optimism provided us by our new plans, we believed we had earned such luxury.

A few days before my departure for Rome, d'Alquen gave my husband a document that had fallen into his hands on the way to Himmler. It was a sketch of our house, complete with all the details, with exact information on every window and every door, with indications as to whether a door was made of glass or wood, and showing the location of our bedroom. At this moment, XY lost his previously steady composure. A stormy altercation ensured, during which XY described this filthy spying in the words it deserved, while d'Alquen hurled long-suppressed accusations against him about his impossible behavior. He called him a traitor and finally, white in the face, he pulled his badge out of his pocket and said he was under arrest. This scene took place in an apartment belonging to Tamara, with whom the Obersturmbannführer was passionately in love. The actress succeeded in defusing the situation and saved XY—this time, at least.

By this time it was obvious that only a life far from the public eye could reduce the unbearable attention now being showered upon us. XY applied to his boss, Reich Film Dramatist Nierentz, for a one-year leave of absence. Nierentz was horrified and refused to forward the application to Goebbels. Apparently it was common in the Third Reich to be sent on leave, but not to apply for it oneself.

XY decided to take daring action. For some time the circle around Göring had been asking whether he, as a former pilot, would be willing to film from the air. He had previously steered away from this project, but now it provided him with a splendid opportunity to secure leave from Goebbels without raising his ire. XY knew that his direct superior in the army ministry was an old regimental comrade of his. He went to him and declared his willingness to enter the air force following his divorce, provided that he would be freed from all other service. According to the law, high military posts could only be filled by irreproachable people's comrades, and even a former officer living in a mixed marriage was automatically demoted to a private. In view of this indignity, which one comrade does not like to impose on another, XY was granted leave until the conclusion of divorce proceedings.

It worked. During my stay in Italy, my husband spent almost a year of voluntary imprisonment in our silent, remote house, which he scarcely left. It was a year of complete peace and quiet undisturbed by any outside events. But this peace and quiet came too late for a man who was broken inside. This constant life in the shadows, the relentless need to scheme and watch his step, to suppress his own opinion and to lead a double life—all of this was more than he could bear. When I saw him again for the first time after many months, I knew that this man was doomed to destruction if we could not find a way to get him out of Nazi Germany.

Then a ray of light fell upon this hopeless situation. It came from the last place we would have expected. One of XY's most beautiful films, the one that first provoked Goebbels's opposition, had had an unusually successful run in New York. The theater owner cabled to ask for an option on the film rights since he hoped to sell them to Hollywood for a remake. This was a clear sign from heaven—for the first time, America seemed in reach. Our minds were made up. XY had to receive an invitation to go to Hollywood; there was no doubt that Goebbels would give his permission to such a leave. Corresponding would have been too complicated and too dangerous. Besides, we did not know anyone in the United States who could have provided us with the affidavits one needed to enter the country. I had to travel there, as quickly as possible, because the situation of the Jews had deteriorated dreadfully over recent weeks and a new pogrom was expected at any moment.

Following endless efforts and after using all our connections, the Gestapo granted me a two-month passport that allowed me to stay in the United States for fourteen days. To be sure, I had to sign a statement that I would emigrate within four weeks of my return. There was no point in renewing our long and expensive rental lease, so before my departure we looked for a flat where my husband and our children could live until I came back. That was as far as we could plan ahead. As pressed for time as we were, we took the first thing we found, namely the lower floor of a two-family house in a Berlin suburb.

I sailed to America, and a miracle occurred. Within those two weeks I found the assistance for my husband that I had sought in vain in Europe for two years. I did not receive one invitation but two. They were pure fiction and of no professional value, but they were convincing enough for Goebbels. They were our salvation. I brought affidavits for my brother, the children, and me. Still astonished by my luck after so much despair, I arrived in Berlin, never suspecting that anything could be wrong. And then I was confronted with a situation that was all the more eerie for its dislocation from the reality outside.

When I rented the flat, I naturally made certain that the landlord was not a Nazi. Of this there was no question, since the house belonged to the widow of the unfortunate radio director K., whom the regime tried to get rid of after 1933 following a failed attempt to try him for bribery. The Nazis brought Herr K. to a sanatorium because he "needed rest." And rest he would have for the rest of eternity, because they put a revolver in his hand and stationed a guard outside his door until Herr K. finally committed suicide. To heighten the effect of this drama, the Nazis chose a sanatorium located directly across the street from Herr K.'s house, so that his wife could follow everything at close quarters.

We thus felt safe in Frau K.'s house. Unfortunately, I had failed to ask about the other tenant. As was discovered while I was still in America, this tenant was none other than a general, the Count von Rocques, president of the Reich Air Defense League and the most dangerous neighbor we could have found.

The situation I encountered upon my return from America was like this: as soon as Herr von Rocques found out that a family with Jewish connections had moved into his house, he demanded that Frau K., the owner, evict them within twenty-four hours. He stated his reasons in a letter that shattered the mold of common courtesy between civilized human beings. He said that it was a blatant insult to expect him and his wife, two "old fighters" of the Nazi Party, to live cheek by jowl with Jews or half-Jews. It was intolerable to be forced to look out of one's window onto the garden and see Jewish half-breeds at play. Furthermore, his position in society had been severely compromised as he could not invite guests to a house in which the latter could risk encountering Jews and half-breeds of both sexes on the stairs.

Frau K. responded that she saw no way of challenging a half-year rental lease, particularly since she had concluded it with the Aryan XY and he had signed it with his own hand. The general's answer was that in the Third Reich an Aryan could not be forced to live under one roof with non-Aryans and if she again refused to evict them from the flat, he would take matters into his own hands and leave. He would make her, the owner, liable for all costs arising from the move as well as for all resulting damages. Through her lawyer, Frau K. refused all such demands. The general in turn threatened that he would sue both Frau K. and the film director XY for concealing the true state of affairs. He argued that XY had rented the apartment under false pretenses, since it had really been intended for his Jewish wife, who had already slept for one night under its roof. When Frau K. refused to give in, the general filed suit with the public prosecutor. My husband, entirely helpless in a situation he saw no hope of salvaging, limited his efforts to drafting a letter in which he utterly rejected the accusation of renting the flat "under false pretenses," and postponed any further steps pending my return.

A number of secondary tragedies occurred alongside this central drama, and they would continue to play out long after we had left Germany. More and more people were drawn in: alongside Frau K., these included the young couple who performed gardening and doorman duties in the house, our cook, and the nanny. All four were Aryans. They committed no other crime besides remaining loyal to us.

As I learned from her later on, Frau K. lost virtually every aspect of her case and was ruined financially. The gardeners drew the general's anger upon themselves when their two lovely children, who were close friends of our own, ignored his aristocratic injunction and continued playing with them. When the general challenged the young woman on this, she exploded and said that her children's upbringing was her own affair and she would let her children play with whomever they liked. Although both my husband and Frau K. did their utmost to negotiate in this burgeoning scandal, the couple ended up losing their position. When during the course of the trial they refused to make false statements on the general's behalf, he arranged for the man to be thrown out of his professional association. The general then put such shameless pressure on the cook to quit her service that I also began to fear the worst and finally persuaded her to leave us. The final player was our nanny, who had acted as a substitute mother for our children during my long absences. She was our only confidante and would not have left us at any price.

In the end, this girl, as an inconspicuous Aryan, brought our children over the border. As a result of the "revelations" the general then made, she did not dare return to Germany. After immense difficulties she crossed the Atlantic with us, leaving all her possessions behind.

The American consulate took note of our dire situation. Thanks to his great helpfulness, we did not have to wait for our immigration visas in Germany, as was customary, but had them sent after us many months later. Thus we now only had to wait for my emigration passport to be issued in order to leave Germany. Since freedom was so near, we decided to risk the general's rage and at least let the children continue living there under our nanny's protection.

XY moved back to the hotel where he had been living before, and I tried to find a place near our flat. This was not possible, since neither hotels nor private pensions were allowed to accept Jews. Thus I finally moved in with some friends who lived an hour away. Although I did not dare enter the flat as anything but a brief guest, nor could I make any preparations for our emigration during those hours, I nevertheless spent some nights there. During these nights, XY patrolled around the house for hours in order to warn me of approaching danger.

In June of 1938 the children left Germany with their nanny, and I followed a few days later. The divorce was formally proclaimed in September. In November, XY received a half-year leave of absence to travel to the United States.

Part V

Through the Eyes of Children

The adults had a hard enough time comprehending what was happening to their surroundings and to themselves. But for Jewish children it was almost impossible to understand why their playmates were no longer allowed to play with them, why they were excluded from swimming lessons and from field trips, why people shouted insults at them or even beat them up for being Jews. It was painful to be humiliated in school by doctrinaire teachers and radicalized pupils and be labeled as outsiders. The increasingly ideological character of the curriculum and the indoctrination of non-Jewish children, which occurred in their presence, affected them deeply. Already in December 1934 a report by the Reich Agency of German Jews reported that many Jewish children displayed psychological disturbances. Of course, in the early phase after the Nazi seizure of power there still were some teachers who paid attention to the situation of Jewish children and sought to protect them, and there were still fellow pupils who refused to break off their friendships. But they were placed increasingly under pressure by Nazis among the faculty or were informed on by other children.

The problems continued for Jewish children after graduation. The number of Jewish companies available for vocational training declined steadily. Many of the apprenticeships still available, for example in the commercial trades, had no future. In addition, in 1933 the German Chamber of Crafts and Trades decreed that Jews should be excluded from craft training. Following Jewish protests this decision was temporarily revoked, but the situation did not fundamentally change.

University access for Jews was also increasingly restricted. The "law against the overfilling of German schools and universities" of April 25, 1933, limited the proportion of Jewish students to 1.5 percent, making exceptions solely for front soldiers. Jewish students lost all benefits, including scholarships. In the fall of 1933 only 590 Jewish students were still registered at German universities.

Stigmatized young people could only find new playmates and friends within the traditional Jewish organizations and sports clubs, whose activities were also restricted by decrees and the overall situation. The Zionist organizations were tolerated until November 1938. Their notions and ideals may have seemed alien to children and young people from liberal families, but they at least helped compensate for their discrimination and offered some protection. Within a short time, membership in such groups doubled. In 1937 around 60 percent of Jewish young people belonged to them. Participation helped transform many new members into conscious Jews and convinced Zionists who were proud of their Jewishness and now began discovering new goals and a new meaning in their lives.

Jewish pupils were allowed to attend public schools until November 1938. But, as at the universities, their proportion was restricted to a certain percentage. However, because of these bad experiences at the public schools, the Jews began developing their own school system in 1933. This meant large financial expenditures that nevertheless paid off. While only a quarter of the some sixty thousand Jewish children in Germany attended Jewish schools in 1933, this share grew to 60 percent by 1937. The 167 Jewish schools may have stood under state supervision, but in regard to curriculum, content, and teaching materials they largely operated independently. These schools also contributed to a new Jewish identity through such subjects as Hebrew, Jewish history, and Palestinian geography. The last remaining Jewish schools were closed on June 30, 1942.

Jewish vocational counselors strove to help Jewish school graduates attain career oriented training. They were allowed to continue their work, and in 1934 they managed to fill some three thousand apprenticeships, most of them in remaining Jewish companies. They also attempted to prepare young people for emigration to Palestine through special training courses in agriculture, the trades, and home economics on special training estates. It was often not easy to convince parents of the need for such training. But in view of the increasing pressure in Germany, this appeared more and more as a possible escape route for children.

Many parents tried different ways of getting their children out of Germany and settled abroad, even if this meant long-term separation. The memoirs of witnesses often report devastating scenes where children boarded trains for an uncertain future and their weeping parents waved to them from the platform. At such moments, no one, neither the children nor the parents, knew if they would ever see each other again. For many of them, this meant good-bye forever.

20

A Child's Suffering

Hugo Wolf

My daughter began attending a convent school at Christmas 1933, and she was very well treated by the Catholic nuns. When this school was outlawed at Easter 1938 and the large building was converted into a factory, she was sent to the secondary school in the nearby large city. My son began his secondary education in another school starting at Easter, 1938.

Before they were admitted [to primary school], I visited the director in order to ask him whether he thought it advisable to send my son to his school. He replied with these words, "I am a good Catholic and have served my profession for more than thirty years. My school is only concerned with performance and learning. The Party does not rule here yet. Go ahead and send me your boy."

From the very first day, my son, who was then nine years old, was placed by his teacher at a desk of his own, while the other pupils all sat two to a desk. When he once dropped his pencil on the floor and another pupil reached down to pick it up for him, the teacher shouted, "Let the Jew pick up his own pencil!" Another time, the teacher asked for help changing a coin. When my son, the only one in the class who was able to, offered to change it, the teacher said angrily, "No, I don't touch Jewish money." My child was not allowed to join in swimming lessons. The teacher said to him, in the presence of the other pupils, "Go jump in the Jordan with your flat feet. I'll not have you fouling German water." He was not called upon a single time in the classroom and his written work was never graded. Only once, when the class was told to write an essay on "Adolf Hitler, the savior of the German people from the Jewish world plague," the teacher called to my boy, "Well, let's see yours." When my son told him that his father had forbidden him to write on such a topic, as I had instructed him to say, the teacher gave up on him altogether. In the eyes of this most excellent of teachers, my son had ceased to exist. However, the other teachers were good to him. When this tormenting of an innocent little child became insupportable, I made the painful journey to the director and reported the situation to him. The director told me, "This is all news to me, and it's hard to believe. When I inspected the little ones a few days ago, the homeroom teacher asked your son a question and received a satisfactory answer." My son confirmed the truth of this, and it demonstrates just how malicious a German teacher could be. Then the director said, "Unfortunately, I cannot take any action against this teacher as he is the chairman of the teachers' association. A protest would cost me my position." When Jewish children were banned from the secondary schools, my ten-year-old son said to me, "Father, if you had forced me to go to school any longer, then I would have thrown myself in front of a train." My hair stood on end and I felt a tingle down my spine. What had happened to the soul of this small, innocent child? How teachers must torment a child in the New Germany to put such thoughts into the mind of an innocent ten-year-old boy!

21

Segregation from a Child's Point of View

HANS WINTERFELDT

I had only negative experiences away from my parental home, because for as long as I can remember there was never a time when we Jews weren't under pressure. Even the conversations at our house between my parents and their acquaintances always sounded negative and did not point to a pleasant future. Although I understood virtually nothing of what was said, I felt that the future that was being painted by these political pessimists did not bode well. I preferred those people who may have been wrong but who at least took an optimistic view of the future. Then I would hear phrases like, "Nothing is ever as bad as it seems." Others were convinced that HE would soon disappear, because things simply could not continue on like this forever.

One Saturday—it was April 1, 1933—two Storm Troopers wearing brown uniforms appeared in front of the Jewish shops in our town. For the first time, I began to understand what the "political" conversations that were being conducted between members of the Jewish community really meant. My father and the other gentlemen spoke of an individual action which was entirely unjustified and which the government had absolutely nothing to do with. The optimists were right again, and they triumphed when the Storm Troopers actually did disappear after a short time. They said this was proof positive that we were living in a state under the rule of law that would not permit such individual actions in the future. The optimists were right, because this was the last large-scale individual action.

When my mother traveled with me to the children's festival in the Eichwald, as she did every year, in the company of two other Jewish women, Dr. Krantz, the dentist, who was already drunk, yelled into the crowd, asking what the Jewish bitches were doing there. My mother went straight home. She gave the sandwiches, which had been intended for me and my sister, along with the torches for the evening parade, to another woman so as not to spoil their fun. Since the family members marched in the rear, I did not witness the incident.

My homeroom teacher, Herr Walter, had recently begun noticing that my classmates were shunning me: no one wanted to sit next to me, no one wanted to play with me during recess. We always had to leave the classroom in pairs to get to the courtyard. To go from the courtyard to the classrooms the pupils also had to walk in class formation and in pairs. I always went alone, and I was always last.

As early as 1935 it was impossible for us to spend time in any public places. It didn't matter if it was the restaurant in Eichwald, the public swimming pool, the station restaurant, or the parks—not to mention "Hitler Square," which no Jew dared enter just because of its name. We either stayed home or, on Sundays and holidays, particularly during the summer, we took bike rides in the countryside around Lippehne, where no one knew us. The only excursion we could take without fear was to the Jewish cemetery. But not even it was spared. One day, when no one was there, Hitler Youth members climbed over the cemetery wall and knocked over the gravestones. It was revealed that dentist Krantz's son knocked over my grandfather's gravestone. My father wrote Dr. Krantz demanding that he pay for the repairs to the stone, which the doctor did without comment.

Of course, we children felt the general ill treatment of the Jews and the exclusion from the community more strongly than the adults. We could only go places where no one else knew us. We could not go to the sledding hill in the winter, we could not go to the public pool in the summer, and on the street we always had to behave inconspicuously, which is to say, no more than two children could be seen together at any one time. This isolation from the rest of the population resulted in the Jews closing ranks and, not least, becoming more aware of their Jewishness.

Since most of the Jewish men in town had taken part in World War I, they all belonged to the Reich League of Jewish Front Soldiers (RJF). The Berlin members of this association organized a trip to Berlin for many Jewish children during Christmas vacation, because they were of the opinion that Jewish youth suffered most under Nazi persecution. Every child from the province was lodged with a Jewish family—these were largely very well-to-do people—over the holidays. The children from Soldin, Lippehne, and Pyritz traveled in a group to Berlin and were met by the gentlemen of the RJF at Zoo Station and then taken to their guest families by car. I twice went to Berlin in this manner, in 1935 and 1936. The first time I was sent to a prosperous family by the name of Böhm. These people owned a belt factory and lived in southwest Berlin.

Herr Böhm, who was a very amiable man, wanted to know what rural life was like under the Nazi regime. I told him how unpleasant it sometimes was. He was amazed at the many restrictions and the chicanery we were exposed to. He told me that people didn't take the Nazis seriously in Berlin. He said that he and his daughter enjoyed looking at the funny pictures in the *"Stürmer* cases" and reading the accompanying hate propaganda.

He advised me not to let myself be intimidated, because the Nazi regime would not be able to hold on much longer. Much of the atrocity propaganda came from the Jews themselves, he said. In Berlin there was little evidence of such things and one could move about with complete freedom.

And as far as I could judge, Herr Böhm proved to be correct in the following days. The lady of the house took us children on evening walks through the city, which was all lit up for Christmas. No one gave us a "crooked" look, we could go into all restaurants, shops, and department stores. In fact, she even took us to the Christmas market. I had two wonderful weeks in which I almost forgot my dismal life in Lippehne.

Our last year in our house and shop in Lippehne was 1937. Our income was so low that my father saw no choice but to sell the house and shop. I had wished for a scooter for my birthday. My father inquired at a toy factory where he could buy the scooter wholesale. But even that was too expensive for him. He called me into his shop and explained all the circumstances. I was proud that by doing without the scooter I could at least help my father save money.

We had always talked about moving to Berlin after selling the shop. Of course, I also suffered from the lack of freedom we were experiencing in our small town, particularly at school. I felt the agitation against the Jews just as strongly as the adults, but I did not suffer so much from the injustice they showed us, because for me the pressure had not suddenly started in 1933. I had never experienced anything else. I was particularly worried about our financial future. I constantly heard my father say that he had to put in his own money. He had no income and his expenses piled up, particularly taxes and his employees' wages. I know that there was one evening when my father had a total of seven marks in the till.

For us children, the years 1935–37 were actually better than the first years of Nazi rule. It was only at school that things grew worse from year to year. We had become accustomed to the fact that we were "non-Aryans" and were not allowed to play with "Aryan" children, so we always kept to ourselves. On Sundays my parents rode with us and with all Jewish children who owned and could ride a bicycle to a lake around 15 km from Lippehne, where nobody knew us. There we could swim, go boating and play ball without being harassed.

At that time it was difficult to find a flat in Berlin. My father had asked a cousin of his there to help us. One evening the cousin called us up and told us to come immediately. My mother departed the very next day. She had no choice but to take the flat that was offered her, since we had no prospect of finding anything more reasonable. It was bad enough that the flat was going to cost us 110 marks a month. The worst thing was that we had to start paying the rent starting November 1 but could not move to Berlin until the end of December.

As the new year 1938 dawned, life took a serious turn. My sister and I were to complete our education in a Jewish school. My sister started at the school in the Prinzregentenstrasse—right next to the synagogue—while I attended the Joseph Lehmann School at Joachimsthalerstrasse 13. The pupils and teachers were very pleasant to me, but the entire atmosphere was alien. Although it was obvious that the children were of Jewish extraction, I didn't really think of them as Jews. They played in the courtyard during recess, talked loudly, and in no way behaved the way one would expect Jewish children in the provinces to behave. I was suddenly in another world I could not accept—it was all too good to be true. In addition, all the teachers were Jews.

My grandmother was very nearsighted. She didn't care for Berlin at all because there was so much traffic that she could not go out on the street by herself. I led her to the nearby Wartburgplatz a few times. After she had become well acquainted with the route, she would go there alone and sit on a bench. But at this time Jews were no longer allowed to sit on all benches. Of course, with her bad eyesight she could not read the small sign saying that Jews were not allowed to sit on a particular bench. One day, in the spring of 1938, she came back home all excited and said that a young boy had chased her off the bench with the words, "Stand up, you old Jewish bitch. You can't sit here, so buzz off." After that, my grandmother never left the house again. A few weeks later she moved back to Lippehne, where she was taken in again by the Bass family.

An acquaintance of my father had an itinerant trade license that permitted him to travel throughout the March of Brandenburg selling textile goods to private customers. After my father failed to find a means of earning a living, he also applied for such a license. His first circuit took him to Brandenburg on the Havel. My father's acquaintance, Herr Happ, took him along and sent him to people—usually bakeries or fish shops—where he had been turned away because of his Jewish appearance. I felt so sorry for my father, having to travel with such a heavy suitcase. He left the house at seven in the morning. He first took bus number 8 to Potsdam Station and went from there to Brandenburg by train. The first evening we thought that my father was spending the night in Brandenburg. We waited until eight in the evening, then my sister and I went to the bus stop. At 8:30 my father climbed out of the bus with his heavy suitcase, completely exhausted. "Well, how was it?" my mother asked. "I sold nothing," my father replied and dropped himself onto a chair. My father was too tired to eat. I was very disheartened the entire evening, and I hoped my father would be more successful the following day.

Aside from our parents' flat, school was the only place where we were allowed to move about freely and without compulsion. The school administration always warned us to behave inconspicuously on the street and never to appear as a group but only in pairs. We should never stand in front of the school. A teacher always stood at the entrance before the first bell and after the last bell to make sure we never formed groups in front of the school.

22

I Want to Become a Nazi

ERNST LOEWENBERG

Over the years an atmosphere developed in which it was virtually impossible to raise children in a consistent manner. They heard daily reports of arrests, only a few of which involved guilty people. On the other hand, those people who succeeded in smuggling their assets out of the country were looked upon as heroes. There is no injustice in a land without justice. But what was to become of children growing up with such a relativist notion of justice and injustice? When our boys traveled to Amsterdam in the summer of 1938, our older son only regretted that he didn't smuggle a million marks since the customs officials didn't even look at him. And on the way back he was proud that he had hidden some packages of meat from the stern eyes of the officials. The boys had a good time overall, even though they were infected with the general nervousness. Our older son had a particularly hard time not being part of the crowd, not being allowed to march with the others.

In my wife's diary there are a few small comments that show how the children viewed the events of that time. Frank asked how the Egyptians knew that Moses was a Jew, "He can't have been stupid enough to tell them himself." Frank went onto the street with a friend of his. Other children came and shouted at his friend, crying "Jew," and beat him up. Then the friend, pointing to Frank, said, "He's one, too." "How stupid of him to say that," Frank said. "I could have helped him otherwise." The census form was delivered to our house. "Father, do you have to write down that you're a Jew?" "Oh my, what are they going to do to you?" At that time, in the spring of 1933, Frank was seven years and four months old. In the summer of 1933 a regulation was issued stating that schoolchildren had to greet everyone with the Hitler salute and sing the Horst Wessel Song in the schools. We had previously forbidden Frank to do either. He was now very happy that this regulation made him part of the crowd. He marched into the room wearing a swastika. "What are you?" "A Storm Trooper." "What do you want, sir?" my father asked. "I want to inform you that you are being released." He listened to the story of Aladdin's lamp. "Oh, I wish I had a lamp like that." "What for?" "Then I would wish to be a Nazi." "And the rest of us?" "Of course I'd wish that for all of you as well." That did not show any sympathy with the Nazis but rather his wish to belong, to be one with the masses. At that time, Frank was just seven years and sixth months old.

In January 1934—Frank was now eight years and two months old—his homeroom teacher told us that he did not believe that Frank was suffering personally from the tensions of the times. However, he had noticed how he often trembled at the raising of the flag. In May 1934 he was physically attacked by the other boys for the first and only time. Four boys of his size punched and kicked him after they tied him to a garden fence together with his lunch box. In the summer of 1935 he observed that the Jews were being excluded more and more. "Wouldn't it be better," he asked, "if we lived in a proper ghetto?" Starting at this time he stopped wanting to go to Langenhorn, where he used to play with Aryan boys every Sunday.

Jacob, who was four years and six months old in September 1933, went to the synagogue for the first time. Before he went he said, "I can't say Heil Hitler, there's nothing but Jews inside."

In June 1934, at the age of five years and three months, he came back from playing in the street, his eyes full of tears. He refused to tell us what happened. It was not until two days later did he finally admit to the following, "The boys said that Father killed Frank's teacher and that we're all bad people." Here I need to mention that Frank's teacher was called Heiland [savior]. Jacob had never before heard this term for Jesus. He was terribly upset to hear his father being denounced as a murderer.

In the summer of 1935, at the age of six years and four months, he said, "Daddy, what would you rather be, a Jew or a Christian?" "I don't know. I've never been a Christian and I don't know what that would be like." "What would you like to be, a boy or a girl?" "I don't know that either because I've never been a girl." "I would rather be a girl, because then people wouldn't know right away that I'm a Jew."

23

Jewish Schools as Refuges

Heinemann Stern

The effects of the so-called renewal were not nearly as profound in the schools as in other areas. Years later, Jewish students still attended the public primary and secondary schools in large numbers. The same was true of the vocational schools, to the extent that they were mandatory. In Berlin, Jewish students at public schools numbered in the thousands. Nevertheless, as early as Easter of 1933 students began flooding into the Jewish schools, which gradually grew to mammoth schools and finally became the mandatory schools for all Jewish students, although they legally remained private schools, all the way up to middle school. This means they were "voluntary" institutions of the congregation, naturally also in regard to funding. Whatever subsidies the city provided were on a voluntary basis. The Jewish public schools, meaning schools as municipal or state institutions, continued in Prussia until July 1, 1939. In the other states—almost exclusively those in southern Germany—this policy was followed on a "discretionary basis." The first ones to abandon their duty toward the Jews with a stroke of the pen were Baden—the formerly renowned liberal "model state"—and Hessen.

The middle school provides a good example of how our schools swelled and then receded. At the end of the 1932/33 school year it had 470 pupils. The big, beautiful building in Grosse Hamburger Strasse was almost deserted. Two weeks later, at the start of the new school year, the number had risen to 840, and a year later it peaked at 1,025. Then it started to decline, slowly at first, then faster and faster. By Easter 1939 there were only around 380 pupils left.

The cause of this decline was not primarily compulsion. There were certainly many pupils who could no longer stand to stay in their old surroundings. A large share of both the young people and their parents were not so strongly linked to Judaism that they did not feel the turnaround as anything else than bitter compulsion. Added to this was a certain prejudice that equated Jewish schools to what some Christians disparaged as the "Jew school." And finally, in many cases the sudden departure from the old traditional school meant the apparently unmotivated rupture of friendly, even close relationships with comrades and teachers. I must emphasize there were also schools where Jewish pupils received the best of treatment, and not only on the part of the teacher but—more importantly—on the part of the pupils. There were pupils who felt it was a question of honor to preserve their Jewish comrades from harassment and insult. But the resentments that many children brought with them to our schools soon vanished when they learned how the situation outside continued to deteriorate and when they consequently learned to appreciate the Jewish schools as a port in the storm.

The development and expansion of the new school system naturally caused all kinds of difficulties, particularly at the beginning, and above all in financial terms. As long as the existing facilities were sufficient, everything went well. But when new facilities became necessary, the community authorities were helpless in the face of the financial task involved. In 1933 the community had one middle school for boys and girls and three primary schools: one for boys, one for girls, and one mixed school. To this were added the schools of the Adass Jisroel Congregation, a secondary modern school and a primary school. In the west, in Grunewald, there were several private secondary schools, which naturally only came into question for a select group, and which, with one exception, did not prove equal to the new situation. One serious problem was the absence of a community-owned secondary school. Those belonging to the Adass were not open to the great majority of parents and pupils, above all because of the high tuition. When the tuition benefits for Jewish pupils—waivers or reductions—were suspended at the public schools, the first crisis was upon us. Crowds of pupils with nowhere to go poured into the middle school. When it was full to bursting, the school administration shunted those who were left off to the primary schools. Of course, the parents protested, leading to scenes that do not bear thinking of.

Whether it wanted to or not, the community had to make a decision to place scholastic necessity before financial concerns, and once this decision was made there was no more hesitation. It is with pride and gratitude that I think back to that time when I appeared almost daily with new demands and never left empty-handed. Our community chairman Stahl never said no. That was up to community director Breslauer and school committee chairman Alexander. But they ultimately resigned themselves to the inevitable. Breslauer just shook his head a little, and Alexander clapped his hands together, approving what could not be changed. In this way we developed and established a school system that was more than a stopgap measure. At the highwater mark, the community maintained a secondary school—the new standard type of secondary school—a middle school, eight primary schools, a special school, the school for the deaf-mute in Weissensee, and finally the school for the mentally impaired in Beelitz—without including the other nontraditional educational facilities. Added to this were the secondary and primary schools of the reformed congregation. I already mentioned the ones belonging to Adass. The Waldschule Grunewald emerged from the private schools along with the diverse school network of Leonore Goldschmidt. When the previously named smaller congregations were no longer able to maintain their schools, the community also took them over, including the Goldschmidt schools. The primary schools remained autonomous, the upper-level schools were joined to the secondary school, and during this whole time no one ever spoke of financial impossibilities. We had become accustomed to spending money—in the other categories, too.

No one whose experience is limited to normal school operations can even begin to imagine the organizational difficulties we had, particularly in regard to the upper-level schools. A middle school has six grades—from the fifth to the tenth school year. At its peak, our middle school had twenty-five classes, some of them containing fifty to sixty pupils. Since the first foreign language in the middle school was English, and French in many upper level schools, two courses had to be set up in the boys' and girls' divisions respectively: an A course with English, a B course with French as a basic language. In addition, there were modern secondary school pupils learning Latin. Thus it happened that no pupil exchanges could occur between two classes of the same grade when one class was overfilled while the other had the proper number of pupils. If one class had forty pupils, then it was divided up into specific subjects, such as languages, mathematics, and girls' handicrafts. Hebrew represented a special problem. Normally only pupils from our primary schools had a basic knowledge of the language. But now hundreds of pupils flowed into the school knowing little or no Hebrew, meaning that we had to set up special remedial classes. This fragmentation of the classes into divisions and groups led to a situation where at times up to six hundred hours a week had to be taught, requiring no fewer than forty-eight teachers, many of whom were employed on a half-time basis (twenty-five hours a week). Schedules, tables, charts, and so on became so voluminous that the standard forms no longer sufficed. The schedules in particular resembled invasion plans. Half a dozen teachers spent two to three weeks creating these genuine strategic masterpieces. When I then submitted them to the administrative authorities for their authorization, I always had to include explanatory notes. Occasionally it turned out that no one even looked at this material because no one could understand it. When the secondary school was established later on, this situation repeated itself.

Of course, the teacher question also represented a problem within this complex organism. For a short time the school risked an influx of unqualified or uninvited elements to the faculty. In Prussia, anyone desiring to give any sort of instruction to school-age pupils, except at public schools, had to possess a teaching permission certificate issued by the district school council. When our tribulations began, students, artists, business people with language skills—basically everybody who thought he could teach jumped on this opportunity to earn a piece of bread, and numerous school councils in Berlin began issuing such certificates, either out of sympathy or indifference to Jewish interests. They were issued "for the instruction of Jewish pupils" and were valid not only for tutoring but also for school instruction. Once this custom had gotten completely out of control, I presented the matter to our school council, whereupon the indiscriminate distribution of these licenses was halted. If we occasionally required such a person for a special activity, then the school administration applied to the city council for a special permit.

In this way we developed and expanded our schools, while everything else fell to pieces around us—with the exception of the old people's homes—and we also furnished them comfortably. For as long as possible we took what the outside world gave us. We made excursions and hikes as often as possible, and with satisfaction I can note that the often expressed concerns of frightened souls about the mass excursions of Jewish children and young people in and around Berlin never proved justified. Neither the field trips nor the hikes were ever disturbed by harassment, let alone worse things. Of course, we could no longer stop at restaurants. It was not until the November catastrophe of 1938 that our hikes, like every other form of public Jewish activity in Germany, came to a halt.

In this time of continual and increasing pressure, a major component of our pupils' physical and mental education lay in athletics. We were fortunate to own a spacious sports field in Grunewald, which our sports clubs gradually transformed into a modern stadium with their own hands. Every fall our schools held tournaments there. In 1938 they did so with the participation of teams from large schools from across the Reich. The community, the Reich Association, and the Prussian State Association sponsored prizes which were competed over with the greatest seriousness. Of course, from an educational point of view the months of training were more important and valuable than the sports festival itself. It was not until 1938 that the field was "confiscated," robbing our youth of their last recreational facility.

Thus the schools were increasingly called upon to compensate for losses in the outside world. Sadly, this included many things the family and the association could no longer provide. The schools had to provide the atmosphere of joy and well-being that young people and children need for the normal growth of their souls, just as they need their daily bread for the growth of their bodies. "Creating joy at school!" was just as much of our teachers' work as providing their pupils with the intellectual tools for a fulfilling and successful life. How did we do it? We put the arts first, and here too we provided for our daily bread ourselves. Alfred Loewy, our excellent music teacher, Frau Elsbeth Lasch, our incomparable drawing and arts and crafts teacher, and Dr. Fritz Wiener, our "director," were in charge of the artistic design of school holidays and the preparation of regular matinees and soirees. Our excellent school choir formed the backbone of our musical events and was soon joined by an orchestra. A radio and a phonograph rounded out our musical equipment. We even managed to put our own trained dancers onto the stage. From the initial planning stage to the last detail of stage design, and particularly in the performances themselves, these events lay in the hands of the students. The fact that these performances often had to be repeated three or four times for the parents demonstrates their high quality.

We complemented these school events with presentations from professional artists in the form of celebrations and as high points in our artistic education and edification through art. Speakers and actors, singers and instrumentalists were regular guests in the middle school. We greeted them joyfully on arrival, and took leave of them with gratitude. And the artists themselves were grateful since our events offered them an increasingly rare opportunity to exhibit their skill, and their success filled them with joy. For here they had the opportunity to give everything they had. Our many hundreds of pupils filled the auditorium three times over, allowing us to present three different programs that were progressively fine-tuned to their audience's expectations. One particularly popular art form—for us as well—was the puppet show. This included not only Punch and Judy shows but also much more serious productions extending all the way to the Story of Doctor Faustus.

But man cannot live from art alone, and you can enjoy it only half as much when you are faring badly yourself. But we were lucky enough to be able to provide for our young people's physical well-being to a large degree. And if I now turn to our school services, it is only to answer my readers' question as to how we found the money to provide such a wide-ranging system. Our two formally autonomous middle schools had access to large charitable foundations going way back to the time when they were the community's only schools. The interest from these foundations was partially spent on scholarships, but the greatest share was used to provide destitute pupils with teaching materials and clothing. After the inflation the community generously replenished these foundations. But when the difficult years came, they began earmarking some of the interest payments for the school budget. I sought and found a replacement for this loss, namely by introducing lending fees for the library, which was so large that scarcely any pupils needed to buy books. As low as the individual lending fees were, they added up to enormous sums that, together with the income from the foundations, allowed us to provide considerable charitable activities. These activities were and remained largely centered on providing clothing to destitute pupils. Hanukkah and Purim provided an opportunity to distribute such gifts in grand style. Our voluntary helpers discreetly began collecting the children's desires weeks in advance. We then made a cost estimate, which the ladies took to the well-known wholesalers, where they could always be assured of a warm welcome. In the end we got what we needed and paid what we had. We always had enough left over for other occasions and purposes. Whenever shoes and clothes were needed over the course of the year, the money was there. And whenever one fund was exhausted, whether it was the money for the community's monthly transit fare subsidy, or the money for breakfast and a hot lunch, the Casper Arnstein Foundation—beneath whose flag our entire charitable work sailed—always helped out. It helped us when the pocket change we collected for the visiting musicians was too paltry, when parents could not pay the fees for a vacation colony or a health spa, even when a child needed special medical examination that no one could or wanted to pay for. Whenever a particularly well-behaved and able pupil was forced to leave the school for financial reasons, he received a modest "educational aid," if it could be of help. Of course, no pupil ever had to forego an excursion because he could not pay for it. And it was just as natural that in our genuine charitable activity only the degree of need counted, not one's educational performance or any other such considerations. When one of our boys was forced to leave school because of his sufficiently proven indifference, he was given a pair of shoes as a parting gift.

Thus our school was a genuine home for our pupils, a refuge from the wretched conditions outside its walls. And, when the genuinely bad days and hours came, making our school, namely the instruction, seem utterly insignificant, then I always insisted on keeping it open—as a place of refuge. Because nowhere, not even at home, were the children better off than there. Did they realize it themselves? One former pupil wrote to me from England, "I am homesick for the middle school." Another pupil, also from there, "I always think back to the wonderful time we had under your loving supervision. . . . because this time will surely never return." And another from Berlin, ". . . and I feel more a part of your school, where I only spent one year, than of the school where I spent nine years."

Part VI

German Culture Is *Verboten!*

The National Socialists consciously pushed the Jews' cultural segregation in their quest for a "pure German culture." While Jewish attendance at public artistic facilities and events was "only" banned in 1938, Jewish artists were driven from public cultural life soon after the seizure of power in 1933. On September 22, 1933, the Reich Chamber of Culture Law established chambers for all fields of culture. Henceforth, membership in one or more of these chambers would be the precondition for any future cultural activity. Although the law did not contain the so-called Aryan section until 1937, Jews were not permitted to join, and wherever Jews were still at work they were removed under government pressure. The Aryan section in the Reich Press Law of October 1933 amounted to an employment ban for Jewish journalists. The only exceptions were for those journalists working for the Jewish press. Many world-famous artists, actors, musicians, writers, and directors subsequently left Germany. But the majority stayed on.

In order to provide them with a field of activity and to enable German Jews, who increasingly stopped attending public concerts and theatrical performances but who still wanted to experience art and culture, to remain active, Jews began developing their own cultural sector. They started in Berlin, where a Jewish Kulturbund (culture league) was founded in June 1933. Just four months later it counted more than ten thousand members. In October 1933, the theater group performed its first play, Lessing's *Nathan the Wise*. At about the same time they founded a symphony orchestra, an opera company, and a cabaret, along with a lecture series. Other such institutions patterned after the Berlin model arose in other towns, so that by April 1935 a total of thirty-six Kulturbünde with around seventy thousand members were active across Germany. They joined together as the Reichsverband der jüdischen Kulturbünde (Reich Association of Jewish Culture Leagues) on August 6, 1935. Their activities, including theatrical and opera ensembles, orchestras, and choirs, provided numerous artists with a new livelihood. At the same time the Kulturbünde provided visitors with a free space where they could enjoy culture without discrimination and gather spiritual strength for everyday life. The Kulturbund's work continued until its dissolution in September 1941, shortly before the Jews were deported eastward.

The Nazis were not unhappy about this development since it seemed to complement their own efforts to shunt the Jews off into a "cultural ghetto." The Kulturbünde were required to report their activities to the authorities and were also subject to state supervision and censorship. The precondition for their tolerance was that they would employ only Jewish artists and that only Jews would be allowed to attend their events. Over the course of time their repertoire was increasingly restricted in order "to prevent the distortion of German culture by Jewish interpretations," as one legal text put it. In 1934 Schiller and the Romantics, in 1936 Goethe and all of classical literature, and shortly thereafter all non-Jewish authors were banned from the stage. The musical repertoire was also restricted to the works of Jewish composers.

This development made life hard for the Kulturbünde. They had to fall back upon the works of Jewish authors or composers, write their own works or commission others to do so. The majority of their audience—people who had been raised on German culture—questioned or even rejected such offerings. In the end, however, they had no choice but to accept these government restrictions in order to be able to enjoy any culture at all. But the public took an increasing interest in the new repertoire. Contrary to the Nazis' intentions, the Jewish cultural establishment, which also included the Jewish press and publishing houses, contributed to the emergence of a new Jewish consciousness and a new Jewish identity.

24

Hitting a Wall

Fritz Goldberg

I attended the dress rehearsal of one of our publishing house's works at the Berlin Volksbühne. Some thirty people sat in the stalls, but I was the only civilian. Everyone else, from the newly installed theater director to the last member of his staff, wore a Party uniform. They rehearsed the play's final scene again and again, but they found no effective resolution. Finally the theater director and Storm Trooper officer turned to me. My recommendation was not a revelation but rather arose from my long experience in the theater. However, the theater director—and this was typical—had no professional experience whatsoever. He did not owe his new position to any professional ability. Instead, he, like so many other dilettantes, was installed because he had belonged to the Party for a certain length of time. In any case, he accepted my suggestion and no one understood the grotesqueness of a situation where he asked for advice from someone whom he had been struggling for years to eliminate from cultural life.

A young Nazi playwright had submitted his first script to me in 1932, filled with attacks on the Republic and ending in a hymn to the Führer state. I have always believed in judging manuscripts objectively, according to purely artistic standards and independently of the author's political views. This man clearly had dramatic talent, even if it was still at an early and amorphous stage. I called the author in, made no secret of my personal distaste for his ideals, discussed his play's weaknesses, and called for changes to which he—my mortal enemy—willingly agreed. Then I recommended that the publishing house accept the work, which it subsequently did. Following the seizure of power, it was a simple matter to arrange the premiere, which was arranged within a special framework, at a celebration for the warriors of the new movement. The author not only asked me to attend the premiere, but actually demanded that I ride in his car and spend the evening in his box as a guest. I had the greatest difficulty in extricating myself from this situation. He simply did not understand that such an arrangement could only harm both of us.

Such experiences were commonplace in the first period of National Socialism, when people still made a clear distinction between principles and individuals. The laws eliminating such distinctions came later. They were frequently preceded by so-called individual actions, which anticipated the content of future regulations. I attended the premiere of a film starring the celebrated actress Elisabeth Bergner. A crowd of civilians marched up and down in front of the cinema, recognizable at first glance as trained Nazis. They howled, whistled, and jeered at the viewers and forced the film to be cancelled immediately. Soon a corresponding law was passed with the following typical justification: Frequent experience has shown that popular sentiment has "spontaneously" arisen against the appearance of alien artists; thus in the interest of preserving law and order, films employing Jewish actors may no longer be shown. Most Germans laughed at the official use of the term "spontaneous." But there were also plenty of previously reasonable people who succumbed to this propaganda.

The Nazis officially allowed Jewish artists to continue working while finding other ways to prevent them from practicing their professions. I was also officially admitted to the newly founded Reich Chamber of Culture, which accepted Jews provided that they had fought in World War I. I was asked to pay a not inconsiderable application and membership fee and was given a pin that bore an unsettling similarity to a Storm Trooper badge. Our situation deteriorated noticeably following the death of Reich President Hindenburg. The Nazis dropped all their previous inhibitions. In place of the tricky backdoor chicanery they had used against us before, they now hit us head-on. Even the special arrangements for front soldiers were suspended since there allegedly had been no Jewish soldiers in the field. It was a proven fact that twelve thousand of them had given their lives for Germany. One morning, the mailman woke me up to deliver a registered letter announcing my expulsion from the Chamber of Culture. It stated that I was neither politically nor morally fit to administer German culture, nor was I even able to do so on account of who I was. I was to return my pin and identification card within a matter of days. However, they never returned my advance membership fees.

This meant the final end of my professional career, as only the organization's members were permitted to be active in the field of culture. However, my company tried to ignore this fact and keep me on its payroll. I continued my old job for nearly a year. But things were no longer the same. My personal contributions were restricted more and more each day as I was progressively pushed into the background. Finally I hit a wall. The official enquiries into my activities mounted. The Chamber of Culture itself appointed my successor, whom I was asked to train. He treated me with respect and consideration, and repeatedly told me how embarrassed he was to be getting his position in such a way. In the end he assured me that he was determined to continue running the director's department in my spirit. We parted as friends. When the door closed behind me, I breathed a sigh of relief—the pressure and tension had become unbearable.

25

The Banning of a Music Critic

Ludwig Misch

National Socialism first touched my destiny on April 1, 1933. On this day, the editor of the *Lokalanzeiger* where I was the leading music critic, said to me, "You are a reasonable man. You can see what is going on, and you will understand that we cannot keep you here." I was paid a settlement amounting to my annual income from the *Berliner Lokalanzeiger* and from the weekly radio magazine *Europe Hour*, where I was also the music editor. I say "income" and not "salary" because I never had a steady position, even though I had been working as a music critic since the end of 1921. Neither my teacher, Professor Wilhelm Klatte, the former chief critic who hired me, nor I myself managed to land a regular job. It was only after Professor Klatte's death, when I moved up to fill his position, that I received fixed wages for my new work as a music editor. For *Europe Hour*, however, I received a regular wage.

I had no financial worries at first, but I was certainly worried about finding a new job. While I was certain that the Nazis would not stay in power long, I saw scarcely any prospects for the future. The loss of my livelihood struck me sooner than it did most German Jews. We, by which I mean my wife, my sister and myself, went to the CV (Centralverein Deutscher Staatsbürger Jüdischen Glaubens) for advice, and also to the Jewish congregation—without any result at first. I consulted a number of musicians. We made various plans, but nothing came of them since some new government regulations thwarted our intentions. When we came to the topic of emigration, Leonid Kreutzer, the Russian Jew who had immigrated to Berlin after World War I, said, "Where could we emigrate to? Where else in the world do people make music like they do in Berlin?"

On the advice of my younger sister, I traveled to Paris a few weeks later to look into the possibility of making a fresh start there. My visit brought no results. I talked to everyone and was usually given a friendly welcome, but as far as my professional prospects were concerned, all I heard was,

"C'est très difficile"—even though I had a letter of recommendation from Furtwängler, who was in Paris at the same time as I. Someone wanted to introduce me to Ravel, but he was not in Paris. Finally, having given up all hope and getting a taste of the fate of an emigré in Paris, I returned to Berlin, swearing I wouldn't make any snap decisions. And in the first years, this turned out to be the right choice for me.

In Berlin the Jewish Kulturbund was founded. House concerts as well as events by Jewish artists for Jews were offered in public concert halls. I founded my own a capella choir, the New Madrigal Association, later called the Jewish Madrigal Association. This meant plenty of hard work at first. I first had to find singers who, like me, were motivated by the pure love of art. Among this group I had to select those who were useful to this purpose. Everyone else dropped out after a few rehearsals. I copied out the choir parts myself and when the little choir seemed concert-ready I had to seek engagements among the events of the "Joy in Winter" program, the Reich League of Jewish Front Soldiers, Jewish lodges, and so on. The "Artists Aid" of the Jewish community took us under its wing. We had to send out invitations for our own concerts and we had to request financial donations for such unavoidable expenses as hall rent, printing fees for the programs, and the like. We began our rehearsals in the fall of 1933 and gave our first concert in March of 1934. Our repertoire had lots of variety. We distributed the proceeds from our engagements and our own concerts equally amongst ourselves, with the exception of renowned soloists like Paula Lindberg, Wilhelm Guttmann, and others, who worked free of charge.

The authorities demanded that all artists be subordinated to the Kulturbund, which was required to submit the programs for approval. In this way, shortly before a concert, I was prohibited from performing the great *Twenty-Second Psalm* by Mendelssohn, whose text the Nazis found objectionable. After this I was in no mood to continue my work and I disbanded the choir. That must have been in the middle of 1936. This decision may have been helpful, because shortly afterward I was called in to the Gestapo to be interrogated about the choir. Since I could honestly say that it no longer existed, they left me in peace.

For me, the Madrigal Association was only a matter of artistic pleasure, since the income that I, like every other member, received from our performances was minimal. Leo Kreindler, the chief editor of the *Gemeindeblatt der Jüdischen Gemeinde* (newsletter of the Jewish congregation) and the Israelitisches Familienblatt (Israelite family paper), found a financially profitable position for me. He hired me as a music critic, for both papers at first and then later—to avoid potential rivalry—for the newsletter alone. I soon ended up doing the same job for the *Schild* (shield), the official paper of the Reich League of Jewish Front Soldiers.

In April 1935 I was hired as the music teacher at the Private Jewish Waldschule in Grunewald. Since I had not been trained as a school music teacher, but had a state permit to work as a private music teacher, school commissioner Spanier from Wilmersdorf gave me permission to accept the job. Together with my journalistic work, it provided me with a sufficient income. While at first a few puberty-afflicted boys and a few spoiled young ladies in their senior year showed nothing but contempt for the "minor subject" of music and caused me my fair share of disciplinary problems at first, I enjoyed my new job. In fact, the hours I spent with the youngest children and the middle grades, with whom I was on an excellent footing from the start, were pure pleasure. I also founded a school orchestra.

I need not bother to tell of the horror the shameful Nuremberg Laws of the autumn of that year brought forth. But it is worth relating my own experiences at this time: we were evicted from our flat in the artists colony at Breitenbachplatz for "racial reasons." As we were leaving the flat, our neighbor from across the hall, whom we only knew by sight, came out of her door and said, "I am ashamed to be a German." Well, back then a Jew could still find a new flat.

I suffered a severe blow when, citing formal reasons, school commissioner Freitag from the Wilmersdorf town hall cancelled my teaching permit, effective immediately. This ruinous decision could only be reversed by the education minister. I asked Wilhelm Furtwängler to intervene on my behalf, which he did immediately. I no longer recall the precise date when I had to give up teaching. I only recall that I suffered greatly from a long period of forced idleness. Finally, on January 7, 1937, I received a letter from Furtwängler, "I recently had an opportunity to remind the minister personally of your case . . . He told me that he had forwarded the matter immediately and it is currently under review." But it was not until I received a letter from the city president dated March 24 that I was informed that the decision had been reversed. On April 13, Herr Freitag had to record the permission to teach again on my certificate. In the meantime, another music teacher had been hired for the Lessler School whom they did not want to lose, but I was hired once more and we shared our duties in a cordial and equitable manner. Starting at Easter 1937 I was also put in charge of musical instruction at the Jewish congregation's Holdheim School.

One day at the Lessler School I received a telephone call asking me to come to a Kulturbund meeting that had been convened by state commissioner Hinkel to discuss choir matters. In my impromptu remarks I said among other things, "The Jews in Israel are proud to have performed Haydn's *Creation,* but here every singer feels compelled to include a few primitive Yiddish songs in his program." Of course, my words were not aimed at Jewish culture as such—I myself once arranged three eastern Jewish folk songs for an a capella choir and performed them with my Madrigal Association—but was instead referring to the lowering of musical standards out of "folkish" considerations. In his closing statement, Herr Hinkel said among other things, "Now that we have heard such beautiful words from Rabbi Dr. Prinz, it seems there are still people here with the stinking eggshells of assimilation sticking to their skin." These were his precise words. Dr. Prinz, with whom I was not previously acquainted, came to me and said, "He means you." I have yet to feel any shame for this accusation.

26

The Kulturbund— Ghetto and Home

Kurt Baumann

One morning I suddenly realized that the Nazi Party program repeatedly made the claim that the Jews in Germany represented an alien economic and cultural element in Germany and thus had to be eliminated from German life. Logically enough, my next thought was that it might be possible to organize a separate cultural life for the Jewish population, at least in the large cities. I based my idea of founding a Jewish cultural circle on some very simple figures: at that time, some 175,000 Jews lived in Berlin alone, and many other large cities had comparable concentrations. I calculated that a city with 175,000 inhabitants could maintain its own theater, opera, symphony orchestra, museums, lectures, even its own university, just like any other medium-sized town.

It was clear to me from the start that it was still questionable whether and how we could receive permission from the authorities. After all, we were uncertain about which branch of the Nazi Party held which positions and how seriously the respective agencies took the Party program. I was also aware that Zionist groups would only give their consent if we would conduct all our cultural efforts in Yiddish or Hebrew. Aside from the fact that the bulk of German Jewry had little knowledge of either Yiddish or Hebrew, and that translations of Yiddish and Hebrew literature were rare to say the least, the Zionists themselves were but a small minority within the Jewish population. I knew that the majority, which was encompassed by the Central Association for German Citizens of the Jewish Faith and by the Reich League of Jewish Front Soldiers, would respond to the idea of a purely Jewish cultural circle in Germany with the slogan, "We will not enter the ghetto voluntarily."

In any case, I was aware that a detailed plan with a budget, artistic and cultural personnel and a membership organization had to be presented in order to prove that such an idea could be realized. So I sat down and in about two weeks I drafted a meticulous plan. The next question was who should be put in charge of such an undertaking. I was aware that with my twenty-six years I was virtually unknown among either Jewish or German officials and was far too insignificant. It would have to be someone who had a good and familiar name in artistic circles and who, if possible, had contributed so much to each side that the German authorities could not reject him out of hand.

It did not take long for me to come up with the name of my mentor and the former director of the municipal opera: Dr. Kurt Singer. He was not only a very well known musician and organizer, but he also had another great advantage: he had been a front soldier in World War I and had contributed greatly to the German folk song as the director of the Berlin physicians' choir, in his writings and on the podium. Even in German nationalist circles he was both renowned and loved, although he himself was a liberal democrat and probably had once been a socialist. So I went to him, presented my idea in general terms, and—after he had promised the utmost confidence—I invited him to take a look at my plan. It aroused his interest at once, and he said that he had previously entertained such ideas but that he had thought no more about it. He promised to make a close study of my plan. Soon afterward, Dr. Singer called me up and asked to see me. We now worked together intensively every day revising the plan. Dr. Singer was excited about the plan and said that if it succeeded he would be honored to become the organization's leader.

Two main problems had been visible from the beginning: where were the Jewish administrators and artists we needed for a cultural undertaking that was intended to encompass nearly all cultural spheres of Western civilization, and how could we discover their current status? We knew that since January 1933 Jewish artists of all kinds had lost their positions or would lose them in the coming months. We also knew that at least a small number of Jewish artists had not yet been officially dismissed because they had served as front soldiers. But the Nazis often circumvented this official rule, which came from Reich President Hindenburg, while others resigned on principle. A list of various professional organizations was easy enough to find, not only for Berlin but for all of Germany. The Jewish administrators, at least those living in Berlin, could be traced through an office the Jewish community of Berlin had set up soon after the seizure of power in order to look after such people.

The second problem was the question of how broad the new organization should be, and above all what agencies would be responsible for evaluating and ultimately approving such a plan. Dr. Singer and I came to the conclusion that we should move slowly and that such an organization should be limited to Berlin at first. It was clear from the beginning that, if we were to succeed in developing such a cultural organization in Berlin, other large cities should follow.

Since our plan foresaw the founding of a theater as its centerpiece, there was no way around the fact that we needed one of the most celebrated men of the German theatrical world. There were many famous names, but the one we thought of first was that of Julius Bab. Strangely enough, he was a distant relative of mine, a second cousin on my mother's side. I had known him since childhood, and from early on he had been one of my most important advisors in my theatrical training and my early career. I will never forget how he reacted when I called him up and suggested that he come and work with me as the new organization's director. He said in his famous high voice, which so many Jewish people in Germany knew from his lectures at the Humboldt, Lessing, and community colleges, "Are we allowed to?"

People later said that we only founded the Kulturbund to provide a few Jewish artists with work and bread, but that is only half true. Of course we were concerned with giving the hundreds of Jewish artists who had been summarily dismissed a modest living until such time as they could leave the country. But for us in those days it was much more important to provide the Jewish public in Germany, which had once stood at the forefront of German cultural life, with a home for as long as possible.

Soon it started to look like the negotiations with the Prussian interior ministry were proceeding positively. One problem was that the other side still feared that the "Aryan" public could be pulled away from German cultural life and that the whole thing could prove to be a Jewish trick to undermine the Nazis' cultural reeducation of the German people.

By the time May came around, everything was set. They permitted us to rent an old theater and create an association in which exclusively Jewish artists would give performances of all kinds for an exclusively Jewish audience. The members had to carry photo IDs and could only attend by subscription. It was forbidden to drop in off the street, even for members. The box office was prohibited from selling last-minute seats. In return, we were promised police protection and guaranteed that no Nazi organizations would bother the association's members on arrival and departure and during the events themselves. Of course, all texts, music, and exhibits had to be approved by the interior ministry's review office in advance. Here I would like to mention that we were "urged" to avoid any and all cultural material of an explicitly "German" character.

It had become clear to us that we had to buy our initial permission by agreeing to work under the strict supervision of the authorities. But the greater price was the fact that the Nazis would use us as one of their strongest propaganda tools whenever harsh anti-Jewish measures made waves abroad.

We really did enter the ghetto, but we brought the Jewish public—at least for a time—a cultural forum with the kinds of offerings to which they were accustomed, and in surroundings that protected them from all sorts of unpleasantness. The great Jewish artists of international standing, particularly the musicians, had all emigrated immediately following the seizure of power. They had no difficulty in finding work and bread abroad.

But in Berlin there were still hundreds of highly skilled and well-trained artists and intellectual workers who could not so easily emigrate because they were not sufficiently well known outside and who could not find work in Germany. In the agreement between us and the Prussian government the German side made it clear that, if the association was to receive official status, official representatives of the Jewish community had to be seated on our new board of directors.

We subsequently began our negotiations with the Jewish community in Berlin, which turned out to be harder than with the Nazi authorities. As I have already hinted at, the struggle first had to be fought between Zionist and non-Zionist forces within the community itself until both factions finally came to an agreement and stated their willingness to send representatives to our board of directors. Dr. Singer's prediction came true. Herr Hinkel's superior in the cultural office suggested to Minister President Göring that Herr Hinkel be appointed the director and supervisor of Jewish cultural affairs in Prussia. We never received any official word of the internal negotiations within the Prussian interior ministry, but in mid-May 1933 Herr Hinkel informed Dr. Singer that there was nothing more standing in the way of the agreement, that he—Hinkel—had been appointed director by Göring, and that he—Singer—would be personally responsible for the smooth execution of all the conditions contained in the agreement. All that remained was to pay a personal visit to Göring and receive his "blessing." And that is what happened. Göring tried to appear friendly and jovial and essentially said, "If you do everything right and Herr Hinkel does his part, then everything will go all right. But if you get out of line, then there'll be hell to pay, as you well know." On May 20, 1933, everything was set. An agreement was formalized, bearing the signatures of the Kulturbund of German Jews and its board of directors and the new secretary in the Prussian interior ministry, Hans Hinkel. Hermann Göring only put down his initials.

One serious and seemingly insoluble problem for our side was the reaction that this new organization would arouse within the Jewish community of Berlin and in radical Nazi organizations. During the negotiations, Herr Hinkel had repeatedly pointed out that he was expecting difficulties since a number of extreme Nazi groups would resist our new organization. After all, the setup demanded that a number of authorities and Nazi offices exert exclusive control over Jewish cultural matters, even though the Nazi Party program banned such activities. But Hinkel always assured Dr. Singer that that was his concern and we had nothing to fear. Of course, we were not informed of the inner Party conflicts, but we knew enough to be able to imagine what kind of battle must have raged among the Gestapo, some circles within the Reich Propaganda Ministry, the radical press, and even some groups of Hinkel's own "Battle Group for German Culture" over influence and control over our new association. In fact, it never stopped until the Kulturbund's disbanding in 1941. But Hinkel always ended up asserting himself. He was and remained the only supervisory authority we ever had; we never had anything to do with other Party and government agencies. I will say more later about these attempts to wrest control from Herr Hinkel's hands. At this point it is important to note that the agreement allowed Hinkel to take anyone he wanted to our events. Since we had declared our willingness to work in complete isolation from the German public, not a single word about our new organization had gotten out. Upon our request, Herr Hinkel finally allowed a small notice to be published in the major Berlin newspapers so that the Jewish public would know that the new organization had been approved by the authorities.

But even with this small concession we had no way of knowing how Berlin's Jewish population would react when they read about it in Jewish and German publications. It could well be that many people might suspect that the whole thing was a Nazi trick designed to disrupt or even arrest large groups of Jews. Furthermore, we knew that there were a great number of people who refused to enter a cultural ghetto and thus would not become members. I should point out that Jews were not yet banned from attending German cultural events and following Hinkel's repeated assurances no such bans were to be expected for some time. That only came after the Kristallnacht in 1938. One can easily imagine how hard it is for a family to give up decades-old subscriptions for the Philharmonic, for other concerts, the theater, and the opera when there was no ban, even if they occasionally ended up sitting next to a Storm Trooper or an SS man in uniform, from whom they heard the occasional negative comment. A great deal depended on how Berlin's Jewish press supported our membership drive.

Dr. Singer's large flat now became a beehive of activity. At least twenty persons now worked in all departments, particularly in the advertising department. Several large and a great many small publicity events had to be planned over the summer in large synagogues and small halls. An orchestra had to be formed under the direction of Michael Taube, a choir under Berthold Sander. The first actors and singers had to be auditioned. All the Kulturbund's associations, particularly the members of the Jewish community council, had to advertise our cause everywhere, both publicly and privately.

The echo among Berlin's Jews was much greater than we ever imagined. The first large advertising event in the synagogue on Prinzregentenstrasse, featuring a choir, an orchestra, and a speech in the middle of the summer, brought 2,500 people together. Half of them became members on the spot, and 90 percent of the others joined up ten days later, once they were assured that there were no disturbances and that only scant police protection had been present, just as for any other cultural events, Jewish or non-Jewish. Our later events were even more overfilled than the first one and with similar results in regard to membership. Our event schedule called for performing one play for an entire month, then an opera for the next month. In addition, there were two concert programs and two lecture series per month. Subscribers could choose their own days and were guaranteed two programs, whatever they selected.

Herr Hinkel had promised to help us find a theater with enough office space and a large enough auditorium to serve as the Kulturbund's headquarters. He finally offered us the Berliner Theater on Charlottenstrasse, which was old but had pretty much everything we needed. It is important to point out that it probably would have been impossible to rent a lot and a building for a Jewish organization without help from the authorities. We did not know that the theater building was located on a piece of ground that was gradually sinking and that the theater would have to be demolished within a few years anyway. We never learned whether the supervisory authorities were aware of this or not.

In late summer 1933 the man who put together our first orchestra, Michael Taube, received an opportunity to emigrate to Palestine. We urged him to do so and gave him all the assistance we could. This meant that we had to refill one of the most important positions on our artistic staff, and Taube was a first-class conductor and orchestra developer. In Mannheim, a rising star called Joseph Rosenstock, the young general music director of the Mannheim Opera, received his dismissal. He came to us and we hired him immediately. He provided the new art institute with immeasurable services not only through his great skill as a conductor but also through his special ability to "educate" orchestra members and young singers in the best sense of the word. Within a few years, the Kulturbund orchestra became one of the best in Berlin, even though it was largely made up of young people, as the internationally famous Jewish musicians from the Philharmonic and the great opera orchestras had already emigrated or were in the process of doing so. Three world-renowned soloists from Berlin's City Opera came to us: my cousin Wilhelm Guttmann, the excellent bass, Fritzi Jokl, who had long been a chamber singer in the Bavarian State Opera and was one of the finest coloratura sopranos I have ever heard, and Lotte Schöne, who had created many of the parts for the composer Richard Strauss. A young tenor, a Hungarian called Feher, who had already sung a number of lyrical parts at the City Opera, served us for years as a lyric tenor. Then there was a young bass, Walter Olitzki, who had a particularly beautiful voice and finally ended up as a bass-baritone at the Metropolitan Opera in New York. Another City Opera singer was the first-class bass Gerhard Pechner, who like Orlitzki would end up singing at the Metropolitan Opera for many years. To this were added a series of young people who were all more or less beginners, but who soon began singing their first lead roles under Rosenstock's direction.

We hired the well-known actor Fritz Wisten, who had a non-Jewish wife, as our chief drama director and as the head of our acting department. I still recall some of the names in our acting ensemble: Kurt Katsch, Siegmund Nunberg, Hans Lennart, Franz Brandt, Wolfgang Bernstein, his mother,

Frau Bernstein, Leni Steinberg, Gina Petruschka, Camilla Spira, and the famous Rosa Valetti. These and other renowned and beginning actors stood on our stage and, through the Jewish and German tragedies and comedies they performed, provided our audience with a cultural home as long as they could.

The Kulturbund's theater was scheduled to open on September 1, 1933. Since the preparations for a play took less time than for an opera, it was clear that we would have to open with a play. There was never any question about which one it would be. There was only one work suited to demonstrating our new situation. It had a Jewish theme, it was part of the German classic repertoire, and at this time its author was not yet banned in Germany, although he was almost impossible to perform. It was Lessing's *Nathan the Wise* with Kurt Katsch as Nathan, Siegmund Nunberg as Pater, Fritz Wisten—who was also the director—as Derwisch and Hans Lennart as Templer. It was an impressive premiere, the house was sold out, Herr Hinkel came with his staff, there were no disturbances, and the audience reacted with feeling and enthusiasm.

And so began a series of cultural events that continued all the way to 1941 with only two small interruptions. In the glory days of the Kulturbund we sometimes had several events a day. There were lectures and exhibitions, together with concerts, theater, and opera performances. There were also matinees. Sometimes the orchestra went on tour, sometimes the theater or the opera hit the road. We later added Max Ehrlich's Cabaret Ensemble and Werner Hinzelmann's Youth Theater, which did not only play in Berlin but also went on tour. We performed every day.

Even at that early date we made a conscious effort to present as much Jewish material as possible, even though it was still acceptable to use German literature and music. Of course we never would have played Wagner, not even Richard Strauss, since both of them were known as Hitler's favorite composers. Nor did we ever touch Schiller, although we probably would have been permitted to at first. Instead, we played a great deal of foreign literature and music. The problem was that in later years we had to pay licensing fees for contemporary foreign authors and composers, and that meant foreign currency, and we knew that the authorities did not approve of this. For the same reason we were long denied permission to set up a film department. We fought for and received one later on under very different circumstances.

On October 1, 1933, we celebrated the premiere of our first opera, Mozart's *Marriage of Figaro*. Like *Nathan the Wise*, it was a complete success.

The first Prussian towns in which Jewish groups and congregations attempted to found their own Jewish cultural associations were in Silesia. Thus it came that in November we attempted our first opera tour to Breslau, Liegnitz, Gleiwitz, and Beuthen. Hinkel's office not only had no objections to this tour but invested a great deal of effort into it. After all, special Reichsbahn trains, buses and above all non-Jewish theater halls had to be organized and coordinated. Of course, that was only possible with the support of a Prussian government agency. This successful tour confirmed our long-cherished opinion that sooner or later a whole range of Jewish Kulturbünde would pop up all across the Reich and work independently, and that the supervision question would lead to a Reich organization in the not too distant future.

Breslau soon received permission from Hinkel under the condition that we in Berlin would be made responsible for the smooth operation of the events. Already in 1934 the Jewish community in Hamburg sent representatives to Berlin in order to find out how they could establish a dependent or independent branch of a Jewish Kulturbund in Hamburg. Hamburg had a special political status. For the moment it was still officially a "free Reich city," and the question was to what extent Hinkel's authority extended to Hamburg. Then came Rhine-Main, ten towns in the Rhine Province that, taken together, had a substantial Jewish population. Rhine-Main had the capacity to put together a good orchestra, and of course it had the opportunity to stage significant lecture series. Frankfurt am Main soon informed us that it would be possible to establish a Jewish theater if the organizational problems could be solved. The same situation soon emerged in Hamburg. The matter of government supervision for Rhine-Main was easily resolved, since it lay in Prussia. Soon Munich was added. They wanted to have permission to function either independently or as a branch organization. That was the moment when Hinkel began to seriously consider the idea of a Reich organization. He seemed to believe that the regulations that had been so successful in Berlin and Prussia could simply be applied to the Reich as a whole. And thus he began long negotiations with us. We were basically happy with the idea of a Reich organization. However, it meant that the personal danger to Dr. Singer would increase, since Hinkel refused to work with anyone else, while we thought that the responsibility for a Reich organization would be too much for Dr. Singer.

The negotiations continued throughout 1935 and into 1936. It had become obvious to us that the only agency that could supervise Jewish cultural affairs on the Reich level would have to be part of the Ministry for Popular Enlightenment and Propaganda, under the control of Goebbels. We did not exactly know how Hinkel would manage to move from Göring's Prussian interior ministry to Goebbels's propaganda ministry. Furthermore, we were well aware that a concentration and "coordination" of Jewish cultural work in the Reich could strangle the cultural variety we had previously enjoyed. Dr. Singer was prepared to take sole responsibility under a Reich agency provided that Hans Hinkel—and only Hans Hinkel—were made the director of such an authority. Whether Dr. Singer's position had any influence in this matter is unclear, and we never learned of the conflicts there must have been between Göring's and Goebbels's ministries. In any case, by the spring of 1936 everything was set. Hans Hinkel became Reich Cultural Administrator, the ministerial director in the new

Division IV-A in the Ministry for Popular Enlightenment and Propaganda. On the other side, we invited all the Jewish Kulturbünde and branch agencies in the Reich to a three-day conference at the Brüdervereinshaus in Berlin for the founding of the Reich Association of Jewish Kulturbünde in Germany.

At the Reich Association's founding convention the authorities pressured us into changing the name Kulturbund of German Jews to Jewish Kulturbund of Berlin. Hinkel explained at the same conference that we should now include more Jewish themes in our programs and that henceforth the approval of German authors would be more closely restricted. We had already foreseen this and had requested a group of first-class Jewish studies experts to start translating some of the classic works of Yiddish literature. This may have been a slow and wearisome undertaking, but two plays and a series of cabaret programs were soon completed. In the meantime, some of our artists and officials had emigrated, along with a growing share of our audience. The Kulturbund of Berlin reached its highpoint in the spring of 1936 with twenty-thousand members, and we were well aware that this number would soon decline. I too gave more and more thought to emigrating. Then Dr. Singer asked me to assume a new position, namely that of censor, officially titled "lector."

All texts, music, and so on which was performed or shown within the Jewish cultural circle had to be approved by the authorities. Since this had to occur on the Reich level, it was absolutely essential that someone should read our programs with the eyes of a Nazi, so to speak, in order to make sure it would not be banned. Dr. Singer offered me this position in the Reich Association of Jewish Kulturbünde. I would stay with the Kulturbund Theater's opera company, but would give up the theater's artistic office. The censorship question became particularly critical starting in 1936 because we were working with a new ministry where we did not know if our potential mistakes would be treated with sufficient humor. Hinkel's pressure had given us fewer opportunities to present German material, but we were particularly uncertain about what German material was allowed and what was not. Although I recognized that the Kulturbund's heyday had passed, I nevertheless did not wish to leave my post, particularly because until that point Herr Hinkel had ensured that no other Nazi agencies interfered with us and that not even a single threatening letter ever reached us.

The guidelines for the Jewish Kulturbünde looked very simple on the surface: material considered to be particularly German, above all the works of the German Romantics, was more or less forbidden. German classic authors, with the exception of Schiller, were acceptable all the way to the end. Themes from the German Middle Ages and the so-called heroic age were all taboo. The issue of the German Romantics was very peculiar. In music the entire German Romantic era was permitted for a time, particularly in symphonic form, while the *lieder* were a more delicate matter. It was hard to know in advance which texts by which authors would be approved and which wouldn't. Of course, the so-called left-wing authors of the Weimar era were off-limits for both the Germans and for us from the very beginning. I have already hinted that the question of foreign authors was never finally regulated. Until 1936 it is likely that the foreign currency issue was the decisive factor.

Part VII

Self-help—
Self-assertion—
Self-discovery

Although many representatives of German Jewry, and also many non-Jews, believed that Hitler would not hold onto power long, they soon began to develop a network of economic and social aid services designed to help people in distress. To some extent they could fall back upon already existing structures that had been set up to help Jewish immigrants from eastern Europe, who largely belonged to the lower classes. Trained and experienced social workers stood ready to help. It was upon this foundation that in March 1933 the Central Office for Jewish Economic Assistance was set up and, on April 13, the Central Committee of German Jews for Help and Reconstruction, which was later incorporated into the Reich Agency for German Jews. It was created on September 17, 1933, as the first political agency representing all German Jews—whether Zionist or assimilated, orthodox or liberal.

Fired and unemployed civil servants, employees, lawyers, and physicians were among the first to seek advice and assistance. Over the years a separate economic sector arose with a Jewish job exchange and a Jewish banking and credit system that helped people build up new livelihoods. Jews worked, produced, and bought for Jews. But perhaps the most important aspect were the newly created educational and training programs. Learning a trade or an agricultural profession became a matter of survival for those who wished to emigrate. People with the appropriate training were of greater interest to potential guest nations than academics or commercial employees who would only have swelled their own army of unemployed. Handicraft and agricultural training were especially important for immigration to Palestine. The Reich Agency financed such training workshops. In addition, Jewish companies offered apprenticeships and the largely Zionist school estates trained farmers.

The increased suffering soon pushed the self-assistance network to its limits. The number of persons dependent on charity steadily increased, particularly in small communities where in the end no one remained but the old and poor, while the young and able either left the country or moved to the large cities. While Jews could claim public charity and the benefits of the Deutsches Winterhilfswerk until 1935, they were often passed over. Thus in 1935 the Jüdisches Winterhilfswerk was founded, an unparalleled example of Jewish self-assistance and solidarity. The first fundraising drive in 1935/36 amounted to 364 million Reichsmarks. Clothing and coal were distributed, but also free tickets to cultural events, presents for children on important holidays, and even newspaper subscriptions for people living alone. But as the Jews became steadily poorer and as more and more of them emigrated, the donations also declined and the self-help system was ultimately doomed by the government's systematic campaign to dispossess and expel the Jews.

The Reich Agency for German Jews ended up playing a tragic role. It fought desperately to gain the state's attention, it appealed in vain to reason and humanity, and it sought assistance against attacks, vandalism, and legal violations. It even met with Hermann Göring. At first, the Reich Agency concentrated on self-assertion and survival in Germany; it could not yet imagine how meaningless such efforts were and that everything would end in the Holocaust. The assimilated Jews, who now became outcasts in their own country, fared particularly badly. In many cases, Judaism meant nothing to them. Now as pariahs, who were no longer allowed to be Germans, they became painfully aware of their Jewishness. Many of them broke down when they reached this point. But others sought and discovered a spiritual home in Judaism, which they rediscovered and of which they were proud. That strengthened their powers of resistance and their will to survive. The rediscovery of their Jewish identity gave them confidence and promoted a form of spiritual resistance that emerged only from Nazi persecution.

27

The Jewish Wirtschaftshilfe

Alexander Szanto

The Wirtschaftshilfe (economic assistance network) began its work at a chaotic time and under chaotic conditions, as thousands and thousands of Nazi victims turned to the congregation for help. Its offices were swamped by a flood of confused and desperate people. No one had any clear idea of how their coreligionists, who had lost their livelihoods and had fallen into distress, could be provided with productive charitable assistance. No one had ever experienced such an extraordinary situation and there were no contingency plans. It is a tribute to the skill and organizational ability of the German Jews that they succeeded within a short time in bringing order to chaos and transforming a stopgap institution into a well-run organization providing effective assistance to thousands of Jews. The necessary funds were provided by the congregation, by private donors, and also by foreign organizations. They were later systematically allocated to the budget of the congregation and the newly created Reich Agency for German Jews. Office space was made available by the congregation.

Over the first months, during which time people virtually stormed the building from morning to night, the situation was grave. The building was like a beehive—the rooms and hallways swarmed with excited people, the staircases were flooded with them, and one could hardly get from one floor to another. I recall with horror the winter of 1933/34, when—the last thing we needed—we also had to house the emigration counseling office known as Aid Association for German Jews, and people crammed into the halls and stairwells. At first we could scarcely keep any semblance of order. The heating functioned badly, the ventilation was poor, and the air was stifling. But we gradually succeeded in bringing the situation under control.

One of our most difficult administrative challenges concerned the hiring of staff. Who would look after these unfortunate people, who would listen to their worries and give them advice and assistance? The congregation's staff were not sufficient—not only in regard to number, but particularly because they were not prepared for such tasks. The congregation's administrators had been effective as long as they were concerned with religious and charitable tasks. In fact, one could even say that the Berlin congregation's charitable work was exemplary. But now new problems were arising for which there was no precedent. Difficulties surfaced that could not be solved with the usual routine. This kind of work could not be handled by people who insisted on their old eight-hour day and for whom "correctness" was often just another word for pedantry.

The Berlin Wirtschaftshilfe was integrated into the framework of the Berlin congregation apparatus in the second half of 1933. In this way we made our way through the first chaotic months. From 1934 to 1940 the Wirtschaftshilfe represented a fixed item in the congregation's budget. The Wirtschaftshilfe's organizational structure was originally planned in such a way that subdivisions would be in charge of the individual economic sectors and/or professions. Unemployed Jewish workers were to be dealt with separately, and business people affected by the boycott would be given their own department. State and local officials would also have a special department, and so forth. We planned special subdivisions for physicians, lawyers, technicians, commercial travelers and door-to-door salesmen, students, and so on. But we soon discovered that these categories often intersected, that many groups shared the same problems and, most of all, that the seriousness of these problems varied from year to year, sometimes even from month to month. It was only by maintaining the maximum flexibility in its organizational structure that the Wirtschaftshilfe managed to handle its various tasks quickly and effectively.

One of the most important subdivisions was "legal advice," later called the legal defense office. Countless coreligionists who had been affected by such Nazi actions as the economic boycott and other threats turned to it for help. At that time, the responsible Jewish authorities took the position that, if possible, no position in public and particularly in economic life should be abandoned without a struggle. This tactic proved successful in numerous cases and saved the livelihood of many coreligionists, or at least saved them from unnecessary financial and material losses.

In the days and weeks following the "seizure of power," and on the occasion of the boycott of April 1, 1933, many Jewish employees, clerks, sales personnel, and other such people were removed from their positions and simply turned out onto the street without notice. In such cases, the Nazi factory cells acted on their own, ignoring the will of the management and without even waiting for directives from Party authorities. In one case the entire Jewish staff of a department store, several hundred people, were given the sack by the Nazi "factory cell," even though the company itself was Jewish-owned. The owners had no influence over the Nazi rank and file, and they were in any case too intimidated to attempt anything.

In this and many similar cases our legal defense office successfully intervened with the authorities and high Nazi Party officials. The factory cells were put in their place and the unemployed Jewish staff could either return to work for a time or else were given the money they were entitled to during the notice period. In this way they were safe from immediate suffering and could either look for a new livelihood or else prepare to emigrate. At that time the Nazis were still eager to maintain at least a veneer of legality, and when the legal defense office turned to the labor courts to help a fired Jewish worker it was usually successful in granting the affected person protection against unlawful dismissal, meaning that he received either the payments owed to him or else a financial settlement. Sometimes National Socialist intimidation made people panic and forego litigation.

In such cases the legal defense office ensured that the affected persons regained their nerves and their self-confidence, and that those Nazi authorities who arbitrarily went farther than the top Party officials thought appropriate were shown their limits.

Not only employees but also the self-employed were frequently saved from the loss of their livelihoods or from severe material loss. This particularly applied to many Jewish market sellers, door-to-door salesmen, and persons plying similar trades. During the first boycott, shocked by the anti-Semitic propaganda, many Jewish tradesmen in the market halls abandoned their stands in panic. The legal defense office saw to it that they later returned to their stalls, that they saved their inventories and continued working for a considerable time afterward.

In individual cases it happened that Jewish shop owners were chased out of their shops or offices by their Christian staff. In such cases it was usually a minority of the staff, namely the Nazi factory cells, who committed such acts of terrorism. Jewish bosses were usually bewildered to find out that they had "nourished a viper in their bosom," meaning that they had given work to their own enemies who now took off their masks and revealed their true faces.

But even then it was clear that such measures shot well beyond the mark set by the Party for the first stage. Thanks to intervention and/or protests from the highest level it was nearly always possible to restore a business's owner to his former rights. Of course, this became more difficult over the course of time, and in all such cases the atmosphere in the company was so poisoned that the boss no longer felt secure. The story usually ended in the company's liquidation or "Aryanization." In many cases the Wirtschaftshilfe's commercial and legal experts intervened and managed the Aryanization in a way that protected its victims from excessive financial loss.

Alongside the legal defense office, the commercial counseling center was heavily frequented by our suffering coreligionists. It continued its work until 1939. This subdivision not only dispensed advice and legal assistance, but it was also the office that supported Jewish merchants and tradesmen through the generous distribution of funds in the form of credits. The commercial counseling center primarily supported the "little people," that is, the craftsmen, small tradesmen, and shop owners. The anti-Jewish boycott pushed many small merchants into financial difficulties. Customers stayed away and income declined while rental and wage payments stayed the same. In addition, credits were cancelled by third parties and creditors demanded quick payments. In other cases, Jews were forced to move their businesses or workshops to a different town on short notice. Sometimes it was possible to save one's livelihood by switching to a different line of work. As always when such situations arose, our coreligionists demonstrated great skill in finding new livelihoods, shifting gears, and opening new employment opportunities in place of those that were lost. But they usually needed some capital to tide them over, and this is where the Wirtschaftshilfe and the commercial counseling center came into play.

There were already agencies concerned with providing Jewish merchants and tradesmen with loans. These included the Jewish mutual savings banks, of which there were two in Berlin: the Ivria and the Jewish Credit Association. But both institutions extended credits only to their members and carried out their transactions according to standard banking practices. Another agency that came into question was the Jewish Credit Bank, which operated on a nonprofit basis but demanded security or guarantees for its credits and was quite ruthless in collecting outstanding interest. In addition, the entire structure of both the credit bank and the mutual savings banks was such that they functioned in a clumsy and time-consuming manner and thus often failed in urgent cases. From the start, the Wirtschaftshilfe worked in such a flexible and nonbureaucratic manner that it could intervene effectively in all genuine emergencies—of which there were now thousands.

The Wirtschaftshilfe fundamentally provided its financial assistance in the form of loans; however, it did not levy interest and did not necessarily demand security or guarantees. Each case was processed individually, and in many cases the money was given *à fonds perdu* even though they kept to the formal structure of a loan contract. It is all the more remarkable that repayments surpassed expectations. It was only natural that virtually no repayments took place in the catastrophic year of 1933. But starting in 1934 the share of repayments steadily rose to 50 percent in 1935, around 65 percent in 1936, and 75 to 80 percent in 1937 and early 1938. Starting in late 1938 the repayment quota dropped drastically, which was also natural. The high rate of repayment in the period between mid-1934 and mid-1938 demonstrates two things: first, the honesty of our coreligionists who saw it as their moral duty to repay the assistance the congregation had extended to them through the Wirtschaftshilfe to the best of their abilities, and second, that during this period many Jewish merchants and tradesmen really were prosperous enough to cover their financial obligations alongside the cost of living.

The amounts represented by these loans varied considerably since, as I have said, each case was processed separately. In many cases small amounts as low as fifty marks were sufficient. But on average the amounts ranged up to five hundred marks. The Wirtschaftshilfe primarily assisted the "little people." In appropriate cases it granted sums of up to a thousand marks. Applications going beyond this amount were directed either to the Jewish Savings Bank or to one of the two mutual savings banks. As far as the loans' running time was concerned, decisions were also made on an individual, case-by-case basis. It usually varied between one year and a year and a half. In emergencies, extension applications were given sympathetic attention.

Although the Wirtschaftshilfe functioned quickly and on a nonbureaucratic basis, the funds were not spent indiscriminately. Each individual case was examined to see whether a loan really matched its purpose, that is, whether it was intended to save someone's livelihood or find a new one or else tide someone over during an existing crisis. Wherever it was possible, the organization made sure that each applicant did not rely entirely on this loan but also provided at least some funds of his own. It often provided so-called merchandise credits instead of cash credits, and for the same reason. This means that the applicant did not receive the necessary sums for the acquisition of machines, tools, goods, or material, but rather that the Wirtschaftshilfe ordered and purchased them directly from the supplier. In this way it sought to ensure that Jewish suppliers were benefited, thus helping not just one coreligionist but many. The same principle was applied when the applicant required labor for his plan. It was then supplied by us through the Jewish Labor Exchange.

Of course, the attempt to form a Jewish economic sector where Jews bought from Jews and worked for Jews within the general economy was not practicable within a highly complicated economic organism like Germany, nor was it genuinely desired by either the Nazi authorities or the Jewish organizations. But steps were taken in this direction, and the Wirtschaftshilfe promoted such attempts in many cases. For example, it cooperated with the Jewish Crafts Association to publish a directory of the names and addresses of Jewish tradesmen and craftsmen, organized according to industry, and made this little book available to all coreligionists. In this way every Jew in Berlin was given the opportunity to make his purchases and orders at Jewish firms, and they tacitly made widespread use of this opportunity. But of course it was impossible to force them to do so, and the Nazis would not have tolerated such an attempt. The rapidly increasing Aryanization of Jewish businesses then restricted this option more and more.

From among the many cases the commercial counseling center processed, I would like to list a few from memory that I see as vivid examples of the steps we took to help some of our coreligionists back then. The Jewish gastronome X had been running a small café for a number of years and served mainly Christians. Although he was personally very popular among his customers, after the boycott they scarcely dared enter his shop, particularly since the Nazis had made that part of town into a Party stronghold.

At the same time, he clashed with the Christian waiters in his employ, and the authorities gave him no end of trouble. He fell into debt, found no buyer for his establishment, and had to shut down. At that point he had no possibility to emigrate. The Wirtschaftshilfe helped him to open an ice cream parlor in another part of town, which sold ice cream cones and other such things in the summertime and sweets at other times of the year. The Wirtschaftshilfe purchased the ice cream machine for him from a Jewish manufacturer. He needed no personnel since his family members helped out in the shop. Of course, this business was much smaller than his previous one, and it also had a highly seasonal character, but it brought in so much money that he managed to maintain his family's living standard. The business kept going until the summer of 1938, at which time the Nazis launched a hate campaign and a new boycott against the Jewish ice cream parlors. But at this point he finally found an opportunity to emigrate, and he took his family with him overseas. He had already repaid his loan to the Wirtschaftshilfe down to the last penny.

The Jewish merchant Y was an accomplished commercial traveler for textiles. Since he was already very well established among his customers, both Christians and Jews, he continued his trips to the provinces with success at first. But he had trouble finding accommodation in small provincial towns, where the hotels and inns increasingly refused to provide Jews with room and board. The Wirtschaftshilfe provided him with a car and later with a delivery truck which made it possible for him to set up his visits without being tied to the train schedule, so that he could drive to larger towns in the evenings where accommodations were still available. When this became impossible starting around 1937, he would sleep in his delivery truck somewhere on the highway and eat the canned goods and such that he took with him. This was certainly not pleasant for him, but in this way he managed to continue plying his trade until the end of 1938, at which time he emigrated. He also repaid his loan to the Wirtschaftshilfe in full.

The press photographer Z was fired from his well-paying position with a newspaper publisher as a non-Aryan. The Wirtschaftshilfe gave him a loan to purchase his own photographic gear with high-quality equipment plus his own studio, in which he continued to work independently as a technical photographer for industrial and advertising purposes for several years, earning a good income for himself in the process. When it was time to emigrate and his loan was not entirely repaid, he gave part of his photo equipment back to the Wirtschaftshilfe, which then used it in its training courses.

There were innumerable cases where Jewish merchants took advantage of the Wirtschaftshilfe because they were now forced to make all their purchases from Aryan suppliers in cash instead of on credit and did not have the needed cash assets. But there were just as many cases where persons who had previously held steady jobs and lost their positions were helped by the Wirtschaftshilfe to become self-employed, working for several years in a related profession and earning a sufficient living. While it was already difficult enough to help affected Jewish merchants, craftsmen, and tradesmen to stay in business, this assistance was much more difficult for persons in the free professions. Because of the racial laws of April 1933 they frequently lost their jobs overnight. In most cases they had no savings and faced utter ruin.

In the case of civil service officials and employees who were hounded from their positions, the legal defense office of the Wirtschaftshilfe first tried to arrange for favorable settlement or pension payments. This was successful in some but not all cases.

It also conducted difficult negotiations with the authorities in regard to the problem of Jewish physicians. If a large number of them managed to continue working and if the Study Group of Jewish Physicians was only slowly and gradually restricted over the following years, this was because even the Nazi government feared a complete collapse of the medical services in Germany if all Jewish doctors were taken out of circulation at once. The Nazis simply could not do without the Jewish doctors, at least not immediately. They thus created "exceptions" and privileged categories such as World War I veterans, and so on, and allowed them to continue working at first. Over the following years, as the number of Christian doctors grew, the circle was systematically narrowed. Jewish doctors first lost their access to the insurance system, then their work was exclusively restricted to Jewish patients, and finally even this was nullified. The doctors organized a sort of self-help activity by which those who could still practice collected money for their less fortunate colleagues. In this way considerable sums were collected and made available to the unemployed doctors. Aside from the regular contributions the doctors made according to a certain formula, considerable amounts flowed from the proceeds of the "physicians' ball" into the doctors' fund every year until 1938. This was a ball the doctors organized every winter, representing the main social event for Jewish circles in Berlin during those otherwise dark years.

Just like the physicians, the Jewish dentists organized their own self-help organization, as did the Jewish pharmacists and the Jewish lawyers. The Wirtschaftshilfe only participated in these actions to the extent of providing the doctors' fund and the lawyers' fund with administrative guidance, meaning that it made payments and disbursements according to the instructions of the doctors' committee and the lawyers' committee. To be sure, this purely administrative function represented a considerable degree of additional work on top of our other responsibilities.

The Wirtschaftshilfe sought to help the numerous Jewish employees who had lost their positions following the Nazi seizure of power find new positions if they were not yet willing or able to emigrate. These people were mostly commercial employees, bank employees, salespersons, clerks, and house servants. Of course, new positions only came into question in regard to shops or firms in which Jewish owners were still in charge of their own businesses. In the wake of the many "Aryanizations," these firms increasingly disappeared from year to year. But until Kristallnacht in November 1938 there were still enough of them to provide a number of Jewish workers with employment.

The first goal was to encourage Jewish business owners to keep their Jewish staff and, whenever possible, expand it. The fact is that during the first wave of panic, many Jewish bosses fired their Jewish employees, particularly in businesses where there were National Socialist factory cells. One outstanding exception was the Berlin department store N. Israel, which had hundreds of Jewish and non-Jewish employees. Although this eminent firm, which had been founded by a Jew more than a century before and which was still in Jewish hands and remained a family-run company, had always shown exemplary behavior toward its staff regardless of their religious beliefs, a Nazi factory cell had been founded there even before the seizure of power and kept to the shadows at first. But it now stood up and demanded that all Jewish employees be dismissed. The company's owners, Berthold Israel and his sons Herbert and Wilfried, refused to fire even a single Jew. They did not let themselves be intimidated, even when high Nazi authorities threatened to arrest them. This brave stance, which was supported by our legal defense office, worked. The firm kept its Jewish personnel and continued to prosper for years until, in 1939, it passed into "Aryan" hands as the last large Jewish business in the Reich capital.

This brave stance served as an example and a model, and after the first panic of April 1933 faded away, many Jewish shop owners felt encouraged to hire Jewish staff. This is where the Wirtschaftshilfe came into play. For several years, that is, even before the seizure of power, there had been a community institution called the Jewish Labor Exchange, which had its offices in the building of the Lindenstrasse synagogue and which had already performed a great deal of useful work for our coreligionists, particularly during the Depression years. This office was now taken over by the Wirtschaftshilfe and acted as its subdivision, although in greatly expanded form, until 1937. It succeeded in finding new jobs for unemployed commercial and shop employees, bookkeepers, salesmen, commercial travelers, craftsmen, household servants, and so on. It succeeded in this because it did not wait for open positions to be advertised but instead intervened personally with Jewish employers—in writing, orally and by telephone, day by day, pressing them to hire Jewish workers. Success was particularly visible among female job seekers, approximately half of whom were provided with suitable jobs. Finding positions for male job seekers was more difficult, but here too the results were good. In many cases, besides our efforts with Jewish business owners, we had to resort to negotiations with National Socialist factory offices, with the German Labor Front and other organizations. Our legal defense office took charge of such cases.

In 1937 the Jewish Labor Exchange had to cease its activity at the behest of the Nazi authorities because at this time all job placement offices were centralized in the hands of the state. But during this period another department within the Wirtschaftshilfe, namely the vocational reorientation and training section, had gained enormous significance and was able to take over much of the old Labor Exchange's activities. It differed fundamentally from the previously mentioned departments. While, for example, the commercial counseling center and the legal defense office primarily served the interests of those coreligionists who at least temporarily intended to continue living in Germany, the vocational reorientation and training department was primarily aimed at preparing people to emigrate from Germany.

Following the fateful month of January 1933, the choice of one's profession—whether one intended to practice it in Nazi Germany or was planning to emigrate—was no longer determined by one's own desires and inclinations but rather by the situation. Jewish young people were prohibited from attending German universities. Thousands of already active academics woke up one morning to find themselves without a job and without any prospects for the future. Opportunities in commerce, finance and industry were restricted and dwindled from month to month. Those who were considering emigration were faced with the fact that the few foreign states that came into consideration only issued permits, affidavits, and visas to trained workers, technical experts, and so on. The need to choose a new profession emphasizing manual work became unavoidable overnight. The new tasks resulting from this were assumed by the vocational reorientation and training department. In practical terms, the professional training was aimed at young people just out of school who had not yet entered the workforce, while the vocational reorientation dealt with adults who had already chosen a profession but who now had to be retrained.

Helping young people just out of school was all the more urgent since after the Nazi seizure of power Jewish boys and girls could only be apprenticed in Aryan businesses for a short time. Thus our professional training department either had to find these young people apprenticeships in Jewish firms, which was difficult due to the rapid decline of such firms, or else create its own training workshops. In this way, a systematic program was established for the training of Jewish young people in industrial and agricultural professions. In detailed conversations, we discussed the inclinations and skills of each one, examined his or her future prospects and set up a training plan. In cases where there was a chance for a young person to emigrate to a particular country, we also gave thought to the economic and specific professional situation in that country. For this purpose the professional training department stood in constant contact with the Aid Association for German Jews, which handled emigration matters and was constantly informed by a network of foreign correspondents on the situation in various overseas areas, as well as with the Palestine Office, which organized the Aliyah to Palestine.

At first the vocational reorientation for adults had greater difficulties to overcome than the professional training for young people. The main reason for this was the antipathy individual Nazi agencies felt toward the thought of Jews flooding into industry, handicraft, and agriculture. Precisely those circles who had previously denigrated the Jews as "parasites" because they allegedly shirked physical labor now resisted the concept of Jewish workers, Jewish craftsmen, and Jewish farmers. Only when they understood that the entire reorientation process was intended as a preparation for emigration did they hesitatingly and unwillingly give their consent. These same circles later had no objections when the last Jews slaved away under the SS whip in basic production and were harried to death.

The Berlin congregation's first reorientation courses were banned by the Gestapo and were only permitted after arduous negotiations. Afterward, on a higher level, it attempted to arrive at a general regulation in negotiations between the Reich Agency for German Jews and top Nazi authorities. Finally, in the spring of 1935 the Reich Economics Ministry decreed that only vocational reorientation courses aimed at emigration preparations would be permitted. In any case, systematic work in the field of vocational reorientation for adults only occurred after early 1935. Earlier efforts in this area, which were undertaken without benefit of official permission, were more or less experimental. Some small craft courses were set up; people were placed in Jewish craft workshops for retraining or sent to agricultural estates placed at the disposal of various Jewish agencies. In the small town of Waidmannslust near Berlin a reeducation center was created. Here, young people were supposed to live under rather spartan conditions and be trained in agricultural and craft work. Waidmannslust was an experiment that failed because it had no trained instructors at its disposal. But the basic idea, namely that retraining should involve the student in his entirety—not only his technical knowledge but also his character and disposition—and that it should place him into an entirely new environment, into a new kind of milieu, was not bad at all. Henceforth, reshaping a former office inmate and desk person into a new kind of person who did his part at the vice and the workbench or in the fresh air of the farm remained one of the principles of vocational reorientation.

The Reich Agency for German Jews and the Central Committee for Assistance and Development working within it developed guidelines for Jewish vocational reorientation work which were intended to be valid throughout the Reich. In theory, these guidelines also applied to the Wirtschaftshilfe in Berlin. But in practical terms, we were largely independent, thanks to the professionals and the funds at our disposal. It was our intention that two-thirds of the costs of vocational reorientation and professional training would be provided by the Reich Agency and a third by the congregations. In actual fact, the Wirtschaftshilfe in Berlin contributed far more than the third that was demanded from it, and it was thus in a position to create exemplary training workshops in which not only our coreligionists from Berlin but also Jews from the provinces were received for training and reorientation. On the other hand, the agricultural training farms in the provinces, particularly those in the vicinity of the Reich capital, were supported by the Wirtschaftshilfe in Berlin to the extent that we assumed the complete costs for room and board for our coreligionists sent there from Berlin. Many of these training farms would not have survived without our contributions. Of course, we were happy to submit our work to the supervision demanded by the Reich Agency. But the occasional inspectors not only found nothing to criticize but usually returned with mostly positive experiences, which they then passed on to other communities.

If managing the labor exchange for unemployed Jewish workers and the professional training for young Jews fresh out of school was already a very difficult task in these critical years, it was even more difficult for the professional reorientation of adults. In this area there were virtually no practical experiences or precedents one could apply to the situation in which we found ourselves. A great deal had been written in theoretical terms about the need to move Jews into different professions where—whether at home or abroad—they would have a better chance to earn a livelihood and simultaneously improve the overall image of Jews. But as soon as we actually tried to realize these plans we encountered serious difficulties.

A great many vocational reorientation courses were called into being in which several thousand men and women received training. The Wirtschaftshilfe maintained three large training workshops of its own, namely a workshop for the building trade, another for the metalworking industry, and a third for woodworking. Training in these congregation-owned training workshops occurred under the supervision of experts using modern machines and devices, whereby the instructors were extremely careful to teach genuinely up-to-date skills. The "reorientees"—we called them that because it would have been somewhat odd to call people the between ages twenty and forty "apprentices" or "pupils"—worked eight hours a day. The courses lasted a total of nine to twelve months. The division of work occurred more or less according to the norms to be found in a corresponding factory. The costs for these apprentices were considerable.

Of course, we did not teach all the reorientation courses in our own workshops. For example, in textiles training it was more sensible and practical to place the "reorientees" as apprentices in existing Jewish businesses than to purchase vast numbers of sewing machines. Of course, we supervised the instruction and reimbursed it properly. In this way a great number of male and even more female tailors, ironers, and seamstresses received training. The training period in these textile courses was generally considerably shorter than in our own workshops as described above. Further reorientation courses conducted over these years included photography, bookbinding, auto mechanics, ceramics, chemical industry, shop window decoration, kindergarten work, nursing, cosmetics, dress design, dietetic and industrial cooking, weaving, leather working, clock making, and many others.

Of equal, if not greater importance than the industrial and craft reorientation was agricultural training. However, in this area the Jewish organizations were in the fortunate position to be able to channel the "reorientees" onto long-existing Jewish training farms where they received solid training in the various fields of farming, animal husbandry, and gardening under professional guidance. This reorientation was not limited to vocational training but encompassed a person's entire personality. Detached from his previously accustomed urban environment, separated from the close circle of his family and neighbors, living in a rural setting under entirely different working and living conditions, a "reorientee" on an agricultural teaching farm had a chance to prepare himself for an entirely new life, a completely transformed existence, both internally and externally. As a rule, younger people signed up for agricultural reorientation, while people over twenty-five and thirty preferred craft training. The age limit for vocational reorientation was generally set at thirty-five, although this was not seen as a rigid law. In practice, it was discovered that in many cases even men up to age forty could successfully complete a reorientation course, and among female reorientees even women up to age fifty could be trained in certain branches of domestic labor, and as seamstresses and cooks. I heard from many instructors, who were in a position to know from their daily experience, that "reorientees" between the ages of twenty-five and thirty approached their new work with greater seriousness and eagerness than the younger age groups, and that they sometimes showed better results.

When I was forced to abandon my position in December 1939 upon my expulsion from Germany, the general secretary of the congregation wrote in my job reference that it was due to me that no delays occurred and no complaints arose in the work of the Wirtschaftshilfe in all the years I worked there.

28

From "German Maiden" to Convinced Zionist

LUISE STEIN

We were a thoroughly assimilated Jewish family. My father was so assimilated into German culture in his behavior, feelings, and thoughts that he never would have said he was a Jew or a German Jew but only that he was a German and an ardent patriot. He had been a noncommissioned officer during World War I and was awarded the Iron Cross, which he displayed with pride. His fatherland was always uppermost in his mind while his family took second place. In our congregation we were equally respected by Jews and Christians, but we participated in no club activities and had absolutely no interest in promoting Jewish life. We only took part in temple services during vacation—that was the least that we did to identify ourselves with the Jews and to live the way people expected us to. It was the most we could do without making ourselves appear suspicious in the eyes of our Christian neighbors.

My early school friends were all Christians, which matched my parents' attitude toward the Jews. Looking back, I think that they were conceited German Jews, the kind the New York Jews say needed a lesson from Hitler. And nevertheless, too many of their attitudes rubbed off on me for me to condemn them. My father in particular wanted nothing to do with Russian or Polish Jews since such contacts would have called attention to him and because he despised their behavior. They talked with their hands. They had a Yiddish accent that sounded intolerable to a "German ear." They were not very particular with their manners and clothing. Of course, they had a heart of gold. That might count for something in America, but not in aristocratic Germany. Even I felt ashamed when one of these Jews addressed me on the street in plain view of my more restrained Jewish or Christian friends.

Jewish girls in my town usually associated with Christian boys. We felt a certain amount of pride about this, and we girls thought we were doing it for the sake of better integration into German culture. Even when Hitler took over the government in 1933 there was no change in the girls' behavior. I felt that if one of us girls was discriminated against, it did not occur because of her religion but because someone took objection to her behavior. We were too well raised to let ourselves be influenced by things for which we were not personally responsible.

In April 1935 I was just about to complete the secondary school or, as it was called, the Mädchenoberrealschule with the intention of studying languages when I had my first personal experience of National Socialism. I assumed that this year, like every other year, I would receive a book prize for the best finishing grades in my class. It would be publicly announced at the annual graduation ceremony in front of an audience consisting of parents, local citizens, and teachers. But this time the auditorium was decorated in an entirely different way than it had been in previous years: a large Hitler portrait stood in the center and all around it stood Nazi flags with swastikas. And then they did not sing "Deutschland über alles," as I in my childish naïveté had expected, but the Horst Wessel Song, "Die Fahne hoch."

Finally they announced the names of the outstanding students. I smiled at my parents, who were creasing their foreheads, encouragingly, expecting them to hear that their daughter would receive the third, perhaps the second, or even the first prize. But all the names were read, and mine was not included. A friend noticed that there were two name tags on top of one another in her book and when she pulled the top one off she saw mine underneath. My fellow students were almost more outraged than I was and began to investigate. The professor, they said, went white in the face and then supposedly said or, more accurately, stuttered, "I don't know what happened. It's the principal's responsibility." The next morning the newspaper headline said, "Jewish boys and girls in public schools receive no more prizes." All of my schoolmates accused the principal of being a coward and a trimmer. In fact, one or two principals of a gymnasium and a girl's primary school had still awarded the Jewish students their prizes.

My father had not been as shocked by the rise of National Socialism as many other Jews were. When my brother once told us about his friends who wanted to join Communist clubs, my father flew into a rage. He was really afraid we could become Communists, and often said that he would prefer Nazism as the lesser of two evils.

My friend Emmy invited me to our usual group hike around Lake Constance, where we would always carry on philosophical discussions about nature and the essence of being human. And it was this profoundly German character trait of mine, this love of nature, a sentimentality and romantic sensitivity for the ideals of Schiller and Goethe, that made me into a spiritually rooted member of this youthful and idealistic hiking and singing circle. We never discussed political issues but simply enjoyed the wonders of nature and hiked from town to town. Once Emmy moved up to me in the grass and whispered in my ear, "You are wonderful, you are just as much a part of us as everyone else." Although I thought that was a very good thing, I sensed she was also aware that I was no longer one of them. She later asked me once more to take part in our usual hike. But I could hide no longer. "No thanks, I can come with you no more." "Why not? We have reassembled our group, and the others won't notice because you don't look Jewish. Please come along!" She did not know how much that hurt me. But this "they won't notice" made up my mind not to go. I never hiked with them again.

In the meantime, the Jewish boys and girls in our town had closed ranks in a group of their own because there was nowhere left where they could go. They formed "study groups." And what did they study? The rebirth of our Jewishness through the study of the Bible and our history to find consolation and a comprehensible reason for all that was happening. We first discussed whether we had violated some law or other, and whether that was the reason for our fate and whether we could justify or improve ourselves. Out of this there gradually emerged the Zionist ideas, namely that we should have a national home where the persecuted could go instead of having to roam about alone.

I went to these meetings quite often since I felt somewhat protected there, but I was never active. I had to force myself to go there because the completely Jewish atmosphere still seemed too foreign. There were a few boys there who spoke Yiddish, which sounded horrible to a "German ear." The others accepted these boys in their group as valued members, but I could not get used to their speech and their manners.

Soon the group turned into a melting pot made up of conceited German, Russian, Polish, Palestinian, rich, poor, loud, "cultivated," and other Jewish youths from Constance. They lost their former ordinary Jewish character and developed into a Zionist group, which turned me off at first. But the others finally convinced me of the need to create a national home for those unfortunates who could no longer remain in the countries they were scattered across. I became a registered member of the Zionist Movement of Germany. That was too much for my father. We didn't talk to each other for weeks. He would become outraged when anyone would ask him if he felt the Palestinian blood in his veins. He would then pull out the family Bible to prove in "black and white" that our ancestors had been living in Germany since before the Thirty Years War, around 1600. The mere fact that Hitler said he was not a German did not by a long shot mean that he wasn't one. Father became even more outraged when he heard people in the congregation saying, "He'll learn one day and maybe he'll become one of us." He never has, not even now.

It was undoubtedly a great victory on the part of a portion of Jewish youth that they found their way to one another. But it was the persecution, the recognition of our fate and our suffering that brought us together after 1934.

I spoke English rather well, and the entire Jewish congregation came together and asked me to give them English lessons with an eye to future emigration to England, America, South Africa, Palestine, Canada, or even Australia. The general trend was to get as far away from Europe as possible. For more than a year I gave English instruction to more than seventy men, women, and children, to the old and the young. In this way I got to know the entire congregation and was very surprised at how many valuable people there were among them and how dramatically this time of persecution had united them. Polish, Russian, and German Jews sat at the same table and repeated the English words I taught them. In view of the hostile atmosphere outside, the small cultural differences such as accents or a more lively manner of expression did not seem to bother most of them.

Part VIII

The Beginning of the End— The Reich Pogrom Night

The Reich Pogrom Night of November 9–10, 1938, which the Nazis cynically called the "Reichskristallnacht" (Reich Crystal Night) because of the shattered glass, introduced a new phase of Jewish persecution in the Third Reich. In this way they demonstrated that civil rights no longer applied to Jews. After the Anschluss of Austria and the occupation of the Sudetenland in the wake of the Munich Agreement, the Nazis now apparently felt so certain of their power that they needed to pay no further attention to foreign opinion. The Reich Pogrom Night also showed that the regime could go to vast lengths without arousing significant protests among the non-Jewish population.

The pretext for the pogrom was an attack on the German diplomat Ernst vom Rath by the seventeen-year-old Jewish Pole Herschel Grynszpan on November 7, 1938. Vom Rath died from his wounds two days later. In explaining his motive, Grynszpan cited the expulsion of his parents, who had been living in Hanover, to Poland. They were arrested on October 28, 1938, along with seventeen thousand other Polish Jews residing in Germany and deported to the no-man's-land between Poland and Germany. Before that, the government in Warsaw had issued a decree stripping all Poles living abroad of their citizenship if they did not return to Poland to receive a special stamp in their passport. However, the Jews whom the Germans deported to the border could not cross it since the Polish government had decided to refuse Polish Jews reentry from areas under German rule. That is why the deportees ended up wandering around in no man's land for days on end.

When the assassination became known in Germany, local Party organizations initiated the first acts of anti-Jewish violence on November 7 and 8, the so-called wild actions. When word of vom Rath's death arrived from Paris on November 9, Reich Propaganda Minister Joseph Goebbels held a speech in Munich, issuing the signal for a nationwide attack. In doing so, he referred to a conversation with the Führer. Upon his suggestion, Goebbels said, Hitler decided that, should anti-Jewish riots spontaneously spread across the entire Reich, they should not be interfered with. This statement was understood as a call to action. The SS and police received no orders. However, the Storm Troopers sent out their own squads. The very same evening, a wave of unprecedented violence and blind destructiveness swept from one end of Germany to the other. With few exceptions, all synagogues were set on fire and Jewish shops and homes were laid waste and pillaged. Jews were pulled from their apartments or picked up off the streets, abused, sent to concentration camps, and killed. A total of one hundred Jews were murdered and some thirty thousand men were sent to concentration camps. Hundreds died there. Although the excesses were officially halted on November 10, in some places they continued for days.

The victims were at the mercy of their tormentors. The police and fire department either looked away or merely watched, their hands in their pockets. Those who tried to help were prevented from doing so. Most non-Jewish citizens also failed to help them. Even if some of them were horrified by these events, only a very few dared to express open protest or to provide the victims with direct assistance. A not inconsiderable portion of the population watched with interest and sometimes with malicious pleasure. Some displayed unabashed enthusiasm and welcomed the terror. Non-Jewish Germans also actively participated in the destruction and plundering of Jewish shops and homes. The Storm Troopers expressly invited them to join in. The Jews, however, had to pay for the damage themselves and even assume responsibility for the final demolition of burned synagogues. In addition, on the pretext of the need to pay damages for the murder of a German diplomat, the Jewish community was billed for a "retribution payment" of one billion Reichsmarks. The state also confiscated the insurance sums owed to the Jews as a result of the damage. The Party and other courts halted lawsuits set in motion by the events of the Reich Pogrom Night, although during this pogrom many things occurred that were considered crimes under the penal code.

To this day a controversy rages over whether the attacks were improvised or planned. Other Nazi leaders immediately criticized Goebbels as the event's initiator. Heinrich Himmler, Reichsführer of the SS and chief of police, declared that the attack order came from the Reich propaganda administration and, in his opinion, Hitler had not been informed. He believed that Goebbels launched this action in a quest for power. Reich Economics Minister Walter Funk was concerned about Germany's image abroad and accused Goebbels of wantonly destroying national assets. Hermann Göring complained to Hitler about "Goebbels's irresponsible actions and their consequences for the economy." While Hitler did not distance himself from Goebbels, he agreed that such incidents should not be repeated.

At a conference called together by Göring, in which numerous ministers, high Foreign Office officials, and police officers took part, a decision was made to confine all actions against Jews to "legal means" since "such actions" could not be controlled and damaged Germany's image.

At first, the powerful reactions on the part of the foreign press did not impress the Nazis. When President Roosevelt recalled the American ambassador from Berlin and publicly expressed his outrage, the German envoy to the United States was also recalled on account of the "American interference in internal German affairs." From America, Ambassador Hans Dieckhoff reported that "decent national circles, who are thoroughly anti-communist and to a large extent anti-Semitic," had begun to turn their backs on Germany. "In this general atmosphere of hatred, the idea of a boycott against German goods has also been given new life, and at the moment economic negotiations are unthinkable." Since more and more merchants and importers joined the boycott movement, numerous contracts were cancelled, which had a profound effect on the economy. In December of 1938 a whole range of companies lost between 20 and 30 percent of their export business.

29

Escape from Hell

Max Moses Polke

When my wife and I returned from Berlin to Breslau in the late evening of November 9, there was no sign of the boiling anger of the people or anything of that sort in the main streets we had to pass through on our way home. But the next morning my second son came home from school shortly after eight o'clock and told us that the children had been sent home because all the windows had been smashed in overnight. On the way home he saw how the Jewish shops he passed by had all been demolished. He was also told that the big new synagogue was on fire.

My wife tried ringing up her shoe shop, but no one answered. I went there immediately. On the way I could already see how entire groups of Jews, many of whom I knew personally, were being escorted away by policemen or else rode past me in police vans. I discovered also that all the Jewish shops I passed had been severely damaged. Of course, the same was true of my wife's shop. I proceeded immediately to the insurance company whose offices were located nearby and reported the damage so that they could not later say that I had reported it too late. Then I went to the nearby train station to call up my wife at our flat. No one answered. The line must have been damaged.

Now that I knew what was going on, I decided not to return home and to head for Berlin instead. I had enough money on me to travel even further and live unrecognized somewhere. The next train to Berlin left at 10:25 A.M. It did not seem wise to spend the remaining hour and a half at the station. So I called an acquaintance with whom I wanted to discuss matters. We arranged a meeting in a part of town where few Jews lived and I headed in that direction.

However, fate caught up with me all the same. On Tauentzienstrasse, directly in front of the American consulate, I was recognized by a man whom I had defended some years before because of resistance to the state. He incited a person standing next to him to start insulting me, with other rowdies joining in. I tried without success to appease these people by pointing out that I had done nothing to harm them. On the contrary, this was a man whom I had helped out in a difficult situation. The insults soon gave way to physical abuse. Covered with blood, I attempted to flee to a house entrance. But the doorman drove me back. These were all civilians. The police, the SS, and the Storm Troopers were nowhere to be seen.

I don't know what would have become of me if a big strong man, a furniture mover by the looks of him, hadn't taken pity on me, grabbed me by the arm, and said to the onlookers, "Stop it now, the Jew has suffered enough already." But to me my rescuer said, "If you don't come with me to the Police Presidium you won't come out of here alive." I offered no resistance, and my companion took me to the nearby Police Presidium, past the burning synagogue. Its great dome stood crooked. Flames shot out of the interior. I couldn't help but think of the destruction of the Temple in Jerusalem. At the Police Presidium I was first taken to a police doctor with the words, "Here's another one who fell into the wrong hands." The police doctor stanched the flow of blood and carefully recorded my name and the nature of my injuries in a book. Prussian order remains Prussian order.

Now I was taken to the courtyard of the Police Presidium, where a number of Jews were standing around, including some acquaintances of mine. They didn't recognize me with my swollen and disfigured face. My lips were so thick that I could hardly speak. Four lower teeth and one upper one were loose. Every few minutes more transports of arrested Jews arrived. I kept encountering acquaintances. So we stood and stood. The monotony was only broken when someone came and took away our pocket lighters, knives, and scissors. We were allowed to keep our valuables.

Standing up like this became more and more intolerable, since most of us had been pulled out of our flats early in the morning and had not eaten anything since. At around five in the afternoon an old policeman appeared and told us the following, "There is something to eat now, containing neither meat nor fat. Jews who live according to religious laws can eat it without concern." And indeed, they brought us bowls of tasty potato soup with well-cooked potatoes. Both I and the others had the impression that it had been prepared with fresh butter. In addition, each of us received a big piece of fresh bread, which I held onto, since I was well aware that a visit to the police begins with a thorough fasting. With this in mind, I had been keeping a large package of zwieback in my flat for months so that, in case of a sudden arrest, I could grab it and stick it in my pocket. Now these "arrest biscuits," as my children always called them, were safely stashed away in my flat. While we were standing around in the courtyards of the Police Presidium, we heard three detonations, as if from a demolition. They came from the nearby synagogue, whose destruction by fire was apparently taking too long for the Nazis. The dust from the explosions flew into our faces.

At 7:30 P.M. we were led out of the small courtyards into the main courtyard of the Police Presidium and lined up in rank and file. Several severely injured war veterans were sent home, while the others were led out in groups of ten and first lined up in front of the horribly ravaged synagogue, of which only the sooty outside walls still remained. Then we marched down Breslau's Tauentzienstrasse to the freight depot. They had transported victims of the action of June 13, 1938, there in trucks, but we had to go on foot. An SS man with a cocked carbine under his arm marched at each end of each row. The streets were sealed off but were lined with people whom—to use the Nazi jargon—one could only call subhumans. These were apparently people who had been sent there and who did not lack for the vilest insults, of which the choruses of "Die, Jews!" were the mildest. The SS men had to defend us against physical assault. On the other hand, they also drove us onward with rifle blows and paid no consideration whatsoever to the weak and sick.

To our surprise, at the freight depot we—that is, about a thousand men—were not loaded onto cattle cars but seated on a passenger train. In each double compartment they placed nineteen men with one policeman carrying a loaded gun. They had already informed us at the Police Presidium that they would shoot anyone trying to escape. The train began its slow journey at 9:00 P.M.

We soon retraced the first part of the journey to Liegnitz that I had taken with my wife twenty-four hours earlier in a nice express train. No one forbade us from speaking, but we spoke little. However, the guards behaved decently. They allowed us to smoke and some of them accepted notes from us which they promised to pass on to our relatives. We were allowed to make purchases at the stations we stopped at on our way, without leaving the compartment. But the trains had not been announced to the restaurants beforehand, so only a few of us managed to buy anything. I soon noted by the stations we passed where we were headed, and at nine in the morning we arrived in Weimar, a town that, from my school days, I knew as the very symbol of German culture—the place where Goethe wrote his immortal works, which has gained notoriety as the train station for a place not to be found on any maps but now known the world over as Buchenwald.

I don't know how long we had to wait in the station tunnel, our faces turned to the wall. Every few moments we heard the screams of men undergoing random beatings. Woe to the unfortunate soul who dared turn around. Finally we were loaded onto covered trucks and after an hour's drive we arrived in Buchenwald, where we were driven out of the trucks with gun butts.

Young SS men appeared and welcomed us with blows to the head. Then we had to enter the gate at a running pace. As we ran, other guards tripped us, so that we fell to the ground and were forced to run on as blows rained down upon our backs. As a souvenir of this welcome I received a sprained ring finger and a kneecap injury that would trouble me for a long time to come. They lined us up on the camp's parade ground and made us stand still for hours. The famous shaving of our heads and beards was almost pleasant because at least we could sit down during the ceremony. It was a strange sight to see good friends in a sheared state. As sad as the situation was, when I saw the Breslau cantor without his beautiful long beard, I couldn't help but laugh. When speaking he always used to stroke his beard, and now he merely clawed at the air.

We stood in rank and file until the evening, continually joined by new arrivals. At that time I became acquainted with the so-called Kapos. They were older prisoners who had a sort of seniority. Our Kapo kept walking up to us, yelling, "Will you stand still in rank and file and shape up!" But at the same time he said quietly, "It's not nearly as bad as it seems. Just behave sensibly and you'll make it through." The first words were for the SS guards who were walking around, the others for us. At the suggestion of a fellow sufferer, I soon made friends with the Kapo by giving him ten marks. But I could have saved myself the expense because the next morning he was gone for good. All in all, those who seemed to be taking it the best were those who were seeing Buchenwald for the second time. They apparently knew how to get out of there again.

A barbed-wire fence separated us from the rest of the camp. We also were given special accommodations. These consisted of five improvised wooden barracks. I precisely calculated that each measured ten meters wide, five meters high, and fifty meters long. Two thousand people had to sleep in this dungeon. That was only possible because the bunks were actually shelves, always five on top of one other, which were separated by narrow corridors so that two people could hardly squeeze past each other. My neighbor, the former civil servant Mandowsky, declared, "I have never seen so many violations of the fire and safety laws." There was no question of receiving a pillow, not to mention a blanket.

On the evening of November 11 I tried to celebrate the start of the Sabbath, even in this sad environment, by reciting the prayers meant for Friday together with another acquaintance from Breslau, Dr. Georg Daniel Fränkel. We had just started when we were interrupted by a burst of screaming. An SS man had walked through the barracks and arbitrarily struck a prisoner. The latter was foolish enough to complain by pointing to his experience as a front soldier. Immediately a second SS man appeared and both maltreated the unfortunate man with wooden clubs. We heard him cry out, "I'd rather be shot right away." The SS men responded, "That would suit you Jewish swine, wouldn't it? You'd feel nothing and the state would have to foot the bill." We heard how they continued to beat him until he made no further sound. Then he was carried away. The next morning he were told that he had died after slashing an artery with a knife during a seizure. A young person nearby called out, "But they took away all our knives." Fortunately, no one heard this statement. But what followed was typical: the camp administration was very upset that it didn't have the dead man's personal details. They kept asking if anyone "knew the bird."

On the morning of the second day we once again had to stand in rank and file. We stood longer than eight hours with nothing whatsoever to do. A person who has never experienced such a thing has no notion of the physical and psychological torment this standing meant. The camp commandant appeared at one point, pulled one of us out of the formation, and said to him, "You Jewish swine killed our *Volksgenosse* vom Rath and will now be punished for it." The poor man protested his innocence, but the camp commandant said, "People always say about the Jews that all of Israel vouches for one another, so now you will vouch for Grynszpan!" After speaking these words, he stuck his gun back into his holster and reveled in the psychological torments he was administering to his victim. This day was also filled with random beatings. We had to watch how several people who had already spent considerable time in the camp, including two Kapos, received the infamous twenty-five lashes on their bare buttocks.

At noon they finally gave us something to eat. The food wasn't bad. We ate eagerly, although we had to eat from bowls like animals, without a spoon or knife and fork. The used bowls were then passed on to the next person without any sort of washing in between. But who paid attention to such things? The food even contained meat, although no one could say from what animal. Some claimed that it was roasted whale. In any case, it tasted pretty good. Even the most devout rabbis among us explained that we were not only permitted to violate the Sabbath regulations but that we were compelled to. As is well known, this is only allowed at moments of the greatest threat to life and limb.

On the morning of the third day we stood again in rank and file, ten men one behind the other. They gave us coffee. Every man in the front row was given a bowl from which he was allowed to take a sip before passing it on to the man behind him. This meant one bowl for ten men. This day I was lucky enough to be standing in second place. The bowl still contained quite a lot and I was not so exposed to the random beatings as the people in the last row.

At noon the camp commandant appeared and ordered us all to sit down. That seemed at first to be an alleviation of our ordeal. But we soon discovered that sitting on gravel was anything but a pleasant experience. No one was allowed to move, not even to relieve oneself. One had to do one's business on the spot and then enlist one's neighbor's help by concealing the evidence with sand and gravel. One prisoner dared to stand up and step to the side. The camp commandant jumped on him and held his revolver against his head, only to put it away again after taking pleasure at his victim's fear.

This was the day that the horrible diarrhea, which one hears about in many reports, began taking its toll. I later read that the tasty food of November 12 contained castor oil. I don't believe it. Instead, I suspect that our constant fear was the cause of our intestinal complaints. I myself was constipated during this time, thus saving me a visit to the latrine for three days. That was very pleasant, because going there required a powerful will. The latrine consisted of a very long, some three-meter-deep hole on the edge of which beams had been attached for sitting on. There were many cases of people falling into the hole. They frequently could not be pulled out and died a horrible death.

This atmosphere drove many to suicide by approaching the electric fence that surrounded the camp. It was impossible to do this by accident, because there was a many meters thick wire entanglement in front of the fence that one had to climb with considerable skill. We in our group later posted guards who would grab the arm of anyone who took the path toward the entanglement. In this way, with friendly persuasion and sometimes with force, we prevented many deaths.

Our treatment noticeably improved starting on the fourth day. We no longer had to stand in rank and file but could walk around the constricted area allotted to us, or even sit down to the extent this was possible. The insults and beatings stopped. We ascribed this to the influence of foreign governments, which must have heard of the events of November 10. However, this was pure speculation on our part since we were entirely cut off from the outside world.

We were fed every so often and the food was never bad. But we had to wait a very long time. One prisoner remarked that he had always kicked up a row with his wife if his breakfast coffee arrived on the table five minutes late. Now he would say, "I have learned to wait for twelve hours!"

The lack of water was terrible. Washing was out of the question. There was no way to change one's underwear. We walked around without collars and with beards that grew more bristly by the day. The ones who looked the worst were photographed for the *Stürmer*. The shortage of drinking water was even worse. Sometimes in the morning there would be some water to drink in a special room, the so-called scullery. We had to wait in line an hour or more to receive a swallow of water. Sometimes, after working one's way to the front of the line, the water supply would be exhausted. I coined the expression "fountain promenade" for this wait! The term soon spread throughout the camp.

The scullery also miserably housed the seriously ill, including many mentally ill people, particularly epileptics. We had to shield these unfortunates from the eyes of the SS, because an epileptic seizure was regarded as an act of rebellion and was punished with a revolver. There were also some who could not stomach the camp food, particularly diabetics and others who had to follow a diet. Hardly any of them made it through. We counted between ten and fifteen stretchers every day, carrying off the dead.

The camp administration informed us of their wishes over loudspeakers, which were set up on the parade ground and in every barracks. Every announcement was prefaced with, "Listen up, Jewish rabble!" They could have broadcast Nazi news to us through this system, but aside from reciting the law compelling Jews to yield their property and a speech that Goebbels delivered in Reichenberg, they told us nothing. Our situation was comparable to that of miners who are sealed in a shaft after a disaster and have nothing to do but wait for outside help.

We increasingly tried to come to terms with our fate. The previously mentioned civil servant Mandowsky had thought to grab a pocket chess set upon his arrest, and it now served us well. In the barracks we held religious services during the week and on Saturdays. We certainly had no shortage of cantors. Finally, even the rabbis began preaching. No one disturbed us in these activities. But we were always troubled by the worry of what would become of us; our inactivity made us think dark thoughts.

We occasionally had the opportunity to make purchases, but the prices were horrendous. A bottle of seltzer water cost a mark. Cigarettes cost five times the shop price. I paid 2.50 RM for a pair of socks that the experts said had a retail value of sixty Pfennigs. Once a not exactly new copy of the *Völkischer Beobachter* was offered to us for ten marks, but there were no takers. I happened to have 450 RM in my pocket when I was arrested, so I was in a position to help out many acquaintances with loans.

In the meantime, our women worked tirelessly for our release. My wife completed the still outstanding formalities for our move to Palestine by traveling to Berlin and sending a telegram to Jerusalem. On November 19 the Breslau Gestapo informed her that they would order my release. But it was not until November 25 that I joined the group ordered by the loudspeaker to assemble at the small gate. There was still a whole series of formalities to take care of.

These included shaving and a medical examination, which was restricted to ascertaining whether we bore any visible signs of physical abuse. I really don't remember what declarations I signed and what they said. Upon receiving our release papers we were all asked to pay a contribution to the German Winterhilfswerk. After I paid a mark, someone yelled at me, "You're supposed to be a lawyer and that's all you donate, you bastard." I took that as a sign of praise and recognition.

An SS man led the hundred of us who were to be released on this day out of the camp and accompanied us for some distance. Suddenly, he vanished. I was a free man again and felt the afternoon sun of a beautiful November day shining down on the gentle Thuringian landscape. After a short hike we came to a lonely village inn. I did not notice the town's name. On a road sign we could see that we were ten kilometers from Weimar.

They seemed to be expecting us in the inn. There was good coffee and they had excellent sandwiches, ready to eat. We were more than a little surprised by the innkeeper's courtesy. He even asked us if the gentlemen wished to take a bus to Weimar. Shortly afterward several very respectable buses appeared. We were also curious to see how the population viewed the Jews now. One of us bought chocolate and offered it to some children playing in the street, and they accepted it with enthusiasm. Some Storm Troopers watched and showed no objection whatsoever.

I took advantage of the express train from Weimar to Leipzig to wash myself finally in the train lavatory. After a stopover in Leipzig, where I cleaned myself up some more, I arrived home on the morning of November 27, 1938. I spent the whole first day passing on greetings to the wives of my fellow sufferers and informing them how they could achieve their husbands' swift release.

The next day I had to report to the Gestapo at eight in the morning, where I encountered a great number of fellow sufferers from Buchenwald. I was afraid that the hours of standing were about to begin all over again, but we were led into a classroom where we could sit down. There they gave us a lecture on our duty to emigrate immediately. Once again we had to sign a paper. But that took place in such a leisurely manner that I had time to make a copy of the document. It bore the reference number B/Nr.Abt. II B 5 and stated the following, "I was informed today that I have been released from protective custody for the time being. I have been informed that I face lifelong imprisonment in a concentration camp if I do not immediately pursue my own emigration and that of my family by all means at my disposal."

Then we had to report to the Gestapo every few days, where we were led into the classroom and asked to show our "homework," that is, show what progress we were making toward our emigration. Since in my case everything was more or less set, my "teachers" were satisfied with me. However, there was still a vast array of formalities to tend to at various government agencies, particularly at the revenue and foreign currency offices. But here the Gestapo proved very helpful. During our lessons they impressed on us that we should tell any authorities who had no time that the Gestapo was prepared to send over "auxiliary officials." And it was true—any reference to the Gestapo always ensured that matters were attended to in a fraction of the time such things would have taken otherwise.

Of course, the state of affairs at home was not very encouraging. My wife had been forced to sell the rest of her inventory to a shoe merchant at dumping prices. According to the new laws, she not only could not have the shattered windowpanes replaced by the insurance company but was actually required to have new ones made with her own money. The Jewish capital levy law, 20 percent of our assets, caused us great difficulties since our means had barely been enough to finance the *Vorzeigegeld* ["capitalist certificate"] we needed for Palestine. But in the end we also overcame these difficulties and on Tuesday, December 13, 1938, at 10:15 A.M., I received the coveted Palestine Certificate from the English General Consul in Berlin.

I also informed my accident insurance company of the incidents of November 10. They immediately declared their willingness to finance the cost of repairing my teeth. The official asked me to make as little fuss as possible concerning the matter. However, only a portion of the dental treatment could take place in Germany, because on December 18, 1938, we left Germany forever. I had to leave my seventy-five-year-old mother alone in Breslau.

30

My Troubles Were Just Beginning

ARTHUR SAMUEL

After a few hours, in the middle of the night, we were again ordered to go up. We were given back the things taken from us. Complete silence. Woe to him who made a noise. We were put back on the trucks. Once again, trucks were standing outside the door. Where were we going this time? Into the nearby forest—the expression "shot while trying to escape" ran through our heads. A short distance from the forest the trucks turned toward the town. No one spoke a word. We stopped in front of the prison, whose gates hung wide open to allow the trucks to drive in with their victims unhindered. They unloaded us in the wink of an eye so that they could go and collect new victims. In the prison we relaxed a bit since the fear of concentration camps was great and, sadly, all too justified. Now we were told for the first time to give up everything. We were locked into individual cells. The manner in which this occurred was worse than the fact itself.

Whom did I see there as a prison guard? None other than an old schoolmate from elementary school, Josef Wald! I start to hope. What can I expect from him? Only a tiny bit of humanity. I didn't want to—I *couldn't* abandon my faith in human goodness. I only saw his pistol and rubber truncheon, insignia that didn't fit him at all. He had always been such a coward at school. How many times did I have to fight for him in the school yard when everyone else, who had little affection for him, beat up on him? Now it was his turn to repay kindness with kindness. Of course, I told myself, he can't risk a word or even a look in the presence of the other guards, not even a quick glance. I so longed for a tender word after all these cruelties. Finally I was called on, "Prisoner Samuel, cell 68!" Now I was led away by my schoolmate. I was standing on the steps alone with him, no one could have heard if he said a quiet word to me, and no one could see our secret glances. What happened? Nothing. I tried in vain to catch his eye, but he looked away. Moments later we stood at the cell door. Not a word. Only a gesture, saying "in you go." I went hesitantly, like a tormented animal, into the horrible cage, and then my school friend from past times, Josef Wald from the Kreuzstrasse, with a swastika band on his arm, slammed the iron door behind me—with such an incredible noise that, leaning on the wall, I first had to recover my senses.

The next afternoon toward three o'clock we were ordered to step out in front of our cells. What a sight the poor people were after a single day! Endlessly sad, weary eyes in hollow, bluish eye sockets; yellowish, unshaven faces of almost exclusively elderly people. An expression of defiance and contempt, acceptance of fate lay in all the faces. I have never seen such human greatness in a facial expression as on that day in prison. Most of these mature and graying men had experienced the horrors of the war as soldiers in the German army. They did not just stand up for themselves on the front. I am proud of all my fellow Jews from Bonn who displayed no weakness or timidity in this time of uncertainty. Would we live? Or die?

We waited endlessly. Toward evening we received our prisoner bag with our personal articles, such as suspenders, collars, and money. "Get dressed," we were ordered. We hoped for the best! We thought that this must have been a tool to intimidate us, they just want to tell us that this is what happened to all Jews who didn't understand that the Third Reich was here to stay. Just see that you leave Germany as quickly as possible, otherwise you'll be exterminated! The government's methods certainly were effective. We hoped that we would soon be back with our wives and children. To be home with our families! We got dressed as fast as a child who has been promised a surprise treat. But our hopes were disappointed. We were sent away again. Outside stood the well-known green trucks, and once again hunchbacked, aged figures climbed into the open trucks, meek as children. Where to? To the penitentiary in Rheinbach, to the concentration camps of Dachau or Oranienburg? I could not follow the fate of my poor deported brothers, because they took a different path from mine. The fact that I was the chairman of the Jewish community was the reason why I was now to be released.

Herr S., the Gestapo hero of Bonn, needed me! The synagogue and the community center had been entirely destroyed by fire. The great stone columns and pillars that bore the synagogue's roof had shattered in the fire like glass, so that the massive roof, which the flames could not reach and which was relatively unharmed, represented a great danger to anyone who approached the temple. Herr S. needed me: he ordered me to have the synagogue demolished in an orderly manner. The community had to bear the costs itself. The demolition was going to cost 8,000 RM. Since Herr S. had forbidden everyone to use the salvageable material, such as stones and beams, for further building purposes, the price was higher than usual. The stones of the synagogue could only be used for roadbeds. They were "Jew stones" and thus unusable for any "decent purposes."

The Aryan German contractor could not simply accept a Jewish commission to demolish the synagogue without further ado. He first had to get permission from Herr S. The property on which the synagogue was located belonged to the congregation. In order to collect the money necessary for the demolition we had to sell our building lots on the Rhine and also the site of the other synagogue. It was up to me to put together the money for the demolition of the synagogue. I offered the agent from Bonn a ridiculous price, but no one wanted to make such a tempting deal with a Jew for fear of getting into trouble with the Nazis. I finally went to the city department of planning and building inspection, which was ultimately responsible for the town's construction affairs. I presented my case to an experienced assessor. He told me to come back. The matter was immediately discussed with the mayor. I came to an agreement with the town. All that was needed was the permission of the Nazis, of Herr S. This was denied at first, then granted, and after various changes we ended up losing all the real estate value the lots had once represented.

After two weeks the broken glass was swept up and the damaged facades were covered with white boards. People had almost forgotten the fire, at least on the outside. But there was also plenty of excitement—not just for the Jews but also for the Christians, for the Aryans, even for the Nazis themselves. Because no one felt really safe. This uncertainty created a splendid breeding ground to spread the whole terrible contagion. I recall a high court official, one from the old days! In normal times he would hardly have spoken to me on the street. Despite his "reactionary attitude" he was still in office with the Nazis. Once, in passing, he shook my hand and whispered in my ear, "Well, doctor, what do you say about people's memories, aren't they amazingly brief? Does anyone talk about the synagogue fire today?"

It was two days after my arrest. We were discussing the demolition of the synagogue. Each meeting we held had to be reported to Herr S. Jews were not permitted to hold any meetings without permission. It would have been a political crime. While we talked, Herr S. would keep calling us up. He checked whether we really were holding a meeting, who was there, and so on. On the way home my car, which I was driving myself, stalled in the middle of the road on the way from town to my country home when the carburetor failed. It was a winter night, with cold rain and stormy winds. I couldn't get my car going again. I was alone, twenty minutes away from my house. I left the car on the side of the road and walked home to inform my wife. I knew how afraid she had been since that terrible night. We considered what to do. Should we leave the car there until the next morning? That was the most sensible thing to do, although if another car ran into it during the night, the Jewish owner could be punished for negligently leaving his car outside overnight. My wife didn't let me walk back to the car alone. We wanted to get someone to tow the car. It was raining and the wind was blowing. We walked to an inn where the lights were still burning. It stood alone on the side of the road. It was twelve o'clock midnight. We saw between six and eight young fellows and two middle-aged men. I ordered a beer and a liqueur and asked the innkeeper, who did not know me and who was very polite, whether he could help us. I asked him to call a garage. No one recognized us as Jews in this strange inn. The innkeeper asked where the car was, what it looked like and what make it was. He rang up the garage and then asked me my name.

The moment the young people and the men heard my name, they realized that I was Dr. Samuel from Bonn. The mood in the room changed instantly. The innkeeper said he regretted he was unable to find anyone to help me. We felt something brewing against us, but didn't quite know what was going to happen. We soon left the inn in considerable distress and hurried to our car in the rain. But what had happened? I couldn't believe my eyes. The car had been wrecked. There was not a soul to be seen. We knew immediately what had happened. The fellows had preceded us in another vehicle and demolished my car. I was very worried about my wife, since I expected even worse to come out there on the lonely highway.

While we lingered out there on the now uncanny highway, a big truck came by. The driver saw the glass shards on the road and thought there had been a serious accident. He stopped and asked what happened. I told him nothing of what had really happened for fear that he too was a Nazi. The man was helpful and began repairing the engine.

But at the moment he started to help the young fellows we had seen in the inn emerged from the shadows. They whispered something in the truck driver's ear. He climbed back into his truck and drove off. Once again, we were helpless and alone, entirely at the mercy of these fanatical young men. We immediately rushed back to town. We reached the nearest telephone in fifteen minutes. We didn't dare call the police. We called an Aryan patient who provided professional help in auto accidents. He arrived an hour later. We told him what happened and asked him to tow the car.

We drove to the scene of the accident. He was just attaching a rope to the axle when the fellows appeared again from the field. They stopped the man from helping us. We were Jews, they said, and he mustn't provide any assistance. If he persisted, they would wreck his car and denounce him as a friend of the Jews in the *Westdeutscher Beobachter*. Our helper made objections. He was a big husky man and was not easily intimidated. It was dangerous to leave the car in the darkness, he said, and he could not let it stay there. Then they said they'd let him pull my car to the next hillside and push it over the edge. He started up his Hauderer and drove off. His car made a horrible noise. I climbed into my car and turned the key. My wish came true: the car started up. The fellows had smashed in the car's headlights, so they didn't see me escape in the darkness. But what a ride I had in this car without windows, and in such weather! I didn't dare drive home for fear they would pursue me. My children were at home, guarded only by our dog. I thought that if I drove home now they would burn down the house and terrify the children. So I drove in the opposite direction to lead them astray, then drove to Bonn and left the car there. Then I took a taxi back home. It was now five in the morning.

31

A Failed Escape Attempt, a Devastated Home

SIEGFRIED NEUMANN

Our Christian porters and our house servants stood alongside us. We watched the sparks fly with dismay. At its rear side, the very slanted synagogue square abuts on the shed of a roofing paper factory. On the roof of this shed stood some SS and fire department men, but they didn't extinguish the flames. Suddenly an SS man strode toward us across the courtyard, his revolver in his hand. With the words, "There's the Jew," he stepped up to me and, before the eyes of my wife and children, forced me into the back corner of the courtyard. I was sure that he wanted to shoot me out of view of the crowds standing along the street. In a fraction of a second, I ran behind our house and jumped over the meter-and-a-half-high wire fence separating the courtyard from our garden. The night was bright from the moon and the flames of the temple. But here there was more darkness because of the shadow of the house, trees, and bushes. I expected him to send some bullets my way, so I lay on the ground for a few seconds. He didn't shoot. For a moment I considered crawling or running straight ahead and then climbing over our side fence into the large garden belonging to our neighbors. But to do that I would have had to cross a brightly lit section of our own garden and would have provided a clearly visible target. And so I decided—all of this happened within a few seconds, I should point out—to run around our house to the left so that the SS man could not shoot at me from the courtyard. I wanted to run around the house and escape into the crowd.

When I sprang over the fence separating the garden from our courtyard, I was grabbed by three persons, including a Storm Trooper, and pulled onto the street. With a call of "Throw the Jew into the fire!" they dragged me onto the sidewalk in front of the street. It was jammed with people head to head, all of them silent. They pulled me past a single policeman and over to the synagogue entrance, some thirty meters all told. The whole time they kicked me in the head and face. At the entrance to the blazing temple they propped me back up on my feet. Then the SS man, who had previously entered our property and who was apparently in charge of the action, showed up. He yelled at me, "Of course you know what this is all about: Herschel Grynszpan." I said, "What can we do if somebody runs wild outside Germany? Our religion despises all violence, particularly murder." He said, "Now they do!" Then I had an idea. I opened my coat and pointed to the Iron Cross and the honorary cross for front soldiers I wore on my jacket. I said, "Anyway, I'm a war volunteer and a front soldier and wear the Iron Cross." He said, "Good for you. Try to see if you can jump over that wall. Then we'll see if you still have a spark of Germanness inside you." He pointed to a smooth, three-meter-high brick wall that separated the synagogue square from my own property.

They didn't allow me back onto the street. I threw down my winter coat and attempted the impossible. Since the wall offered no purchase, I naturally failed. I scurried across the synagogue square, which was now as light as day in the gleam of the flames, to the opposite side, which was only separated by a wooden fence from the property where we had been living since November 1935. Everything happened in full view of the crowd assembled on the street. Next to this fence we had built the Sukko, a hut made of boards for the religious rites of the Feast of Tabernacles. Running behind it, I climbed over the wooden fence and now found myself on the property where we had lived for seven years. I considered fleeing across the adjoining school property of the girls' primary school toward the freight depot and then bypassing the barriers and escaping on some train or other. But then I would have had to cross the broad school courtyard, which offered no cover on this bright night. Furthermore, I didn't know how the school property was enclosed on the other side. Since I knew the cellar door on the rear side of the house we formerly lived in was always open, I ran toward it half bent over. It was open.

Fortunately, the inner cellar door, which was also the entrance to the doorman's flat, was unlocked. Behind it lay a dark passage onto which the doors to the doorman's living area and the cellars opened. I opened the door to the kitchen. It was empty. Since there was no key sticking in the kitchen door, I couldn't lock it from the inside. I placed some pieces of furniture in front of the door to grant myself a reprieve in case I were followed. I quietly opened the kitchen window at the rear wall of the house so that I only needed to push it open and escape if someone came through the kitchen door. I myself crouched on the floor so as not to be seen through the window, which was at ground level. I wiggled my feet in my shoes so as to stay spry and ready to jump, because if someone broke into the kitchen then I would be left with mere seconds to escape through the window. I felt like a hunted criminal—and my only crime lay in the fact that I was a Jew.

My distrust of the SS man's permission to escape was soon proved to be all too justified. Suddenly I saw an SS man patrolling the courtyard outside. They apparently had not observed my escape into the cellar. Instead, he was apparently looking for footprints heading toward the adjoining school property. Then I heard the sound of heavy boots in the cellar passage outside the kitchen door. All that separated me from the SS was this unlocked door. Another SS man stood behind the house. At attempted escape through the window in this bright night and under these conditions would have had little chance of success. If only they don't open the kitchen door, I prayed. My prayer was heard. I heard the landlord's voice saying, "You see, nobody's here." I breathed a sigh of relief when I heard the footsteps disappear. Now I felt safe.

Soon I heard the doorman's wife, who knew us from our long tenancy and whose little boy used to play with my daughter on a daily basis. She opened the kitchen door. I whispered to her to be quiet, for God's sake. I was afraid she would scream out in fear. She merely said, "For God's sake, Herr Doctor, you look terrible. Let me wash off the blood." In my excitement I had not noticed that my head and face were covered with blood from the kicks of the SS man's boot. But as she tried washing it away, my wounds started to bleed in earnest. She gave me a sip of water and led me into the smoking room, which she then locked. Now I heard that they had arrested the landlord, who was an Aryan but, as an old German nationalist, not popular in the Party. The lieutenant colonel's wife, our successor in the upper flat, with whom we were still on good speaking terms, had seen everything and was sitting upstairs crying. The lieutenant colonel had run into the street half-dressed and had said only, "What's going on here?" The SS responded, "Go back to your flat." When a similar question rang out from the house asking what was going on, the SS shot twice at the window. The lieutenant's son only dodged the bullet by ducking in time.

The firemen were not permitted to extinguish the fire. Finally, a Reichswehr officer in uniform appeared and gave them strict orders to start extinguishing. Only then did the fire department go into action. Now that I thought I was out of danger for a moment, this mention of the two shots made me start worrying about my wife. She must have thought they had been meant for me and that I was now dead. Since her heart wasn't the best, I was terribly worried whether and how she would withstand the excitement of this night. But for the moment I had to stay in hiding.

The doorman's wife peered through the curtains. The SS men were still outside. The night just wouldn't end. Finally the new day dawned. The black SS car had left. We sent the doorman's seven-year-old son ahead to my flat to tell my wife that I was still alive. He came back and said that the street was now empty. Now I raced back home. My wife sat with the children in the smoking room behind closed blinds. One of her relatives had come as well. I now learned that during the night all the men in the community had been taken into protective custody by the police. The police captain—not the one I mentioned before, but a Nazi from the Storm

Troopers—had come to pick me up too and had been very upset when he couldn't find me. My wife had told him I had been shot and that she had heard the shots. But he strictly denied that I had been shot. I asked my wife if she had packed a suitcase so that we could travel back to Berlin. She replied that the captain had expressly warned her against doing so. This action had been carried out throughout the entire Reich. We should call immediately when I arrived so that he could take me into protective custody. That was the only way he could protect me. If we stepped onto the street alone then he could take no responsibility for the consequences. My wife promised she would call the police immediately after my return. I had to agree that I wouldn't get far with my bloody face.

We called the police. The officer on the telephone said, "The captain isn't here yet. Do you want to take a trip?" That was a hint. Soon afterward the police captain appeared with another officer. "Do you have any guns in the house?" I honestly said no. He didn't ask any further. "You look great." I said that was only external. "Where were you all night?" I replied, "I would like to remain silent on that." He didn't ask any further. He merely said, "I can't drive you through town in that condition," and ordered the police officer to drive me first to the hospital to get bandaged. The medical attendant in the hospital who bandaged my wounds knew me. Beforehand, in the corridor, I asked the police officer if the police would really protect us from the SS. He said that as long as we were in the hands of the police we were safe from the SS. The doctor in the bandaging room asked me if I had any internal complaints. If I had just said yes, then I would have stayed in the hospital. But I imagined that the SS would pick me up from the hospital anyway. So I said no and landed in police custody. As strange as it sounds, since none of us knew what was going to happen and really believed in "protective custody," I felt very relieved when the cell door shut behind me and I found myself together with the male members of our community—they were all personal acquaintances. They said they had lost hope of ever seeing me alive again.

In the evening hours we had to assemble for departure. The accompanying police officers loaded their guns in our presence. One of the older officers had tears in his eyes when he bade us farewell. Three of us, including me—all three of us front soldiers—were to ride in the captain's private car on his express orders, the others on large omnibuses. When we stepped onto the street to board the vehicles, a crowd of people stood there shouting anti-Semitic curses and threats, apparently on command since we later heard the same thing from other towns as well. Then we headed for Oranienburg.

[For reasons of space we must do without the narration of Neumann's weeks of imprisonment, which are similar to those depicted by Max Moses Polke. The report rather abruptly resumes with Neumann's release from the concentration camp.]

I hurried to the station so as to reach Berlin as soon as possible. The suburban train finally left at seven. When I reached Friedrichstrasse station and was about to take the escalator to the other platform, someone behind me whispered, "Do you come from Oranienburg?" The Gestapo already? I thought. Then he continued, "I'm from the Jewish Assistance League. Do you need anything?" I thanked him. Some people didn't even have the train fare to travel home. I first went to my brother who had been released earlier. My wife had left Berlin this same day. I made a telephone call.

I wanted to go home the next day anyway. My wife greeted me at the station the next morning. Back at the concentration camp I often thought I would never live to experience this moment. "I've got to go home and change my suit." The one I had on looked like a corkscrew after going through disinfection. "Leave it," my wife said. "I'm living at my mother's house with the children. I'll tell you everything later. The main thing is that you're back." "Then let's take a taxi and go first to the police where I have to report myself." "No taxi will take us Jews anywhere," my wife replied.

But the trams that links the new town and the old town let us on board. How strange this city, where I had worked as a lawyer for fifteen years, where I had started my career and my family, seemed to me now. I shivered, but not from the cold. People looked at me as if a corpse had risen from the earth. On the way my wife told me that she had sold the house the day before and had purchased tickets to Shanghai for the family with a departure date at the end of March. That was all right with me, just as long as we didn't have to stay any longer in a country where we were fair game for everyone. I reported to the police. We also immediately applied for our passports on the basis of the ship tickets which my wife had with her. Then we went to my mother-in-law's flat.

Bit by bit, my wife informed me that our house had been demolished, our furnishings destroyed, and everything stolen. All I still owned was a summer suit my wife had taken with her. I didn't even have a nightshirt. My mother-in-law was happy to have me back in one piece. The revenue office had seized everything the poor woman had, even jewelry and furniture, to pay for the Jewish capital levy and Reich escape tax. She could not defend herself since her son, who was the only one who understood her affairs, was still in the concentration camp. I learned that the landlord of the house next door, who according to the camp adjutant was dead, would give me a call. He wanted to buy the synagogue square. I was on the board of the Jewish congregation. So the adjutant had lied to make it easier for me to give false information. The lieutenant colonel had long since been released. I felt a weight drop from my soul. Thus I no longer needed to fear an affidavit. The children could not show their joy so openly. The little one was even a bit afraid. Later she told me it was because I had a shaven head. She kept asking, "Papa, when are we going to Berlin?"

That afternoon we went to our house. The missing front door was boarded up, the blinds were drawn. We entered through the cellar door. The doors to the two office rooms had been hacked out of their frames. The shelves had been tipped over. Books and files lay in heaps on the floor. Of the four large office typewriters, three were destroyed and the fourth had been stolen. Someone had tried to break open the safe but without success. I managed to reach in and pull the till out of the inner chamber. So we at least had some cash. All the windows were smashed. The pictures, all original artwork, had all been yanked down and most of them had been slashed. In the parlor the red silk curtains hung in shreds from the high windows leading to the conservatory. The valuable hand-painted lemonwood furniture had been smashed up and my violin had been stolen. As far as the grand piano was concerned, only the lid was smashed. Apparently someone had played on it and let it live. The carpets and runners were still there. In the smoking room the shelves of the bookcase were all smashed up. The books lay all over the floor. All the other furniture was smashed. Only the couch and the chairs were smeared with ink and nothing more. They had apparently sat down here and helped themselves to our supplies of cigars, cigarettes, and wine. We found the broken blade of a big spade they had apparently used for their smashing. Both of my cameras, including a very valuable stereoscopic apparatus with two Zeiss-Tessar lenses, had been stolen. The dining room was full of crystal and porcelain fragments. They had simply tipped over the display cabinet with everything in it. Two large candelabra of Meissen porcelain, representing the four seasons, an old family heirloom belonging to my wife, had been shattered. The ten chairs and the two dining room armchairs were so damaged that they were utterly irreparable. Thus all our expensive furnishings, each room worth several thousand marks, lay in ruins. There was no trace of our kitchen appliances. In the bedrooms everything was equally broken and overturned, even our beds. All our linen and clothing, even the children's school bags and toys, had been stolen. All they left was my evening coat without the trousers. They had spent three days robbing our house, much of it in full daylight.

Our doorman said that he called the police but they just yelled at him. There were stones in the bathrooms. My wife said that eight-year-old boys, egged on by their teachers, had bombarded the house with stones and other missiles. When she called, the police appeared with rubber truncheons. Finally my father-in-law's former chauffeur drove the children, with police protection, through the mob since no taxi would come. My office assistant and our house servant had already begun to save some of our things before the plundering started. But the police forbade it, saying that everything had to be investigated first. I first straightened up the office to pull out the files I needed to take to Berlin to finish up. Beneath the files I discovered the house door.

My wife ended up having to sell this house, which had attracted so many prospective buyers, to a colleague who was a Storm Trooper leader. As he said, the police captain would also be happy if he received the house. He then got it for nine thousand Marks less than the others had been asking. The labor exchange would allegedly have got it for half that sum. The Jewish seller just had to sign on the dotted line. Besides, if my wife had refused I wouldn't have gotten out of the concentration camp so easily. At the revenue office I quickly paid the first installment of the Jewish levy in order to avoid the high late payment penalty. After three days I had also finished up with my files to the extent that we were able to move to a Jewish pension in Berlin where my wife had already been living in the interim.

In addition, they had wanted to torch my mother-in-law's house in order "to smoke the bitches out of the Jewish castle." The Hitler Youth also came marching with drums. But the big dog in the garden had a deterrent effect. They also wanted to destroy everything belonging to the poorer Jews. But the army threatened to intervene if the police didn't finally re-establish order. Finally there were a few days—after Herr Goebbels's action had already been officially halted—when our town was peaceful again.

In Berlin we moved into a little room in the pension together with our daughter. Our boy remained with my mother-in-law. After a few days the boxes with the selected files arrived. I now had to liquidate my practice from here. In addition, I had to provide our family with clothing and linen. The currency office immediately released the desired sum. But our money was all tied up in securities, which were now classified as Jewish holdings according to the November laws. Thus we needed permission from the securities office so that the bank could sell the securities. After considerable delay we were informed that we had to submit the bills for our purchases beforehand. In this way we were forced to buy from the large firms at one central place. Then we had to present the bill and leave the merchandise there for several weeks until the securities office approved the sale of the securities at an equivalent sum. Only then could the bank transfer the money and we finally received our merchandise.

Part IX

Farewell to Germany

The events of November 9, 1938, and the occurrences in the first days thereafter induced many of the still approximately 360,000 Jews living in Germany to prepare for emigration. They had to admit to themselves that their belief that the Nazi madness could not last forever was nothing more than wishful thinking. In addition, the conviction many had that despite everything Jews and non-Jews would still find a way of living together was broken forever. The terror of the Reich Pogrom Night had shaken the identification many profoundly patriotic German Jews had felt with their fatherland.

At first, emigration had not been an option. The first wave of terror immediately following January 30, 1933, had driven some three thousand Jews across Germany's borders, many of them to neighboring countries. After the situation seemed to have settled down somewhat, some of them came back. It was not until the promulgation of the Nuremberg Laws that a renewed flood of refugees left the country.

There had long been hot debates on emigration among the leaders of German Jewry. The Zionists had no doubt that resettlement in Palestine was the only solution. They developed meticulous plans for this, establishing language classes and agricultural and vocational training programs. Between 1933 and 1936 almost thirty thousand people moved to Palestine. By contrast, the Reich League of Jewish Front Soldiers pleaded for Jews to remain and carry on in Germany. For its part, the Reich Agency was not fundamentally opposed to emigration. Above all, it wanted to avoid a chaotic mass escape. Emigration should occur in and through orderly channels. Whoever wanted to leave Germany could rely on assistance from the Jewish self-help organizations. The Aid Association for German Jews had four hundred correspondents all over the world who collected information on living conditions, vocational prospects, and the political situation and immigration and currency regulations in those countries that could serve as new homelands. Between 1933 and 1939 the Aid Association supported more than ninety thousand Jewish immigrants.

The Palestine Office in Berlin was responsible for emigration to Palestine. It was allowed to continue its operations until the beginning of the deportations of Jews to the east in 1941.

Persons desiring to emigrate soon discovered that they were not welcome everywhere. Over the years, most target countries closed their borders to refugees from Germany by arguing that they could not absorb any more immigrants. The Swiss slogan was typical of this: "The boat is full!" A whole series of countries introduced quotas for immigrants. This also applied to Palestine, where the British mandate authorities even reduced the existing quotas. Many countries only took selected immigrants and were particularly interested in refugees who had a specific educational qualification or vocational training that was currently in high demand. The search for asylum was easier if the refugee could point to a certain sum of money or other assets that not only made his or her new beginning easier but also benefited economic development in the country of exile. In addition, a so-called affidavit was required for emigration to the United States. This was a guarantee by an American who had to commit himself or herself to pay for all costs that could otherwise accrue to the United States through the insolvency or illness of the immigrant. In this way the authorities tried to keep refugees from becoming a burden to the American government. However, Great Britain loosened its strict immigration policy somewhat following the Reich Pogrom Night and took in more than ten thousand Jewish children who travelled to the island in unaccompanied "children's transports." Finally, Shanghai, which was under international administration, was the only refuge for which one needed neither a visa nor a certificate, neither *Vorzeigegeld* nor special vocational skills. Thus the Chinese metropolis became a sanctuary for some seventeen thousand Jews. The journey there was adventurous to say the least.

After the deportations began, the often protracted search for a refuge frequently led to situations where entry permission to foreign countries only arrived after people had already been transported to the extermination camps.

The German Reich made a vast profit off of the expulsion of the Jews. According to government guidelines, refugees could only take a small portion of their previous property out of the country, an amount that was further reduced by various levies and also the "Reich escape tax," which had been introduced in 1934 and was regularly increased afterward. Furthermore, they were required to sell things they could not take with them either to the state or to non-Jewish Germans at ridiculous prices. Emigration efforts represented an agonizing and wearing steeplechase that grew continually longer and more difficult because of constantly changing regulations.

32

Freedom!

"Aralk"

On that memorable day of November 10 we were hunted like animals. After the Gestapo repeatedly came to my girlfriend's flat to make inspections, the fourth time around we fled through the garden and onto the street. Since we didn't look particularly Jewish we thought we would be safest in the crowd. Upon reaching the train station I tried to find a way to get to my mother. I was still hoping that she had been spared all these things. She lived together with an old uncle, and I reached her on the telephone. She answered the phone in a deeply agitated voice. I stepped out of the public telephone booth and what did I see? Two civilians were arresting a Jew who happened to be standing next to my husband in the public terminal hall. I thought they were going to arrest my husband too, and so with the presence of mind that danger often brings I spoke to my husband in English, loudly and firmly. We hastily disappeared into the crowd. My little one, who was extremely surprised by this, hurried after us. The three of us raced to a taxi stand and, in our excitement, we each named three different destinations. The stolid old taxi driver replied with the greatest aplomb, "You know, folks, I can only go one place at a time." Despite our great agitation we couldn't help but laugh, and that was a good thing. We felt like ourselves again. We now drove to my mother to see how she was.

When our car pulled into the street where my mother lived, what did we see? The Gestapo was just putting my old uncle into their car. I couldn't believe my eyes and hurried to my mother. I left my husband in the car just to be on the safe side. The house was a terrible sight. The old woman was sick and miserable after all the excitement and we all stayed with her. As you can imagine, that night was an ordeal.

In the meantime we learned from our Anna that our house had already been searched twice. They were searching for my husband and our elder son. Our Anna saved my husband from arrest. I never learned whether it was from incomprehension or a certain cleverness. After they—I mean the Gestapo—came back to search the flat again and asked if my husband was there, she gave the correct answer, namely that she expected us back for supper. Later in the evening three men appeared once more, and then the good girl asked them what it was all about, what they wanted from her master. Then the SS men explained to her the following: We had to leave Munich and Bavaria within the next twenty-four hours since they could no longer guarantee our safety in any form. Since Anna couldn't remember all that, she asked the men to give it to her in writing. And she received the following paper, which we still have in our possession, "The National Socialist Party hereby demands that you leave the city of Munich and Bavaria within twenty-four hours since no guarantees can be provided for your safety."

I don't think I need to emphasize that this message caused us considerable dismay. In addition, they railed against the poor girl, saying she shouldn't work for Jews and that she ought to be locked up. Of course, the poor dear cried and was terribly upset. The next morning, greatly uncertain what would become of us, I hurried home with my little one to make the most essential of preparations. We packed twenty-four large and small pieces of luggage in such a short time that I'm still amazed how we managed it. We slunk out of our house like a couple of criminals and Anna took the luggage to the next corner in a hired car. Then we drove off to pick up my mother and my husband. In the meantime, my husband had arranged for a car for the next stage of the journey.

My husband guided the chauffeur while we women sat squeezed amongst the baggage. We reached Augsburg in less than an hour. There we wanted to look up a war comrade, a good friend of my husband. He reported that the same thing had happened there and that the general atmosphere was very tense. He gave us a key to his private quarters where we should remain until he came for us. Our friend was a hotel owner, and he said we would be able to wait here until he could see more clearly how he could help us further. My mother was exhausted from the fast journey and we wondered whether we should accept this generous offer for her sake. As strong as our friend's love of his fellow man and his true friendship clearly were, we did not want to place the good man in such danger on our account.

So we had to move on, but where to? Time was marching on, and we could not hesitate long. The car with the many pieces of luggage drove through the winding streets. We raced toward Ulm. We wanted to reach the Bavarian border quickly and reach Stuttgart before dark.

As we were racing down the Autobahn, we saw large transport trucks full of SS men and prisoners. A cold shiver ran up my spine. We knew that this was an operation that had the entire country in its grip. We all tensely observed every car we passed or that followed us. Suddenly, my husband and I discovered a small, very familiar police car racing behind our heavy Mercedes. We exchanged glances for just a second and instantly realized what this could mean. My husband ordered the chauffeur to take the car up to 120 km per hour. It was a mad chase, my mother fainted, my little one begged her grandmother to wake up and calm herself. I myself sat there like a pillar of salt, staring at the car in pursuit. Our loyal chauffeur, rightly suspecting that things were afoot that were beyond the bounds of the usual and normal, spoke not a word. He drove the car so safely, so well, that I—a driver myself—felt the greatest respect. This devilish ride, during which I kept thinking I would rather die than be captured with my family, is something I will never forget for as long as I live. This ride filled us with fear and shaking—when would it ever end? The much lighter police car seemed unable to hold our speed. And look! It pulled off onto an Autobahn exit. At first we didn't believe our eyes. It took us a long time to find our voices again. We raced on, in constant fear that we would be pursued from station to station. Finally we crossed the border. Exhausted but at the same time with a sense of liberation, we gradually slowed down.

Leaving the main road, we found a narrow lane where we could pull off and take our first rest. After this eerie ride we finally found time to look after my mother, who sat there in her seat, as pale as a corpse. We did not speak of the fear that tormented us, we did not speak of the danger in which we still found ourselves. All we spoke of was the quickest way to get a roof over our heads before sundown and, above all, how to get Mother into a bed so as to spare her further exhaustion. We remained true to our decision to head for Stuttgart. We wanted to reach our relatives. The last stage of the trip continued in the same atmosphere of fear. We continually encountered transports that, we knew, would end in concentration camps. After withstanding the hostility of the Third Reich for five years, we knew its methods. If I believed that this was the highpoint of our experiences, then I was the more deceived. Things would get much worse.

Unfortunately, when we reached our relatives, they were stuck in the same calamitous situation. The husband of one of my cousins had already been picked up, and the other cousin, a widow, was not happy to receive us. She was essentially a very clinging, weak-willed woman, and we refugees were a great burden to her, particularly with my ill seventy-four-year-old mother. My cousin informed us that she would much prefer it if my husband would report voluntarily to the National Socialist Party since all other Jewish men had already been arrested.

On the fifth day of our stay there, a repetition of the Jew raids took place in Stuttgart in order to capture those Jews they didn't get the first time around, it was said. They also searched my cousin's flat and my husband fled over the garden wall and hid himself until they left.

When everything seemed to have returned to normal outside, we still had to face my cousin. Since she absolutely insisted that my husband should enter the lion's den voluntarily, we had no choice but to put an end to this cruel game. I now looked for an opportunity to send him and our little one on their way. An aunt in Frankfurt declared her willingness to receive the two of them for the time being. I had to decide to take leave of them for Mother's sake. I couldn't leave the woman alone in her condition since I couldn't know how things would develop. Having learned that they had both arrived safely at my aunt's flat in Frankfurt, I went about preparing my mother's return to Munich. Various people had indicated to us that the expulsion of the Jews from Bavaria had been repealed, and so I decided to risk the journey home. In fact, it turned out that the expulsion was one of those laws that one section of the Party issued without informing the others. We experienced that over and over again. And when I attempted to request information on this or that matter from the competent authorities, I always received contradictory information. It was often extremely difficult for us to obey the law.

So I took my mother back to Munich and placed her in the care of our loyal Anna. I myself did not want to appear in public out of concern for my husband. By now, it had become common knowledge that we had been expelled. Other acquaintances believed that my husband had been taken directly to the concentration camp along with everyone else. So I fled to a friend for whose heartfelt hospitality and warmth, friendship and love I will always carry the deepest gratitude in my heart. Like so many other women, she bore the sorrow of having a husband in Dachau. I tried to ease her suffering and that of her children in any way I could. She was a very brave woman. In her grief she offered an entire family refuge in her home—four people, total strangers to her, who had come from Ingolstadt with nothing but the shirts on their backs. Although she was greatly concerned as to whether her husband was equal to the strains of Dachau—since he was a secondary school teacher by profession and of a weak constitution—she always smiled when she stood among her children. Only at nighttime, when we shared her bedroom, did we ponder and plan what we could, should, and wanted to do.

In my house, our loyal Anna attended to everyone who asked for shelter, food, and drink. She cared for them all week long, twenty to thirty people daily, some of them relatives, some of them friends, who came to us after being driven from their homes. These relatives included my sixty-eight-year-old uncle, who—after three weeks—was one of the first to be released. The poor man had suffered terribly. Together with hundreds of others, he had been forced to stand, stand and stand, for hours on end, without being able to relieve himself. It is understandable that at that age his sufferings were particularly grave. In tears, my uncle told us that he had often been on the verge of despair. It was a miracle that his strong constitution helped him survive this inhuman strain.

Since we Jews had had all of our accounts frozen, our Anna advanced the money to pay for the groceries and our daily needs. In addition, she lent money to the others, all of whom came to us without a penny. Only she knew that I was in town and she had my instructions not to breathe a word about it.

During this time my friend and I undertook everything we could to expedite our emigration, and at great expense. We did all we could at the official agencies, running up and down the steps from dawn till dusk: my friend in order to free her husband from Dachau, and I to escape with my family as quickly as possible. Nothing else mattered under the circumstances. The only important thing was to rescue our families and ourselves. Telegrams to our children's sponsors moved things along so quickly that we were promised the necessary affidavit.

A letter arrived from our sons' protector in America. It more or less stated that he was happy to make the acquaintance of these splendid boys' parents. He was of the opinion that parents should be united with their children and that the family should not be torn apart. He was particularly pleased that he could make this possible. His only request was to have the three of us come on February 12 as a "birthday present" for our second son. The boys shouldn't know when we were coming! Tears of joy streamed down our cheeks. We owe our lives to them, the children. They, who are so young, appeared to these strangers to be so mature and superior that they automatically assumed the same about their parents! I give them my pride and my love, and I thank the generosity of our protectors!

I now pushed the preparations for our emigration with tireless energy. For safety reasons I decided not to let my husband come home. The city was simply too dangerous. Wherever possible, I avoided everyone I knew only slightly. I didn't want to give away any information about my husband and thus attended to my plans without interference. It was only many weeks later, when they started releasing the Jews from the concentration camps, that I brought my husband home. It was remarkable the way friends and acquaintances silently and sympathetically shook his hand in the belief that he also had been freed from a camp and had been given a new lease on life. To avoid any further explanations, my husband tacitly accepted their professions of sympathy.

The sale of our shop building, the settling of all the formalities at the revenue and notary offices took all our time from dawn to dusk. While I had wide-ranging power of attorney, for some things I still required the signature and presence of my husband. I then found time to take care of home matters and bought whatever I could in the short time remaining to me.

The officials sometimes treated my husband rudely, sometimes with respect. But not a single day passed on which we did not struggle against adversity. He saw these things through, grim and bitter, his fist in his pocket. Those state agencies still staffed by the old guard promptly provided him with the needed papers. But those officials who had risen to authority in the Third Reich exhibited unbelievable brutishness and chicanery. One new authority was the special department for emigrating Jews at the currency and customs office. Armed with fourteen identification documents, we went out to face these final authorities. Unfortunately, we ended up falling into the hands of the city's infamous "Jew officer." He was known among the Jews as a sadist of the absolute worst kind. Thus began a time of hardship. This official was a former haberdasher who had risen to one of the leading positions in the currency office thanks to his long-standing Party membership. His high salary and perhaps also his special skill in mistreating Jews made him so conceited that he strutted around like a peacock. It was up to this comrade to decide what one could take along and what one couldn't. Our dealings with him were extremely unpleasant. He took a great dislike to my husband and insulted him with obvious glee. But he failed to realize that the chicanery he inflicted no longer meant anything to us. The loss of our fortune? Returning to our children, the thought of saving their father was so powerful that the loss of material things was secondary. We did not know what we still faced, we didn't know how we would feed ourselves, and we didn't know how my husband, now fifty-five years old, would begin a new career without any foreign language skills whatsoever. Back then we knew only one thing: We wanted to live for the sake of our children, not for our own sake!

Time was pressing, and we would only receive our American visas if we could present all our other papers, down to the last one. I spent almost ten days as the guest of this currency office until our friend finally decided to take another look at our case. We reached the train for Stuttgart at the very last moment. They even wanted to send an officer with us, as if we were criminals, to make sure we came back. It was only after my husband agreed to let himself be arrested immediately if he did not return our passports within twenty-four hours that they finally let us travel. That was just one of their ways of keeping Jews in suspense, harassing them as much as possible and with obvious pleasure. So there we sat in the train, my husband, my daughter, and I, dripping with sweat, with just one thought in our minds: we've survived this torture, too!

Upon our arrival in Stuttgart we rushed to the consulate. With the stamp for America in our pockets we were so elated that we started hugging and kissing each other right there on the busy street. It was like a fever! We felt like princes and princesses! We took each other by the hand as a sort of palpable sign of our solidarity. To this was added the realization that we would soon see our boys again. We raced back to the station to catch the next train back to Munich. The sword of Damocles hung over our heads. We had to return the passports before the stated deadline. Such brief moments of happiness are quickly lost in the turmoil of emigration.

We had to pack our furniture under the surveillance of the SS, but the stolid Bavarian who was attached to us preferred to educate himself in cultural matters. He presented himself to the shipping people as a guardian of national assets, only to vanish for two whole days behind his newspaper. He read it with such intensity for hours on end that I'm convinced the good man must have memorized it. He was required to sit there eight hours a day. One should never underestimate the Third Reich's efforts in regard to the education of its officials. However, I gained a better understanding of the Third Reich's tax burden. After all, our emigration kept an enormous staff of officials busy. In addition, these officials were extremely distrustful of one another. It was often downright ridiculous the way none of the gentlemen ever wanted to take responsibility for anything. Everyone—and I mean everyone—tried to keep his backside covered. What had become of their manhood?

We had finally put everything behind us. How empty and lonely and abandoned the rooms looked! Now came an unspeakably difficult day, the day we had to bid farewell to my mother! How terrible, how ghastly to leave this seventy-four-year-old woman behind in a country that offered her no security! My mother had enough to live on, but for how much longer? And I, her only child, was about to leave her. She had lost her other two children through death—her son was killed in the war and the other, a daughter, died at a young age. And now I was leaving her, too. It was a fate that cried out to heaven. We couldn't take her with us because her number was much too high. In addition, taking her to such an uncertain future was too much of a responsibility for us. This emotional conflict wore on me greatly. And so we departed, without telling anyone when we would leave, without farewells, our hearts broken.

Only our loyal Anna was present at our departure from home. With tears in her eyes, she hugged us and kissed my hands, filled with gratitude and love. When the train started moving I felt a rigidity in my heart that pained me. I remained very quiet in these difficult hours. My husband, pale and excited, sat in the corner while my little one waved to our good Anna from the window. She stood shaking on the platform, scarcely in control of herself. After a six hour journey we crossed the German border. As the train passed over the bridge at Kehl my husband grabbed my shoulders, wailing and crying. He clung to me as we cried and cried. It was only in Strasbourg, where we made our first stop, that we started to think clearly about what was happening to us.

33

A Final Round of Theft

SIEGFRIED NEUMANN

Since I knew that lawyers, who are dependent on the laws of their own country, make notoriously awkward immigrants, I began retraining myself as quickly as possible. I learned to make handcrafted ladies' belts and to manufacture liquid soaps with all the chemical knowledge that entails. I also busied myself with English lessons. I had reached the point where I could read an English newspaper more or less fluently, whereby my Latin skills came very much in handy. My wife, who had always made clothes for our daughter, took lessons to develop her skills further.

Since the theft in our house had only occurred after the official end of the "action" and since theft supposedly wasn't supposed to have been part of it, I reported the matter to our insurance company. The manager said our home sounded like a whole warehouse. I was first informed that discussions on this matter were under way at the ministry of economic affairs. Then the insurance company refused to pay on the grounds that the theft stood in connection with the action. By now it was high time that we received permission from the currency office for our packing permit. To receive this we had to submit a list of all the things we were taking along with special columns for acquisitions from before and after 1933. Even the most trivial object, such as a handkerchief, had to be listed. Without this packing permit we couldn't even take a suitcase. With the great volume of emigration, the currency office was unable to handle its workload. So as not to make a poor figure in the gold discount levy, I informed the currency office official of all the property that was destroyed and stolen from us. He couldn't believe that the insurance company had refused to reimburse us because of the "action." When, upon his request, I showed him the official letter he merely shook his head.

Back then one could still take one's silver out of the country. A large portion of our dining room silver had survived because it had fallen down to the bottom of the cupboard. We had submitted a precise list. Jewelry—we didn't have very much—including gold watches had to be valued and sealed by an officially licensed assessor.

We had just submitted the assessment—which was within the permitted amount—when new regulations appeared demanding that Jews give up all objects made of gold and silver. That was our bad luck. In keeping with standard procedures, the currency office passed our list on to the customs inspection office, which was to have the things inspected by an agent and make a report to the currency office. The inspection occurred promptly. But the report was not sent to the currency office. This was scarcely a week before our departure. I ran to the currency office, I ran to the customs inspection office. Finally it turned out that the official at the customs inspection office refused to issue the report before we surrendered our silver and other valuables. My wife then had to go to the delivery office and give up everything we still had of any value for our emigration in exchange for a wretched sum that was calculated by weight, even though the deadline had not yet been reached. By telephone—it was now four days before our departure—I finally found out that we had to pay a gold discount of five thousand marks. I had reckoned with one thousand marks. I had no time to appeal the decision. So this was the concession the currency office was offering me on the basis of my service as a war volunteer and for the destruction and theft of November 9!

We had been forced to purchase a whole new wardrobe for our family. Now I had to hurry and trade in five thousand marks worth of securities. We had to leave Berlin on Sunday to reach our ship in Genoa. On the Friday before that I finally learned from the currency office that the exact amount came to 5,300 marks. I quickly took care of the remaining three hundred marks. On Friday morning the shipping agent came to fetch our things for the customs clearance. I still didn't have the packing permit. The shipping agent was supposed to wait for me and the packing permit at the loading dock. It wasn't until afternoon that I finally received it and I took it there straight away. But the customs office was already closing for the evening. At least we could get my things into the customs area so that we could be sure that they would be cleared on Saturday, when they only worked a half shift. At Saturday noon we were finally able to load our baggage onto the train.

A few weeks beforehand there had been other difficulties. My wife had naturally only been able to make partial payment on the considerable amount for the four steamer tickets from Genoa to Shanghai. The currency office had immediately approved the payment of this sum upon presentation of the tickets. However, the securities office suddenly demanded the submission of a tax clearance certificate. The deadline for full payment of our steamer tickets was approximately six weeks before our departure. If we defaulted we would lose our tickets and, with the ships as full as they were, we would have had difficulty arranging for new tickets before the autumn. I had already applied for the tax clearance certificate in January and fulfilled all the requirements for it, including the payment of all four installments of the Jewish levy. Now, when I reminded the revenue office in my hometown of this, it turned out that I should have submitted my income and sales tax declarations for 1938 and 1939. My ledgers were gone from the office. After enquiring at the police, they were returned to me with the exception of one ledger that could not be found. I completed the tax declarations, then drove to my hometown that same evening so that I could submit them first thing the next morning. The officials, who had known me for years, were accommodating enough to process my case as quickly as possible. By noon I had all the tax documents and the tax clearance certificate ready and even received the rebate I had been collecting from the legally prescribed advance payments. I reached Berlin on the noon train and hurried from the station to my bank in order to submit the tax clearance certificate. The bank first had to present the document from the securities office and receive its permission before it could sell the securities and send payment to the Lloyd Triestino. But even that worked out at the last moment. On March 26, 1939, on a Sunday morning, we departed from Berlin. Jews were no longer permitted to ride in the sleeping cars.

Biographical Information

"Aralk" (pseudonym)
The author, a businessman's daughter, was born in Munich in 1896. She attended private middle and secondary schools, married a factory owner, and became the mother of three children. After 1933 she succeeded in sending her children abroad. Following the Reich Pogrom Night her family was ordered to leave the city of Munich and Bavaria within twenty-four hours since "their security could not be guaranteed." After hiding out for weeks in southern Germany, the family secretly returned to Munich. In 1939 the family succeeded in immigrating to the United States. Aralk was forced to leave her seventy-four-year-old mother behind.

Kurt Baumann
Kurt Baumann was born in Berlin in 1907. His father ran a plumbing business. He studied theater and between 1928 and 1933 worked as a director's assistant at the Volksbühne, the State Opera, and the City Opera in Berlin. In April 1933 he initiated the establishment of a Jewish Culture League in Berlin. It was then created in the summer of that year under the management of Dr. Kurt Singer, the director of the City Opera. Kurt Baumann worked there as director of the opera department. Between 1936 and 1939 he also worked as the "censor" of the Reich League of Jewish Culture Leagues in Germany. In 1939 he immigrated to the United States, where he worked as the librarian at Cornell University in Ithaca, New York between 1946 and 1972 and also founded a small opera company. He died there in 1983.

Mally Dienemann
Mally Dienemann was born as the daughter of a well-to-do merchant in Gollub, West Prussia, in 1883. In 1904 she married Rabbi Dr. Max Dienemann, a leading figure in progressive Judaism. She followed her husband first to Ratibor, Upper Silesia, and then to Offenbach on the Main. In 1939 the family immigrated to Palestine, where Max Dienemann died soon after arrival. Mally Dienemann later immigrated to the United States. She died in Chicago in 1963.

Karl Friedländer

Karl Friedländer was born as the son of a merchant in Pless, Upper Silesia, in 1882. Following his law studies he was admitted as a lawyer at the Berlin District Court in 1910. In 1919 he became the company lawyer of an industrial conglomerate and was appointed a notary in 1924. Although he had not been a front soldier, he was allowed to continue working as a notary after 1933 as a so-called old lawyer, since he had already been practicing law before August 1, 1914. However, he lost his status as a notary. As it became more difficult for him to practice his profession, his clientele dwindled and he was forced to give up most of his board seats. He accepted a client's offer to become the trustee of a large company in Vienna. He left Germany in the summer of 1937.

Fritz Goldberg

Fritz Goldberg was born in 1898 in Stettin as the son of the theater director Jacques Goldberg. He spent his youth in Colmar, Alsace, studied theater in Berlin and Cologne, fought as a soldier in World War I, and was active in the first postwar years as an actor, journalist, and instructor at an adult education center. Starting in 1929 he worked as a scriptwriter at a theatrical publishing house in Berlin. At first he was admitted to the Reich Chamber of Culture, then excluded again after the special regulations for front soldiers were eliminated. This exclusion meant the end of his career. After retraining, he worked for a time as a clerk. Arrested in the wake of the Reich Pogrom Night, he was released upon presenting an invitation to the United States. In late 1938, Fritz Goldberg and his family immigrated to the United States via England.

Leo Grünebaum

Leo Grünebaum was born in Wenings, Upper Hessen, in 1888. Following his teacher's training at the Alzey teaching college and additional studies at the universities of Frankfurt and Cologne, he taught in the public schools of Cologne, ending up at a Jewish school. At the same time, he was active in leadership positions at the synagogue congregation of Cologne, as the business manager of the Cologne "Teachers' House," and as a board member of the Religious-Liberal Association of Cologne and its national organization. In December 1938 he and his family immigrated to the United States.

David Grünspecht

David Grünspecht grew up in the little village of Wüstensachsen/ Rhön, where Jews and Christians had lived together in harmony since 1640. But during World War I the first signs of anti-Semitism became visible there as well. After 1933 the relations between the butcher and livestock dealer David Grünspecht and the local peasants remained good. But his clientele shrank more and more, and government chicanery became part of everyday life. When the withdrawal of his trade permit brought his business to a halt, David Grünspecht decided to immigrate. In the summer of 1938 he left Germany for the United States.

Martin Gumpert

Martin Gumpert was born in Berlin as the son of a doctor in 1897 and grew up in a household that had become completely alienated from the Jewish tradition. He studied medicine and joined a socialist student group. At the same time, he belonged to various poetry circles, the Council for Intellectual Work and the Reich Association of German Writers. In 1917 his first literary work, the poetry volume *Verkettung*, was published by Kurt Wolff. He worked at the Rudolf Virchow Hospital in Berlin between 1923 and 1927 and became director of the municipal dermatological hospital in 1927. Upon his dismissal in 1933, he tried in vain to find work for himself in France and returned to Berlin. Over the next years of his unemployment he published further literary works. Witnessing a Jewish pogrom in 1935, he realized that the situation was hopeless. In 1936, assisted by an American with whom he was only moderately acquainted, he immigrated to the United States. In New York he began a new life as a doctor and writer. He died there in 1955.

Hans Kosterlitz

Hans Kosterlitz was born in Breslau in 1906 as the son of a traveling salesman. The family moved to Berlin a year later. After completing the gymnasium he completed a business apprenticeship and worked his way up to become managing director of a fixed-price shop in Singen, Baden. After the shop had to be sold in the summer of 1938 and he lost his position, Hans Kosterlitz and his wife decided to leave Germany. They succeeded in traveling to Italy, and from there they boarded a ship for Shanghai.

Edwin Landau

Edwin Landau was born in Deutsch-Krone, Western Prussia, in 1890 as the son of an ironmonger and plumber who raised him entirely in the spirit of "the German virtues." After being awarded numerous medals in World War I, he founded a local branch of the Reich League of Jewish Front Soldiers and became the chairman of the local Jewish congregation. As a trained plumber, he took over his father's business and expanded it to a company employing twelve men. The boycott against Jewish businesses in the spring of 1933 shattered the world he knew. He became a Zionist and decided to immigrate to Palestine. He succeeded in November of 1934. He built up a new plumbing business in Ramat Gan, where he died in 1975.

Joseph B. Levy

Joseph B. Levy was born in Kiel in 1870. His family had lived in Schleswig-Holstein for generations. He became a cantor in Hamburg and in 1895 he became the cantor in the synagogue of Rabbi Marcus Horovitz in Frankfurt am Main. At the same time, he taught at the Philanthropin, a school belonging to the Jewish congregation. He was deeply involved in the reform of Jewish religious instruction. In 1924 he became the chairman of the General German Association of Cantors, was a member of the Central Association of German Citizens of Jewish Faith (CV), assumed additional functions within the congregation, and was also active as an author. He immigrated to the United States in 1939 and died in New York in 1950.

Ernst Loewenberg

Ernst Loewenberg was born in Hamburg in 1896 as the son of the school principal and writer Dr. Jakob Loewenberg. He became a member of the German-Jewish Youth League and studied German, French, and Spanish in his hometown. From 1921 to 1934 he taught at the progressive Lichtwark School in Hamburg, and between 1929 and 1931 he also managed his father's private secondary girls' school, which he dissolved in 1931. He was sent into early retirement in 1934, even though he had been a front soldier. He had already been a board member of the CV group of northwest Germany, then assumed further duties in the congregation until 1938, became active as an advisor for the Jewish aid organization, taught at the Talmud-Thora secondary school in Hamburg, and became a member of the pedagogical committee of the Reich Representation of German Jews. In 1938 he and his family immigrated to the United States. There he continued to teach, finishing his career at Brandeis University in 1965.

Raffael Mibberlin

Raffael Mibberlin was born as the son of a merchant in a small town near the Franco-German border in 1879. His family had lived there without interruption since 1743. Following his medical studies, he volunteered for military service and in 1906 he opened a doctor's office in a central Franconian town. During World War I he worked as a military doctor. Since he had been a front soldier, he was allowed to continue treating patients within the health insurance system, but he increasingly became the target of both professional and personal attacks. In early 1939, he and his family immigrated to Palestine.

Ludwig Misch

Ludwig Misch was born in Berlin in 1887. After seven years as a conductor in various towns he joined the staff of the *Berliner Lokalanzeiger* in 1921, where he worked as a music critic. From 1922 to 1931 he also taught at the Sternsches Konservatorium Berlin and in Jewish schools after 1932. In 1933 he was fired by his newspaper and founded the New Madrigal

Association a capella choir, which continued as the Jewish Madrigal Association until 1936. He wrote for the Berlin *Jüdisches Gemeindeblatt* and the *Jüdisches Nachrichtenblatt* and continued to work as a music teacher. In 1941 he was hired by the Jewish congregation in Berlin, and in 1943 he was forced to catalogue books that had been confiscated by the Nazis. Married to a Christian, he was spared deportation and survived the war in Berlin. There he became a teacher at the City Conservatory in 1946. In 1948 he went to New York, where he died in 1967.

Hugo Moses

Hugo Moses was born in a small town in the Rhineland in 1895. He lived there as a respected businessman until his home was demolished in the Reich Pogrom Night and he himself spent several weeks in custody. Afterward, he and his family immigrated to the United States via Holland.

Henriette Necheles-Magnus

Henriette Necheles-Magnus was born in 1898 and moved to Wandsbek near Hamburg at age ten. She became a doctor and practiced in her local community. Her husband was also a doctor. It is not known when the family immigrated to the United States.

Siegfried Neumann

Siegfried Neumann was born in a medium-sized East Prussian provincial town in 1895. He was raised in the spirit of true Germanhood, in which the military played a central role, and volunteered for World War I. Following his university studies, he worked as a lawyer and notary in a small town in the province of Brandenburg. His notaryship was revoked in 1933, but in spite of great difficulties he was allowed to continue practicing as a lawyer until 1938. His house was totally demolished during the Reich Pogrom Night, and he himself was seriously abused and confined to a concentration camp for many weeks. Following his release, he pursued his family's immigration. In the spring of 1939 he and his family immigrated to Shanghai via Genoa.

Gerta Pfeffer

Gerta Pfeffer was born in 1912 as the daughter of a merchant in Chemnitz. Following her training as a textile designer, she found employment in a north German weaving mill in early 1933. Fired in 1938, she immigrated to England.

Max Moses Polke

Max Moses Polke was born in 1896. He studied law and established himself as a lawyer and notary in Breslau. As a front soldier he was allowed to continue appearing before the court, but as his clients steadily abandoned him he had to reduce his legal practice considerably. His wife's shoe shop became the main source of the family's livelihood. In 1935 he lost his license as a notary. During the Reich Pogrom Night his wife's shop was totally destroyed. Max Moses Polke was imprisoned at the Buchenwald concentration camp for several weeks and only released when he consented to immigrate immediately with his family. In late 1938 the family immigrated to Palestine. They had to leave his seventy-five-year-old mother behind.

Kurt Sabatzky

Kurt Sabatzky was born in Köslin, Pomerania, in 1892. He studied law and fought in World War I as a front soldier. In 1922 he became the attorney of the Central Association of Citizens of Jewish Faith (CV) in Magdeburg, and from 1923 to 1932 in Königsberg. He first joined the German Democratic Party (DDP), and after its dissolution in 1930 he joined the Social Democratic Party (SPD). He openly opposed the Nazis and survived an assassination attempt in 1932. Forced to flee from Königsberg, he became the attorney for the CV branch in Saxony and Anhalt between 1933 and 1938. Following the Reich Pogrom Night he was imprisoned for a time in the Buchenwald concentration camp. In 1939 he became the managing director of the synagogue congregation in Essen, but immigrated to England that same year. Starting in 1943 he was active for various Jewish organizations, worked at the Wiener Library in London following the end of the war, and founded a Jewish search service. He died in London in 1955.

Arthur Samuel

Arthur Samuel was born in Bonn in 1886 as the son of a merchant. His family had lived in the Rhineland since the middle of the eighteenth century. After the end of World War I he established himself as a doctor in his hometown, where he also served as the chairman of the Jewish congregation. In 1938 he lost his physician's license but was allowed to keep practising as a "Jew healer" in the Bonn synagogue. All of his medical apparatus was destroyed there during the Reich Pogrom Night. This was followed by several arrests, house searches, and interrogations by the Gestapo. He and his family immigrated to the United States, where Arthur Samuel died in 1974.

Hettie Schiller

Hettie Schiller was born in Berlin in 1906 as the daughter of an executive bank employee. She studied biology and psychology in Zurich and Berlin and later worked as a teaching assistant at the University of Berlin. She published numerous articles on nutritional issues and also the book *Nutrition and Diet*. Dismissed in 1933, she opened a school for dietary cooking in order to prepare Jewish women for emigration. In 1935 she expanded this training to include psychology courses. Her husband, a lawyer, lost his license in 1933 and was forced to make do with casual work. He also ran an advisory office for Jewish judges and lawyers. In September 1938 the family was allowed to immigrate to the United States, where Hettie Schiller underwent supplementary training and established a new practice.

Luise Stein

Luise Stein was born in Konstanz in 1914 as the daughter of a lawyer. She grew up in a thoroughly assimilated middle-class family and her friends were almost exclusively non-Jews. In 1933 she traveled to Italy for several months and noticed upon her return that many of her former friends had been transformed into Nazis. She joined a Zionist youth group. In 1935 she gave English instruction at the request of the Jewish congregation to prepare Jews for immigration. Finally, she too immigrated to the United States.

Heinemann Stern

Heinemann Stern was born in Nordeck, Hessen, in 1878, where he also spent his youth. After training as a teacher he worked for more than forty years at Jewish and non-Jewish schools, concluding with his position as principal of the Jewish middle school in Berlin until 1938. He was a member of the executive board of the Central Association of German Citizens of Jewish Faith (CV) and chairman of the Reich Association of Jewish Teachers' Associations. He worked as a school inspector and pedagogical expert in the education department of the Jewish congregation in Berlin and was active as a scientific advisor to the CV in the CV's counterintelligence department. He immigrated to Brazil in 1940 and died in Rio de Janeiro in 1957.

Alexander Szanto

Alexander Szanto was born in Budapest in 1899 and moved with his parents to Berlin, where the family assumed German citizenship. He became a journalist and joined the SPD and the Berlin reform congregation. Beginning in 1930 he served as its delegate at the representative assembly of the Jewish congregation in Berlin and in 1933 he assumed the chairmanship of the financial department of the Jewish Wirtschaftshilfe (economic assistance). Following the revocation of his German citizenship in 1939 he was expelled and returned to Budapest. There he was interned but survived the war as a forced laborer. He took part in the popular uprising in 1956, fleeing to England after its defeat. In England he worked in lawyers' practices and as a journalist. He died in Manchester in 1972.

Friedrich Weil

Friedrich Weil was born in Schmieheim, Baden, in 1877 as the son of a wine merchant and entered the same profession himself after undergoing the required training. In 1900 he founded his own wine export business in Frankfurt. He was arrested in 1934 and sentenced to eleven months in prison for alleged customs violations. Following his release he attempted to continue his wine business, but was arrested once more in the summer of 1938 as a "Jew with previous convictions" and imprisoned in the Buchenwald concentration camp for several weeks. In the fall of 1938 he immigrated to France and from there to the United States. He died in New York in 1953.

Hans Winterfeldt

Hans Winterfeldt was born in Lippehne, Brandenburg, in 1926 as the son of a textile merchant and ironmonger. Since the business was going from bad to worse, the family moved to Berlin in 1937. In 1940 Hans Winterfeldt became an apprentice cook in the Jewish Old People's Home and in 1941 he worked as a forced laborer in a painting business. In 1943 the entire family went underground. Hans Winterfeldt was arrested by Jewish Gestapo spies in 1944 and, under torture, betrayed his parents' hiding place. They were arrested and deported to the Auschwitz concentration camp but survived. Hans Winterfeldt was also taken to Auschwitz and took part in the death march to Mauthausen, but was freed by the Allies and rejoined his family in Berlin. He immigrated to the United States in 1948, worked as an army cook in Korea, caught up on his schooling and higher education and later worked as a professor of German and Spanish in New York.

Eva Wysbar

Eva Wysbar was born in Berlin in 1900, grew up in a prosperous family, and studied music and theater in Berlin, Freiburg, and Zurich. Her circle of friends and acquaintances included renowned actors, directors, musicians, and intellectuals. She failed in her attempt to found her own music magazine. She worked in the phonograph record and press department of the German-Dutch Küchenmeister group, later in the music department of the Tobis film company, and finally became the managing literary and artistic director of an independent film production company in Berlin. She married the well-known non-Jewish film director Frank Wysbar. After 1933 they were able to continue their mixed marriage for a time, but because of her husband's growing professional difficulties the couple arranged a mock divorce. In the fall of 1938 Eva Wysbar and her children immigrated to the United States. Two months later, Frank Wysbar took advantage of an approved foreign vacation to follow. No further information is available on Eva Wysbar. Frank Wysbar first worked his way through various temporary jobs and then achieved growing success in television before returning to the Federal Republic of Germany in 1956. There he directed several cinema films, including *Hunde, wollt ihr ewig leben*. He died in 1967.

www.ingramcontent.com/pod-product-compliance
Lightning Source LLC
Chambersburg PA
CBHW051432290426
44109CB00016B/1524